KARL MARX

The Evolution of His Thought

KARL MARX IN 1848

KARL MARX

The Evolution of

His Thought

by ROGER GARAUDY

GREENWOOD PRESS, PUBLISHERS
WESTPORT, CONNECTICUT

Library of Congress Cataloging in Publication Data

Garaudy, Roger.
    Karl Marx, the evolution of his thought.

    Translated from the French.
    Reprint of the ed. published by International Pub-
lishers, New York.
    Bibliography: p.
    Includes index.
    1. Communism--History. 2. Marx, Karl, 1818-1883.
3. Communists--Biography.
[HX39.5.G3513 1976]   335.4'1   76-43305
ISBN 0-8371-9044-4

Translated from the French by Nan Apotheker

(*Originally published as* Karl Marx *par Roger Garaudy,
Seghers, Paris, 1964.*)

Originally published in 1967 by International Publishers,
New York

Reprinted with the permission of International Publishers.

Reprinted from a copy in the collections of the Brooklyn
Public Library.

Reprinted in 1976 by Greenwood Press, Inc.
51 Riverside Avenue, Westport, CT 06880

Library of Congress catalog card number 76-43305
ISBN 0-8371-9044-4

Printed in the United States of America

10 9 8 7 6 5 4 3 2

Foreword to the American Edition

The weeks I have just spent in the United States and the warm welcome extended to me by several universities gave ample evidence of the great interest in Marxism that exists among many American intellectuals.

There is no doubt in my mind that they seek, beyond the dogmatisms and pragmatisms of the short-term view, a constructive system of thought and action to help build a better future for their great country.

Marxism, rooting itself in the appropriate institutions and the national traditions of each people, is the most exciting experience of our time—a vital ferment in society as it moves toward a future of prosperity and social justice.

May this little book contribute to such a consummation by evoking anew the essentials of the creative work of Karl Marx—the father of 20th-century man's greatest hope!

ROGER GARAUDY

New York, December 14, 1966

Contents

FOREWORD TO THE AMERICAN EDITION   5
PREFACE   11

I. MARX BEFORE MARXISM   15
   The Sunrise of the French Revolution   15
   The Faustian Dream   20
   The "Stream of Fire": "*Feuer-bach*"   24
   The Fichtean Heritage and the Heresy of Prometheus   33

II. MARXISM: A REVOLUTION IN PHILOSOPHY   45
   The Three Sources   45
   The Alienation of Labor   52
   Practice and the "Reconversion" of Speculative Concepts   64
   Historical Materialism   68
   Marx's Materialism   78
   Marx's Dialectics   89
   Dialectics and Freedom   99

III. MARX AND POLITICAL ECONOMY   111
   Marx's Method in *Capital*   112
     1. Historical Materialism and Political Economy   122
     2. The Alienation of Labor and the Fetishism
       of the Commodity   124
     3. The Dialectical Method in Political Economy   127
   Marx's Great Discoveries and Their Significance   141
     1. Labor Value   146
     2. Surplus Value and the Pauperization of
       the Working Class   151
     3. The Contradictions of Capitalism and Crises   158

IV. KARL MARX AND POLITICAL STRUGGLES   169
     From Utopia to the Class Struggle   169
     Strategy and Tactics   177
     The State   186
     Marx, Founder of Communist and Workers' Parties   190

CONCLUSION   199

REFERENCE NOTES   209

INDEX   219

KARL MARX

The Evolution of His Thought

Preface

Today Marx and his work polarize the hopes or the hostilities of all mankind.

There have been times in the past when philosophy concerned itself with man's environment, but it remained for Marxism—as politics, as philosophy, as economics, as conception of the world with its hopes and perspectives for the future—to penetrate the minds and hearts of millions of men and women who had previously been slaves or serfs, people for whom a life of toil had seemed foredoomed and not susceptible to being changed by consciousness.

Today Marxist thought poses for all men, classes, nations—more or less clearly, in love or in furious hatred—a question, a promise, a challenge.

Why is this so? Because it is a philosophy that concerns itself with changing the world, not only with thinking about it. Theory and practice, thought and action become one in the Marxist thesis. Marx revealed the philosophy implicit in man's labor and struggle; he also tore the mask away from the philosophers who professed to move on a plane above man's labor and his struggles. He exposed the true nature of the practices and policies which such philosophers, consciously or unconsciously, served to legitimize or obfuscate.

Marxist thought has become the effective consciousness of a century. It teaches us to understand the law of historical development of our epoch. It helps everyone to take cognizance of the meaning of his life, of the future he bears within him and his responsibility toward that future. It throws down a militant challenge to those who profess to negate the meaning of human life and history, or refuse to accord any meaning to them.

For its partisans, as for its enemies, Marxist thought today would seem to be the leaven in all the human ferments of five continents. On the one hand, it arouses hatred and violent opposition, the persecutions of barbed wire and crematories, on a scale never before known in history. On the other, it arouses the most prodigious waves of heroism and sacrifice, from the Altai to the Cordilleras of the Andes, among the multitudes who have found in it a cause and a home.

It is this tremendous phenomenon that the present volume will try to explain.

What was the nature of the philosophy which, in the middle of the 19th century, kindled this ever growing flame? Who was this man who was able to become within a century the vital leader not only of the workers of the entire world but also of those to whom the heresies of Prometheus are today imputed?

This book aims to answer these questions.

It is far from being a simple task, because of the very nature of Marxist thought. The true "Copernican" revolution in philosophy was effected far more by Marx than by Kant: In placing man and his struggles at the center of the world rather than regarding man as an abstract "subject," in making philosophy come down from heaven to earth and observe the toil and the struggles of men, Marxism became an active force—a weapon in the hands of some, a menace in the eyes of others. It has molded, developed and sharpened itself in constant intense, dramatic polemics. It has exposed too many special interests and privileges for them not to have sought first to crush it and, when that was not possible, to corrupt it.

To attempt to present the living thought of Marx is, at the outset, to rid it of the revisionisms which, for three-quarters of a century, have sought to drape themselves in its prestige, while grafting Marxism on to other, "inoffensive" philosophies. Thus, attempts were made to "rethink" Marx in terms of neo-Kantism, Bergsonism, neo-Hegelianism, phenomenonology, existentialism, even theology, in the hope of domesticating it and turning it into something quite unlike what it is—the demand and the means for transforming the world. The revisionists preferred it to be, more respectably, one interpretation of the world among others—which would leave the world as it was.

In the reaction to such attempts, there were some Marxists who, in their anxiety to prevent the castration of Marx's philosophy, turned rigid in negation and refutation. In their efforts to defend themselves against neo-Kantism, they ended by underestimating or denying the precious heritage of the Kantian critique, so highly esteemed by Marx; in their opposition to neo-Hegelianism, a long-standing ostracism was decreed against Hegel. In combating the tenets of existentialism or theology or Marxism distorted by subjectivism or transcendentalism, or by attempts to "complete" Marxism by endowing it with a specific brand of subjectivism or transcendentalism, there was at times a tendency to mutilate Marxist thought by robbing it of some of its dimensions, instead of proceeding along the lines of Marx's own method, which was to "put back on their feet" real but confused discoveries and to make them a starting point for the dialectics of his own thinking.

Our undertaking in this book is not without risk and, even with the help of those with whom we have consulted, we do not claim to have accomplished it without any error. But the stakes were too high for us not to have taken the risk. It was a matter of exposing the variety of the revisionist attempts, ceaselessly renewed, to falsify Marxist thought, to rob it of its offensive power. It was a matter of putting an end to the dogmatic distortions engendered or fostered by some of Stalin's interpretations, which took Marxism back to the infantile stage of precritical philosophy. It is a task that demands a long breath. At this new stage of history, Marxist thought is vibrant with fresh vitality. Conditions of struggle for a long time kept Marx and then his most faithful followers from developing Marxism in all its dimensions—for example, the dimension of subjectivity or that of artistic creation—whereas Marxist thought contains the seed for such development. The new potentialities created today by the material and intellectual progress of socialism permit a new development of Marxist research that would lead to the full flowering of two of Marxism's major contributions: a total and militant humanism and an incomparable methodology of historical initiative.

I. MARX BEFORE MARXISM

The Sunrise of the French Revolution

> Never before had man been known to base himself on the
> Idea and to build reality on it. . . . It was therefore a
> superb sunrise.
>
> — HEGEL[1]

Karl Marx reached manhood at a turning point in history. When he enrolled as a student at the University of Berlin in the autumn of 1836, he was 18. His youth, like that of all men of his time, bore the stamp of the great epic of the French Revolution and the profound impact of its influence and its ideas throughout Europe.

His father, Hirschel Marx, was, according to one of his intimates, a "true Frenchman of the 18th century, who knew his Voltaire and his Rousseau by heart," and who had imbibed from Kant the principle of the autonomy of man and the right of all the people of a nation to participate in the conduct of public affairs.

These principles led him in 1834 to organize a banquet in honor of the liberal deputies. Karl Marx was then 16. He heard the Marseillaise sung at these celebrations as a rallying cry for all partisans of freedom; later he became aware of the ominious suspicion with which his father was regarded by the Prussian government— which had annexed, in 1815, the Moselle country. Wyttenbach, the director of the high school Marx attended in Trier, also belonged to a group of Kantians inspired by the concept of French liberty. In 1837, Marx became engaged to the Baroness Jenny von Westphalen, a descendant of a noble Scottish family (the Dukes of Argyll). His future father-in-law. the aristocrat Ludwig von Westphalen, to whom he dedicated his doctoral thesis, inculcated in him a love for not only Shakespeare and Homer but also for Saint-Simon.

At the University of Berlin, the teachers Marx liked best influenced him in the same direction. Notably, there was Gans, a liberal, a

15

disciple of Hegel. While accepting the Hegelian idea of development, he did not seek to stop history in its tracks in order to justify the existing regime by attributing to it an absolute value; on the contrary, Gans projected the rational deployment of such "development" into the future. After Hegel died, Gans initiated a series of lectures on the history of the French Revolution. He declared that he was in favor of democratic progress and even of Saint-Simonian socialism.

In 1837, the year when Karl Marx was attending these lectures assiduously, Gans wrote:

"The followers of Saint-Simon have correctly observed that slavery has not disappeared; that if it has been formally abolished, it nevertheless persists in a most unmistakable form. Just as master and slave once confronted each other, then the patrician and plebian, and still later the lord and vassal, today we have the parasite and the worker. One has only to visit the factories to see hundreds of ill-fed, destitute men and women sacrificing in the service and for the profit of one man their health and all the pleasures of life, in exchange for a meager pittance. Is it not pure slavery when man is exploited like a beast, when he is left nothing but the liberty to die of hunger? Is it not possible to awaken in these proletarians their moral consciousness and lead them to take a conscious part in the work they now carry out like machines? The belief that the state should provide for the needs of the poorest and most numerous class is one of the deeply-held views of our time. . . . Future history will have to speak out again and again on the struggle of working men against the middle classes. . . ."[2]

Thus young Marx lived, with his family and at the university, in a Germany which was at that time economically backward, divided as a nation and politically dominated by Prussian reaction. In this Germany, the French Revolution, begun nearly a half-century earlier seemed like a dream of the future to liberal youth.

At the celebration of Hambach in the Palatinate (May 27, 1832), 25,000 liberals, inspired by the Paris revolution, organized a demonstration for German unity and constitutional government. In 1834, Mazzini's "Young Europe"* issued its manifesto against the Holy

* Young Europe was an association "of men believing in a future of liberty, equality and fraternity for all mankind," based in Switzerland.—*Ed.*

Alliance: "This is the Young Europe of the people who will replace the old Europe of royalty. It is the struggle of young equality against old privilege, the victory of new ideas over old superstitions."

Gans, Marx's beloved teacher, was in 1837 the guiding spirit of the Friends of Poland Club, founded in Berlin after the defeat in 1831 of the Polish insurrection against Russia.

This liberal bourgeois movement existed alongside a sturdier democratic and social movement, in which Saint-Simon's concept of the necessity for man's full emancipation by a rational organization of production and a just distribution of wealth was developed. In the light of this ideal, and following the great historical initiatives of the French people, the middle-class stabilization brought about by the 1830 July revolution which deposed Charles X seemed almost ludicrous. "If God made the July revolution for the shopkeepers of the rue Saint-Denis," wrote Gans in 1837, "I will give up my devotion to philosophy and history, because I could not reconcile them with this accomplishment."

 In Germany itself, moreover, the acceleration of economic development stimulated by the Customs Union of 1834 had created the conditions for more and more active struggle by the workers. If the working-class risings of Solingen and Krefeld in 1823 and 1828, and at Aachen and Ruhrort in 1830 had been swiftly crushed by the government, they had nevertheless signalized the earliest class confrontations between the bourgeoisie and the working class.

The consciousness of this new antagonism, even while the conflict between the German bourgeoisie and feudalists was still in process, manifested itself while Marx was still an adolescent. In his native town of Trier, the Fourierist Ludwig Gall wrote (1835): "The moneyed, privileged class and the working class are fundamentally opposed to each other by reason of their contrary interests; the situation of the former improves to the degree that the situation of the latter deteriorates, becomes more precarious and wretched."

Unlike his future friend Engels, Marx had not experienced direct contacts with the working class. Engels, although he was the "son of the boss," had observed and come to understand the misery and the anger of the proletariat. He had spent his youth among them in the Rhenish industrial section of the valley of the Wupper, in the congested slums where his father's workers lived, where the weavers and their wives and children worked 16 hours a day and died of hunger and tuberculosis. Marx, on the other hand, was born in a farming region, where, as it happened, the bourgeoisie did not greatly fear the working class. Indeed, there had been a certain amount of cooperation between the liberal middle class and the winegrowers of the Moselle who had been driven from their land and thrown into the rural proletariat by the fall in the price of wine. Certain common aspirations had emerged; the struggle against absolutism and privilege, against internal taxation, and the fight for a constitutional government and freedom.

In the course of the year he had just passed as a student in Bonn (1835), Marx had seen the repression imposed on the liberal students; he had seen stool-pigeons, arrests, expulsions multiply— unmasking the face of the European Holy Alliance and of Prussian reaction.

In Berlin, under the influence of Gans and his fellow disciples, Karl Marx experienced, still in a somewhat uncrystallized form, the pangs of a world in process of dying and the contradictions of a world in process of being born.

In a series of epigrams in which he blasted oppression and bourgeois philistinism, the young student exalted the lofty humanism of Goethe and Schiller, the noble characters of Wallenstein and Faust.

The letters and poems he sent to his fiancée Jenny expressed decidedly romantic sentiments; told of his dissatisfaction with the hateful world which failed to correspond to his aspirations; voiced his thoughts on revolution, personal suffering and, at times, on his hopes and dreams. He felt within himself the power to defy fate. "With contempt, I will fling my gauntlet in the world's face and I will see the pygmy giant crumble. . . . Then, like the gods, drunk with victory, I will march into the midst of the ruins, and by endowing my words with the power of action, I will feel myself the equal of the Creator. . . . But how to encompass in words . . . what is as immeasurable as the aspirations of the soul, as you yourself are, and as is the universe."

This romanticism was an expression of the contradictions against which the great bourgeois humanists had hurled themselves, Goethe in particular. From Werther to Wilhelm Meister, and from Prometheus to Faust, Goethe expressed the basic contradiction of bourgeois humanism. The generalization of the division of labor, in tending to make a single system of man's universality—an organic whole functioning like a single human being—had greatly expanded the power of the human species over nature and given birth to the Promethean dream of the omnipotence of man. At the same time, however, the system of private appropriation of the wealth and power wrested from nature—in an anarchy comparable to the savage assaults, the selfishness and greed of the jungle—had fragmented and undermined man's power and led to the mutilation and degradation of the majority of men. The very system that opened endless horizons to man's aspirations condemned the majority of men to live a life unworthy of men.

That is why, at that epoch, the "harsh melody" of the Hegelian dialectic inspired a profound revulsion in Marx. The thing he could not accept was the "reconciliation" of the idea with the real. "I have come," he wrote to his father (November 10, 1837), "to seek the idea within the thing itself. If the gods once floated above the earth, they have now become the center of it. . . .

"Robust traveler that I am, I set myself to this task, to a philosophical and dialectical development of divinity as it is shown to be a concept in itself—like religion, nature, history. My last preoccupation was with the beginning of the Hegelian system. . . . This work, like a false siren, drew me into the arms of the enemy."[3]

Then we have Marx reading "Hegel from one end to the other," and turning one he had hitherto disliked into his "idol," as he put it.

Actually Marx was never to be a true Hegelian—at first, because he did not accept the reconcilation of the idea with the real; further because, even after he had penetrated still deeper into Hegelianism, he would never be able to see in the absolute idea the achievement and the sanctification of the established order, but rather the distant projection of a future order that man had still to encompass through practice, action, struggle. For him, Hegelianism was still not the truth—it had to be made the truth; it was not reality, but a program. As he wrote in his doctor's dissertation[4] on the differences between the philosophies of Democritus and Epicurus:

"Just as Prometheus, having stolen the fire from heaven, began to

build houses and settle down on earth, philosophy, having embraced
the world in its totality, rebels against the world of phenomena. Thus
it is now with Hegelian philosophy."

The Faustian Dream

Lo, the hour has come to prove by deed
That manhood to the Godhead will not cede.
— FAUST, I, 1.

For young Marx, as for all youthful Hegelians, Hegel's philosophy
was the promise of the fulfillment of the Faustian dream of "divine
wisdom." So far as "aboslute knowledge" was concerned, the finite
self of man was equal to the infinite power of God.

In Kant there was the dualism of man and God, of nature and
man. In Hegel, Kant's tragic thesis is transcended. In his religious
 critique, Hegel already considers Jesus less as God-become-man than
as man-become-God. Religion for him was only "'man raising himself
from finite to infinite life."

This Promethean ambition characterized Hegelian humanism, the
philosophy of confidence and pride in the self. Morality is man
made divine. And science is the act by which man discovers himself
in every object, in a world perfectly transparent to reason.

In terms of this philosophy, man is only part of the totality of
existence; there is nothing exterior to him which escapes the sovereign
legislation of his own dialectical thought, neither a transcendent God,
nor the external world.

Such is the central insight of Hegelianism and the key to it.

Marx and the Young Hegelians, in making this grandiose ambition the point of departure for their thinking, were here too acting
as the heirs of the French Revolution, since Hegel's philosophy, as
Karl Marx was soon to write, was "the theory of the French
Revolution."

The victorious French middle class, by breaking down the obstruc-
tions to a tremendous release of the forces of production, by giving
a formidable impetus to the sciences and technology, felt itself

capable of consummating the Cartesian dream of becoming masters and possessors of nature. Besides, their struggle against "divine right," against transcendent religious justifications for the feudal order, and against monarchic absolutism, had led them to putting man in the place of God.

In a country where the revolution could not be achieved because of economic backwardness and political fragmentation, the Germans had to confine to the realm of thought what others had accomplished in action.

Heine, in his *Religion and Philosophy in Germany*,[1] very consciously described the following parallel: According to him, German thinkers—especially Kant, Fichte and Hegel—had accomplished on the intellectual plane a revolution comparable to that of Danton and Robespierre on the political plane. The work of the French Revolution and of German philosophy, he felt, must be realized in a more profound and complete revolution, no longer only intellectual and political, but also social—one that would radically transform society all the way from its economic to its religious life.

Some years later, in 1874, Engels emphasized the importance for Marxism of the heritage of German philosophy: "If German philosophy, particularly that of Hegel, had not previously existed, scientific socialism would never have existed."[2]

In a form that still remained profoundly idealistic, Hegel's philosophy evoked a conception of the world corresponding to the spirit of his time and to the aspirations of German youth: the noble concept of the unity of the material and the intellectual, of their reciprocal action, of their interdependent development; the sovereignty of reason, which was capable of penetrating and mastering the totality of the real world in its contradictions and its movement.

The Hegelian system, to be sure, winds up in an eventual reconciliation with the world as it is, giving its "rational" blessing to the bourgeois order, as in other days the theory of "divine right" gave its blessing to the feudal order and to absolute monarchs.

But to the Hegelian conservative interpretation of the "right," which placed the emphasis on the system and justified the policy of immobility, the "left" Hegelian could easily oppose to the *constituted* Hegelian *system* the *constituting* Hegelian *method*, and discover in this dialectical method of the exploration of *becoming* and its contradictions the best critical weapon against the existing order. As young Marx was soon to write, this method was capable of compelling "these petrified relations . . . to dance by singing their own tune back to them."[3]

This "algebra of the revolution" fascinated the Young Hegelians, although it was conceived by them in a speculative form. All the more since, under the repression of the Holy Alliance and of Prussian reaction, their political aspirations readily accepted a philosophical protective coloration.

In an article written in his youth, Marx's friend, Engels, wrote: "The question is posed: What is God? And German philosophy answered: It is man."

But Engels soon added that if man is God, the task that remained was to organize a world worthy of him.

This attitude was characteristic of the young Hegelians. They found in Hegel the evangelist of the apotheosis of man, the exaltation of their Faustian desire to become God themselves. In the introduction to his doctoral thesis, Marx wrote (1841):

"Philosophy makes no secret of it. Prometheus's admission: 'In sooth all gods I hate,' is its own admission, its own motto against all gods, heavenly and earthly, who do not acknowledge the consciousness of man as the supreme divinity. There must be no god on a level with it . . .

"Prometheus is the noblest of saints and martyrs in the calendar of philosophy."[4]

But if Hegel held out such promise and could inspire such hopes, his system could not long satisfy the Young Hegelians, because historical reality was already overtaking Hegel's philosophy and cracks were appearing everywhere.

After having raised the self to absolute spirit, that is, to God, and after having identified God with the totality of being, the Hegelian system arrived at the point of considering that nature was God manifested in space and that history was God manifested in time. Nature and history could thus be reconstructed speculatively and in an absolute manner.

Now, the progress of the natural sciences made the speculations on "the philosophy of nature" fall apart, just as the uprising of the silk workers of Lyons, the Chartist movement in England, the revolt of the Silesian weavers had made speculations on the "philosophy of history" fall apart. These first reverberating underground fore-runners of a new class struggle showed that the rule of the bourgeoisie was not the rule of the rational, that perhaps this rule was not to be eternal, and that history was (not) yet completely written.

The first fundamental challenge to the Hegelian system was that of Strauss, in his *Life of Jesus* (1835).

Starting with the theological problem of how to reconcile the personal and historical character of Christ and of the Revelation with the Hegelian absolute concept identified with the totality of being, Strauss actually exploded that tenet of the Hegelian system which rested on the positing of God, nature and history at the heart of dialectical reasoning.

Altogether beyond the original intent of the author, this book had profound repercussions. By disassociating philosophy and religion, it led the "Hegelians of the left" toward atheism. By disassociating logic and history, rendering to history its own reality and autonomy, it led the Hegelians of the left no longer to limit the task of dialectics to "understanding that which is," as Hegel put it, but to "extend into the future the dialectical movement of the idea which Hegel had frozen in the present."[5]

Thereafter, for the Young Hegelians (and this was to be the first important turning point in philosophy since Hegel), Hegelianism was no longer a solution but a program, and the password now was "the realization of philosophy." Philosophy was no longer, as with Hegel, harmony with oneself, reconciliation with the world, but rebellion against the world.

This was a point of departure for young Marx, as attested by the preparatory notes for his doctoral thesis (1839–41):

"The theoretical spirit, having been liberated, is transformed into practical energy; it willingly emerges from the kingdom of the shadows of Amenti and turns toward the material reality that exists independently of it. . . .

"The becoming-philosophy of the world is at the same time the becoming-world of philosophy. . . .

"In liberating the world from nonphilosophy, we are liberated from that philosophy which, as a fixed system, has burdened us with chains!"[6]

It was then that true criticism began, that is, "the act by which philosophy is turned outward to the world."

It remained only to make the revolution in the consciousness of man, to destroy the old values in the minds of man before destroying them in substance.

Idealism remains; the rebellion of reality against a philosophy which attempted to eternalize one phase of its own development is still reflected as fantasy in the minds of our Young Hegelians, in the form of the revolt of the idea against the world which is its image.

Hegel led them to the threshold of the promised land, but only in thought. The Hegelian idea remained, but only as a program. This speculative illusion was destined to leave profound after-effects, even in the *Manuscripts of 1844*,[7] in which the idea of the "total" man in its speculative form was still to serve as a measuring rod by which to evaluate existing "estrangements" and to arrive at the eventual goal—communism.

The Stream of Fire: "*Feuer-bach*"

> Philosophy should not begin with itself but with its antithesis, nonphilosophy. . . . Thought arises from being and not being from thought.
>
> — FEUERBACH[1]

In 1841 Marx finished his doctoral thesis on "The Differences between the Natural Philosophy of Democritus and the Natural Philosophy of Epicurus." Although this thesis took its cue from Hegel's *History of Philosophy*, it did not reflect Hegel's hostility to the materialism of Epicurus. Marx admired Epicurus for having preserved (as against the determinism of Democritus) the possibility of the freedom necessary to action; but he criticized Epicurus for having opposed freedom to necessity without seeing their dialectical interrelation. The problem of freedom, as Marx had already pointed out, would be resolved only if the dialectical relation between necessity and freedom was encompassed; or, to put it more concretely, the relation between man and the world, instead of considering man in isolation and in his abstract autonomy.

Marx had already vigorously affirmed, in opposition to the other Young Hegelians, that he considered the dialectical movement as integral to reality and not separate from it. At the same time, however, in opposition to Hegel, he insisted on substituting concrete history for abstract speculation.

Marx received his Ph.D. on April 15, 1841. Several months afterward Feuerbach's *Essence of Christianity* appeared, the outstanding philosophical event since Hegel's death. In the course of the following two years, the *Provisional Theses for the Reform of Philosophy* (1842), and the *Principles of the Philosophy of the Future* (1843) were published.

Feuerbach, extending and deepening Strauss's criticism, established in the first place—in opposition to Hegel—the incompatibility of philosophy and religion, of reason and faith.

Then, generalizing his criticism, he denounced Hegel's assumption of the unity of mind and matter, of man and the world, while attributing to the spirit the totality of the real. "The path followed up to now by speculative philosophy—from the abstract to the concrete, from the ideal to the real—is the path that leads to misunderstanding. . . . Being, with which philosophy begins, is not being that is separated from consciousness, nor consciousness that is separated from being."[2]

Nature exists independently of consciousness; beyond nature and man, there are only imaginary and illusory representations.

Thus the Hegelian system is reversed: Where Hegel says "spirit," Feuerbach says "matter"; where Hegel says "God," Feuerbach says "man." It is not God who is estranged from man; it is man who is estranged from God.

Feuerbach summed up his thought in a formulation that Marx was to use later in the text of his *Contribution to the Critique of Hegel's Philosophy of Right:* "putting the predicate in place of the subject and the subject in place of the predicate." Being is the subject, thought is the predicate; that is, the idea, according to Feuerbach, is a reflection of the world and not the other way around.

The effect upon the Young Hegelians of this reversal was prodigious. "We all became at once Feuerbachians,"[3] wrote Engels.

Marx then declared: "I advise you, you theologians and speculative philosophers, to rid yourselves of the concepts and prejudices of the old speculative philosophy if you want to deal with things as they are in reality, that is, in truth. And there is no other road for you toward truth and freedom than this 'stream of fire' ('Feuer-bach'). Feuerbach is the purgatory of our time."[4]

Marx's enthusiasm for the reversal wrought by Feuerbach should not lead us to the serious error of identifying Feuerbach's reversal of the Hegelian *system* with Marx's reversal of the Hegelian *method*.

There can be no doubt that Feuerbach's work constituted a decisive stage in the development of post-Hegelian thought. For example, before that time the Young Hegelians, especially Bruno Bauer and Karl Marx, had considered Hegel as being opposed to Christian theology; Feuerbach, on the contrary, defined Hegel's philosophy as Christian philosophy decoded by dialectics and, revealing the close kinship between absolute idealism and religion, he wrote: "If one does not renounce Hegel's philosophy, one does not renounce theology."[5]

Feuerbach's basic idea was that of *alienation*.

For man, alienation consisted in regarding what was in truth his own work, the fruit of his creativeness, as a reality exterior and superior to himself.

In the *Essence of Christianity*, Feuerbach defines alienation thus: "Man transforms the subjective, i.e., the actuality of which exists only in his mind, his perception, his imagination, into something existing beyond his thought, his perception, his imagination. . . . Thus the Christians detach the mind and soul of man from his body, and make of this detached spirit, deprived of a body, their God." In his VIIth Lesson, he characterizes this inversion thus: "To deduce nature from God is like wanting to deduce an original from a copy of a picture, or a thing from the mere idea of the thing."

In the perspective of Hegelian idealism, the entire material world is an "alienation" from the soul. For Feuerbach, the transcendance of God is an alienation: "Man projects his being beyond himself . . . the opposition of the divine and the human is an illusory opposition . . . all divine decisions are the decisions of a human being."[6] In a word, it is not God who created man in his own image; it is man who created the gods in his image.

According to Hegel, says Feuerbach, man is an alienation from God. One must turn this formula around: God is an alienation from man. Man is the subject; God, the predicate. Man is not individual man but species-man, and God is the ideal he projects in a heaven beyond himself. This alienation is the consequence of the division of man within himself. It can only be resolved by knowledge, which dispels the transcendance of God as, in Hegel, consciousness dispels the exteriority of the object.

Thus the goal of history is changed. For Hegel it is the realization of God in man; for Feuerbach, it is the realization of man when he ceases to project himself in God. The goal of Feuerbach is to liberate man from religion and to arrive at the unity of man with man. It is this humanism that Feuerbach calls communism; man divested of religion will find his unity in communism.

This philosophical "communism" is no more identified with the struggle for the interests of the working class than it is with a radical transformation of bourgeois society; it deals solely with substituting for traditional religion, humanism that is called materialist and atheist in the consciousness of men.

Thus we have here only a "reversal" of the Hegelian *system*. To reverse the Hegelian system is not to change its nature; to reverse an idealist system into a materialist one is to build a dogmatic materialism, analogous to Hegel's dogmatic idealism. Hegel's ghost haunts Feuerbach's materialism, which is naturalized Hegelianism. The dialectic attributed by Hegel to absolute spirit is now introduced into nature in dogmatic form. The metaphysics of Hegel becomes anthropology, and real man is an alienated religious man.

This anthropology is, according to Feuerbach, the truth about religion. He does not succeed in liberating himself from theology; he finds a human justification for it—man, according to him, is human; God is his ideal. The reconciliation of man with other men, in love, is humanism realized. Feuerbach has thus replaced one religion with another, deifying love, the dialogue between "me" and "you."

Hence we remain with Feuerbach on the inside of ideology. We have not emerged, even while reversing it from what Marx called "the cage of the Hegelian idea." The Hegelian idealist system inverted into a materialist one similarly emerges into theology.

A true reversal would be of quite another nature, and it was Marx alone who was to accomplish this. For this purpose, he had not only to upset the cage, the system, but also to shatter it, to reject it entirely, and enter into the real world of men, their work and their struggles.

As Engels wrote later in *Ludwig Feuerbach*, one does not pass from Feuerbach's abstract man to real, living man unless one knows him in action, in history.

Marx was not to arrive at this conclusion immediately; indeed, he was to make a long detour before arriving at it. He began by applying the method of Feuerbach to the critique of the state as well as to the critique of religion. This he does in his "Manuscripts of 1843" (generally referred to as *The Critique of Hegel's Philosophy of Right*).

As criticized by Feuerbach, religion is only the theoretical form of alienation. Practical forms, however, do exist. Marx understood how to pass from the critique of heaven to the critique of earth, from religious alienation to political alienation ("Manuscripts of 1843"), and from political alienation to economic alienation (*Economic and Philosophic Manuscripts of 1844*).

It would be a profound error to reduce Marxist thought to this single movement, this transition from one alienation to others, religious, political, social, economic. R. P. Calvez commits this error in his book, *Marx's Thought.*[7] All this was Marxist thought before Marxism, that is, it was speculative thought seeking a philosophical base—not yet having found its historical, class and scientific bases.

The "Manuscripts of 1843" are only one stage in Marx's development toward materialism and political radicalism. The method of the work is borrowed from Feuerbach. It is based on a materialist application of the theory of alienation.

Feuerbach had made his criticism of Christianity from a materialist point of view, that is, he had shown that the image and the need of God were celestial projections of terrestrial reality by man—in his sensuous, natural reality. Generalizing his thesis, he regarded Hegelian philosophy, both idealist and speculative, as the last form of theology; "speculative philosophy," he wrote, "is true theology."[8]

Philosophy, having become materialist, should take its point of departure from nature and not from the idea. Extending the traditions of the English and French materialists still further, he asserted:

"The real, considered in its true essence, is the real only in being an object of the senses, of sensuousness. The sensuous, the true, the real, are identical. It is only through the senses that the object is truly given."[9]

This naturalism and empiricism were criticized by Marx from the very outset. "The only point," he wrote in a letter to Ruge (March 13, 1843), "where I depart from Feuerbach is when he attributes too much importance, in my opinion, to nature and not enough to politics. It is only in allying oneself with politics that an actual philosophy can be fully achieved."[10]

To Feuerbach, the environment of which man is the product was nature and not society. Even if Marx had not yet arrived at clearly discerning one of the fundamental concepts that he would later express in his *Manuscripts of 1844*, i.e., that the relations between man and nature are not direct, but pass through society by the mediation of labor, he had already advanced beyond naturalist, empiricist, or mechanistic forms of materialism.

The link between man and nature, according to Feuerbach, is direct; it does not consist of labor but of contemplation. Such materialism does not make possible the resolution of historical and social problems. "As far as Feuerbach is a materialist he does not deal with history, and as far as he considers history he is not a materialist,"[11] Marx was soon to write, at the time when he would be developing the grand design of his own historical materialism (1845).

Thus, for example, Feuerbach conceives of surmounting religious alienation only by a form of purely natural communion, the universal love of species-men; while for Marx alienation could only be overcome by the active intervention of man in his environment.

Feuerbach could not find the key to the question of the Hegelian "left," i.e., how to make of philosophy an instrument of political and social action:

"Feuerbach starts out from the fact of religious self-alienation. . . . His work consists in the dissolution of the religious world into its secular basis. He overlooks the fact that after completing this work, the chief thing still remains to be done. For the fact that the secular foundation lifts itself above itself and establishes itself in the clouds as an independent realm is only to be explained by the self-cleavage and self-contradictoriness of this secular basis. The latter must itself therefore be understood in its contradiction and then, by the removal of the contradiction, revolutionized in practice."[12]

Nevertheless, the work of Feuerbach had given an impetus toward materialism and the critique of alienation, and this was to enable the Young Hegelians to proceed from that point to materialism, to political radicalism, and to "philosophical" communism. Engels freely acknowledged this debt when he said that among the German theoreticians of socialism and communism "almost none . . . arrived at Communism otherwise than by way of the Feuerbachian dissolution of Hegelian speculation."[13]

In a letter dated August 11, 1844, Marx wrote to Feuerbach: "You have given to socialism—I don't know whether by deliberate intention—a philosophical base."

It is, incidentally, in this sense that Moses Hess, who in 1843–44 exerted a great influence on the evolution of Marx's thinking, developed a conception of utopian communism based not on the idea of class struggle and the proletarian revolution, but on the Feuerbachian idea that the fundamental issue was that of the surmounting of alienation. But, for Hess, the primordial alienation was not that of religion, it was that which is engendered by the system of private property. This speculative conception of communism left its imprint on many passages of the *Manuscripts of 1844*.

In his *Critique of Hegel's Philosophy of Right* Marx limited himself to applying to the critique of the state the method applied by Feuerbach to the critique of religion. But already the first contacts Marx was having with workaday reality, as well as the historical studies to which his *Notebooks of Kreuznach* (1843)[14] testify, enabled him to go beyond Feuerbach's horizons in his critique of Hegel.

Having become, after completing his thesis, co-editor, then editor in chief, of the *Rheinische Zeitung*,* young Marx had to deal with problems which his philosophical formulations alone did not enable him to resolve. Analyzing the debates that took place in the Rhenish Diet (May to July, 1841), Marx took cognizance, in an article on

---

* A new liberal journal, published in Cologne, which represented the industrial, Protestant interest as against the feudal and reactionary Catholic influence. Marx took up his editorial duties in 1842.—*Ed.*

freedom of the press, of the fact that the bourgeois representatives were not, as they professed, expressing the general interest but rather the specific interests of their own class. In another article on the law on thefts of lumber, if he did not as yet recognize the legal reflection of the struggle between the old feudal social relations (which had tolerated the gathering of wood on the old communal lands) and the rapacity of the new proprietary capitalists, nonetheless he did discover that the law was the instrument of private interests. Taking his stand not on historic and social grounds but rather on juridical and ethical grounds, he invoked the ancient right as the right of the destitute. It was in this spirit that he approached the *Critique of Hegel's Philosophy of Right* (1843).[15]

The problem was to determine the nature of the state and its relations with civil society, that is to say, with the totality of economic and social interests.

Moses Hess had already applied Feuerbach's method to the study of political and social organization and had shown that men in alienating their generic qualities, as citizens, in the state were reduced to the situation of isolated, egocentric individuals in civil society.

The younger Marx denounced the mystification of the state in Hegel, who, by constructing a rational system for the Prussian state—the incarnation and standard-bearer of reason—justified the monarchy and its institutions. By the same token, the state as ruler and creator of society in its totality was rationalized, together with its reactionary political institutions, its private property in bourgeois forms such as primogeniture, and so on.

In a minute criticism, paragraph by paragraph, Marx revised the Hegelian schema by establishing that it was not the state that gives rise to civil society but, on the contrary, it was civil society that gives rise to the state. Far from existing above class interests, the state is the expression of class interest. "Here," he wrote, "the political system is the political system of private property."

Generalizing this reversal, Marx established the fact that Hegel's speculative method not only reversed the relations between "civil society and state, but the relations between subject and object as well." Referring to paragraph 262 of *Philosophy of Right,* in which Hegel made the family and the property system the products of the state, rather than the other way around, Marx wrote: "In this paragraph is buried all the mystery of the philosophy of right and *Hegelian philosophy in general.*"

Which is to say that Marx rejected not only the creative role ascribed by Hegel to the state so far as civil society was concerned, but also the creative role attributed to the concept in relation to sensuous reality. This work by Marx signalizes an important stage in the transition from idealism to materialism, as well as in the genesis of historical materialism.

Fifteen years afterwards Marx was to draw up a balance sheet on this research. After having recalled that his functions as editor of the *Rheinische Zeitung* had put him "for the first time" in the embarrassing position of having "to take part in discussions on so-called material interests," he adds, "The first work undertaken for the solution of the question that troubled me, was a critical revision of Hegel's "Philosophy of Law." . . . I was led by my studies to the conclusion that the legal relations, as well as forms of state, could neither be understood by themselves, nor explained by the so-called general progress of the human mind; but that they are rooted in the material conditions of life, which are summed up by Hegel after the fashion of the English and French of the 18th century under the name of 'civil society'; the anatomy of that civil society is to be sought in political economy."[16]

These methodological conclusions, the first step toward historical materialism, touched mainly on the provisional political conclusions of Marx. After having established the fact that the system of private ownership, with the conflict it engenders of all against all, prevents man from leading a collective life in conformity with his "true nature," he did not as yet dream of surmounting this alienation by the class struggle and the proletarian revolution, but rather by the establishment of a "genuine democracy," by replacing the monarchy with a republic and universal suffrage.

The extension of these perspectives, which were those of bourgeois radicalism, would require the transition to another, a class point of view.

The decisive step that led Marx to the threshold of Marxism was to be the understanding that the conquest of alienation meant the

abolition of private ownership, and that the proletariat alone, through
its struggles and its revolution, could bring this to pass.

Marx advanced beyond this stage not by theoretical investigation
alone but by a profound contact with the working class.

The Fichtean Heritage and
the Heresy of Prometheus

> Humanity rejects blind chance and the power of fate. It
> holds its fate in its own hands.
> — FICHTE, *A Report Clear as Day*

An error that might lead to a dogmatic and precritical interpretation of Marxist philosophy is that of reducing the heritage of
German philosophy to Hegel and Feuerbach and underestimating the
importance of what Marx learned from Kant and Fichte and then
incorporated into his own conception of the world.

A letter Marx wrote his father (November 10, 1837) * already had
indicated that his first philosophical reflections were nurtured by
"Kant and by Fichte." This was not merely a passing intellectual
phase. At the end of his life, Engels was to recall that Fichte was one
of the sources of scientific socialism. "We German socialists are
proud of the fact that we are derived not only from Saint-Simon,
Fourier and Owen, but also from Kant, Fichte and Hegel."[1]

Auguste Cornu, in his great work on Karl Marx, points out the
essential concepts that Marx borrowed from classical German philosophy: the unity of intellectual and material reality and their reciprocal action, the fundamental immanence of intelligence in history,
the idea of becoming, contradiction as the motive force of becoming.[2]

Fichte, more than anyone else, integrated man into the world: Man
could achieve self-consciousness and develop fully only in the process
of building the future of his world. Marx, from the time of his earliest studies, strove to give a concrete character to this conception of

* See p. 19.

the world. "Liberating myself from the idealism I had imbibed from certain elements in the thinking of Fichte and Kant," he wrote his father (November 10, 1837), I arrived at the point of seeking the idea in reality itself. The gods, hitherto enthroned above the earth, now became the center of it."

The intellectual environment in which Marx worked out his conception of the world was imbued with Fichtean thought.

It is worthy of note, for example, that the idea of "praxis," to which Marx was to give concrete historical-social-materialist meaning was indubitably of Fichtean origin. In his *Preface to the Philosophy of History* (1838), Von Cieszkowski evolved a philosophy of praxis that Fichte borrowed—the basic idea of which was that action determined the future, in opposition to being; in other words, in opposing to being (i.e., the existing world) the ideal that it still must realize, i.e., "the ought-to-be."

Thus philosophy adopted, with Von Cieszkowski, in Utopian form, the character of a weapon in the political struggle, but only insofar as its aims were set in accordance with the principles of bourgeois rationalism. It was the first breakthrough from Hegelian philosophy, which up to that point had deduced only the laws of development of past history. Von Cieszkowski's philosophy of action required that these laws be applied to building the future.

This transition from a philosophy of speculation to a philosophy of action was expressed even more clearly by Moses Hess. He linked Fichte's primacy of action and the individual man to Feuerbach's conception of alienation and the need to conquer it so that the individual would no longer be separated from the community, the real autonomy of man being realizable only under communism.

Going beyond Hegel, Bruno Bauer adopted the Fichtean thesis according to which consciousness makes progress only by constantly surmounting the reality it has already encompassed. Thus he rejects the conservative aspects of Hegel's conception of mind. But this criticism takes place on the purely intellectual plane and remains there, abstract and impotent: The mind, alienated from the world, opposing what ought to be to being, was the motive force of history.

What Marx adduced that was new, in relation to all these idealistic and utopian conceptions of communism, was above all the idea of the indissoluble unity of mind and matter. He was grateful to Fichte who, defending the principle of the autonomy of the individual, rejected all religious authority and posed the atheistic and Promethean premise of a great bourgeois humanism, of which communism would constitute, from the viewpoint of a new class, the highest form.*

Marx considered Kant and Fichte the representatives of the grand bourgeois humanism whose fundamental principle was to treat man always as an end and never as a means, although to them this axiom remained still abstract, external to history. To no one more than to Fichte does Marx's definition of German philosophy apply ("It is the German theory of the French Revolution").

The French Revolution appeared to Fichte as the attempt of a great people to base its political life no longer on tradition or authority but on reason. His ambition was to systematize the philosophy implicit in this revolution, which had revealed dynamic aspects of existence, such as the role of free and creative activity by man, and the autonomy of reason. "My system," he wrote, "is the first system of liberty. Just as the French nation delivers humanity from material chains, my system delivers it from the yoke of the thing-in-itself, and from outside influences; its first principles make an autonomous being of man. The *Doctrine of Science* was born during the years when the French nation, by dint of its great power, brought about the triumph of political liberty . . . and this conquest of liberty helped to give birth to the *Doctrine of Science*. . . . While I was writing a book on the revolution, the first signs, the first prophecy of my system arose within me as a sort of reward."[3]

Fichte's philosophy, in a somewhat mystical, idealist and metaphysical form, reveals the source of the three great philosophical

---

* The influence exerted by Fichte on Marx's thinking is thus put on the plane of philosophy, of the conception of man and his practice, and not, as Jaurès thought in his Latin thesis on "The Origins of German Socialism" (1890), on the plane of collectivist theory.

It is Fichte's *Doctrine of Science*, with its reflections on the creative action of man, on the primacy of action, on the necessity of the transcendance of the individual in the rational totality, which left its mark on young Marx.

On the other hand, the state capitalism, on which Fichte theorized in "The Closed Commercial State," in trying to introduce into Prussia certain of the economic measures of the bourgeois revolution in France, had nothing in common with Marxist socialism, founded on the history and struggle of classes.

themes that concern Marxists: the development of Marx's counsel to put back on their feet a theory of freedom, a theory of subjectivity, a theory of practice.

1. *Freedom* is the keystone of Fichte's system, the source of all action and of all reality. Marx revealed very early what was profoundly progressive in this affirmation of the greatness of man and this optimistic conception of the world. In his "Remarks on the Regimentation of Prussian Censorship" (1843),[4] Marx invoked the intellectual heroes of morality, Kant, Fichte and Spinoza, for example. All these moralists subscribed to the idea that there is a contradiction in principle between ethics and religion, since ethics is based on the autonomy of the human spirit and religion on its heteronomy.

Against traditional conceptions of religion and of feudal and monarchical regimes, Fichte proclaimed that freedom is the right to refuse to recognize laws other than those one has imposed on oneself, and that such freedom ought to exist in every state.

Marx saw in this attitude the true Copernican revolution in ethics and politics; the law no longer gravitated about God or king but about man, every man. Evoking this "law of gravitation of the state" —which he compares to Copernicus' discovery—Marx wrote in an editorial (*Neue Rheinische Zeitung*, 1842, No. 179): "Machiavelli and Campanella at first . . . and later Hobbes, Spinoza and Hugo Grotius followed by Rousseau, Fichte and Hegel, began to consider the state with the eyes of man and to develop its natural laws from reason and experience, not from theology, any more than Copernicus let himself be influenced by Joshua's supposed command to the sun to stand still over Gideon and the moon over the vale of Ajalon."[5]

The governing idea of Fichte's system is that of man the creator, the idea that man is what he does. For the first time in the history of philosophy, the primacy of essence was advanced vis-à-vis the *a priori* theological or anthropological "definition" of man, with the emphasis on free creative activity.

The first principle of existentialism may no doubt be discerned here[6]: In man, essence precedes nature; as well as the theme of the Fichtean Lequier, so often embraced by existentialists, to act and in that action to create oneself; to be nothing other than that which one creates. But Marxism follows the lessons of Fichte more faithfully than this, since for the rationalist Fichte—at the opposite pole

from the irrationalist Kierkegaard, father of existentialism—the relation between nature and essence is dialectical. To exist, for Fichte,
is to act, to create. This activity, this creation transcends all that
has already been created and tested by the laws of knowledge, which
is a secondary reflection from man's initial action and creation. This
creative activity in no way nullifies man's previous work; it constitutes the totality of conditions imposed on and limiting man's
action, just as it constitutes the essence of man—not *a priori*, not
even established but always in process of development, always being
enriched. The rationalism of Fichte, giving consistency and reality
to those rational gleanings that human creativeness leaves behind
in the furrows of its plow, suggests, at least in abstract form, what
happens to the principle of historical materialism itself in the process
of being made concrete by social and historical practice. "Men make
their own history, but they do not make it just as they please; they
do not make it under circumstances chosen by themselves, but under
circumstances directly encountered, given and transmitted from the
past."[7]

In accepting Fichte's discovery and putting it on its feet, i.e., in
materialist perspective, Marxism similarly accepts and transcends
one of the valid themes of existentialism. Human existence is not a
thing which *is given* but a thing to *make*. But the existentialists developed this theme one-sidedly—abandoning not only Marxist materialism but Fichtean rationalism.

Existence is not *given* in the sense of "nature," as the empiricists
and pre-Marxist materialists understood it, nor in the sense of an
"essence," as dogmatic rationalism and pre-Marxist dialectics understood it.

It is because existence is characterized by *making*, by creation,
that history ensues, that the new constantly emerges. It is because
this creation is rational, because freedom is not opposed to either
reason or necessity that this history is not arbitrary but meaningful.

Doubtless Fichte's conception of history, like the conception of
freedom that gave rise to it, is idealist and metaphysical. Idealist,
because of the *goal* that it ascribes to history—the realization of
freedom and reason; metaphysical, because of the *means* it suggests
toward this end, i.e., the motive force of human evolution is for
Fichte a purely rational development of consciousness.

Nevertheless, what remains is that Fichte had the merit of proclaiming, in the face of all theologies and all forms of religious or
metaphysical or political oppression, the heresy of Prometheus:
"Humanity," he wrote, "rejects blind chance and the power of fate.
It holds its fate in its own hands; it accomplishes freely what it has
resolved to do."[8]

2. Fichte's conception of *subjectivity* arises from his conception
of freedom. In *The Holy Family*[9] Marx contrasts the abstract
Fichtean "ego" to the egoistic individualism of Stirner. This is a
necessary distinction if one is to understand Fichte's "ego." Neither
the ego with which he begins nor that at which he finally arrives can
be confounded with egoistic individualism.

The ego from which he begins is not that of individualism since
it is not a thing *given* but an act: the active subject who virtually
carries within himself the law of reason. Thus the subject is an
abstraction, capable of being isolated only by reflection as a pure
form of subjectivity.

The ego, which is the idealist term of the system, is the subject
who has fully realized within himself and outside himself (in nature
and society) a world entirely amenable to reason, and who has
therefore ceased to be a specific individual.

The ego of Fichte is the law of reason, at first in the guise of the
seed, the promise; then under the guise of the ideal, of total
rationality. In principle, as well as in terminology, the ego of Fichte,
far from being isolated in its sensuous particularity and being controlled by it, expresses the demand for the realization of rational
universality. It is the act of taking part in universal history. This
ego is, primarily, the terrain occupied by virtually all humanity. It
is the reflection of all humanity—not only of its past culture, but
of what it will be called upon to become in the totality of its history.
Far from teaching man an existential individualism (with all that
this implies—from Stirner to Heidegger—of solitude, impotence,
despair, of absurd, casual factitiousness)), Fichte presents the ego as
the very act of passing from the particular to the universal, from the
finite to the infinite.

In *The German Ideology*, Marx emphasized this transition from
the individual to the universal in Fichte: "Saint Max [Stirner]
admits that the Ego receives an 'impulse' (in Fichte's sense) from

the world. That the communists intend to gain control over this
'impulse'—which indeed becomes an extremely complex and multi-
farious 'impulse' if one is not content with the mere phrase—is, of
course, for Saint Max much too daring an idea to discuss."[10]

What is characteristic in Fichte's conception of the ego is its
continual transcendence. At every moment the ego sets a limit and
simultaneously leaps over it, as if the infinite were calling it; its
present is never defined except in terms of its future growth. The ego
is always project: What I have been and what I am only assumes
its full meaning in the light of what I am about to be. Existence
is therefore never a *given*, but a creation. It is always on the way
to making itself. In contrast to existentialism, nothingness is not
considered freedom; it is, on the contrary, the "non-ego," while
freedom is identified with actual being, that is, with the act of
creation. In Fichte, existence is not, as with Kierkegaard and his
existential offspring, the lonely and despairing dialogue between
subjectivity and transcendence, but a free and creative act.

That is why this theory of freedom and subjectivity results in a
theory of practice.

3. *Practice*, according to Fichte, has, in the first place, a historical
dimension: Each particular subject being potentially the absolute
subject, the life of subjectivity, like human history, has this contradictory unity as its content. What is created and encompassed
in the world is the passage from the individual to the universal in
man, the elevation of the finite to the infinite, the transformation of
necessity into freedom.

The task of philosophy, the highest expression of self-consciousness,
is to raise each man to the level of a fully rational and free human
life. The *Doctrine of Science* teaches us that the goal of existence is
to establish the dominion of the rational within ourselves and outside
of ourselves, in nature and in society.

Fichte transcends Kant's notion of practical reason. In Kant, the
"field" of practical reason is that of a duel between the sense of
duty (discovered by each of us in the solitude of his own conscience) and nature (of which our bodies constitute a part). Fichte
goes further: In practical reason he includes all the creative activity
of man. Reason is theoretical when a representation of things is
given; it is practical when it submits things to its own concepts,

when it molds or creates them according to its own laws. Thus there is in Fichte, in embryo and in abstract form, the idea of the unity of theory and practice, and the idea of freedom as conscious necessity.

Fichte's idealism is a philosophy of action. Authentic reality for him is in the act and not in being. That is why he does not conceive of history as an accomplished whole. In order to render intelligible the act by which each man participates in the collective enterprise of species-man, disregarding his own limitations and exceeding them, Fichte does not need to posit himself at the end of history to have the entire panorama of being spread out before his consciousness. Each of us, from the very fact of his participation in the common task, is capable of an "intellectual intuition," which is not. as in Kant, the hypothetical divine act, of being totally in the grip of the absolute, but the characteristically human act of the grasp of the absolute as the grasp of freedom, of the creative act. Thus one escapes from the choice between dogmatism and scepticism, restoring—in an idealistic form, to be sure—the unity of theory and practice.

In this dialectical, contradictory unity, the mind recognizes the non-ego, and the will affirms the ego. The contradiction is insurmountable since its solution is projected into infinity. The world is a reflection, the expression of formal freedom, the arena of conflict between being and non-being, the absolute internal contradiction.

Religion itself is for Fichte—at least in his *Doctrine of Science*— merely the promise and the description of the ideal goal of the progressive movement, at the end of which practice would be definitively victorious. The struggle being interminable, intellectual intuition is always militant, never triumphant; it is the revelation of the meaning of that which forever remains the absolute contradiction. understanding the signification of all that is apparently given, of all limitations, as a provisional negation of creative activity. This theory of science puts an end—in an idealist frame of reference— to the myth of a thing-in-itself, forever unknowable, which constitutes, from without, an absolute limit to the understanding and the activity of man. The absolute which Kant posited outside the human world is now identified with the movement of history, with the march of progress, with the effort that undermines all limitations from within.

Hence the philosopher is inseparable from the man of action, from the militant, a fact of which Fichte's life affords many examples. In spite of his Kantian vocabulary and his idealism, to Fichte practice is definitely the engagement of the whole man in the collective effort to make history, to transform nature and to build society.

Fichte has not only extracted the "active side of knowledge," but has posited man's activity on the highest level; above all, the transformation of the subjective into the objective by human activity. He discovered the dialectical relation between the subjective and the objective, the essential dialectics of historical and social development— in spite of the fact that for him Nature (idealistically mystified) may be the work of the ego; that the subject (metaphysically mystified) may be outside of history and time; and that objectification and alienation are confused with each other.

Since he advances beyond Kant's metaphysical dualism, which dug an unbridgable gap between nature and mind, Fichte saw in practical reason the crowning moment in the slow ascent which— from inert matter to the living, and then to the thinking, being— raises man to the consciousness of action by means of which he extends indefinitely the limits imposed by the non-ego on freedom.

Fichte also perceived—even if he presented the idea in an extreme form of idealism in which all nature is the object that the ego gives itself to support its activity—that nature, the most important factor in historical development is not "contemplative" (as the old materialism saw it), but rather a "second nature" created by man, in which he objectifies his own powers. This constitutes for man, as Marx points out in *The German Ideology*, the environment in constant development in which his activity, his work, his practice operates.

Fichte goes beyond Kant in still another respect: Practical reason for him had not only an ethical character, but also a social one. Man is destined to live in society; he is not wholly a man and there is a conflict within him when he is isolated. The individual is not a man except among men.

"The man who isolates himself," writes Fichte, "renounces his destiny; he detaches himself from ethical progress. Morally speaking, to think only of self is not even to think of self, since the absolute goal of the individual is not within himself—it is in all mankind. The sense of duty is not satisfied, as some believe and actually turn into a merit, by sequestering oneself on the heights of abstraction and pure speculation, by leading the life of an anchorite; it is satisfied not in dreams but in acts, acts accomplished in society and for it."[11]

The ethics of Fichte is differentiated from Kant's in the same way as the will to build humanity in history, by depending on nature in order to transcend it, is differentiated from the subjective effort toward individual sainthood.

The "negation of the negation," the act of transcending nature, which is only the first limitation set for the ego, is a collective act; it is all mankind that participates in this effort—the realization of the absolute, that is, freedom without limit within ourselves and in the outer world, is the goal of species-man.

Moreover, in advancing beyond the dualism of Kant, Fichte put an end to the ascetic conception of Kantian ethics; the body becomes doubly important since, in the first place, it expresses the action of the subject on things, and since it permits communication between each and all.

Thus Fichte went beyond both Kantian individualism and asceticism.

Hence, right is determined not only in terms of the individual but also in terms of the community. For example, the absolute individual right to property does not exist—which does not at all mean that Fichte conceived a socialist society. He opposed only the feudal absolutism of property and economic measures which he could not foresee as going beyond those that the French Revolution had conceived and realized, including the transfer of properties required by the national interest, such as the Jacobins had ordered.

Nonetheless, in the working out of his theory of the state and the contract and in spite of the exaggerated powers he attributes to the state, Fichte believed that man, driven into a corner by misery or hunger, is thereby freed from social obligation. He therefore goes beyond the conception of a formal freedom and moves toward the redemption of a real right.

Finally, he undoubtedly remained prisoner of a historical bourgeois conception of property (as a disciple of the French Revolution), and this gave him a metaphysical viewpoint: Property is the necessary background for the exercise of freedom and the essential material basis for action; but even when influenced by the very movement of history that had just put property in its feudal form to the test, he refused to identify property with the possession of inherited wealth. Here again, in accordance with the spirit that inspires his entire philosophy, he opposes the *act* to the *thing*. Labor remains the substance of property; according to the Fichtean theory of right, the only thing that belongs to me is that portion of matter to which my freedom is applied.

It would also be necessary to set aside the part of Fichte's work in which the Promethean titan of the *Doctrine of Science* is transformed into a docile subject proclaiming that philosophy "recognizes that everything is necessary and good and reconciles us with all that exists, such as it is, since this is the way it must be, in the final analysis."[12]

This would be radically to reject Marxism by presuming, as did Lassalle, to substitute Fichte's philosophy for dialectical materialism as the basis of socialism.

But what remains is the necessity for all Marxist philosophy to extract the "rational kernel" of Fichte's thought; to put back on their feet the lofty reflections on the creations of man, to integrate into Marxist thought the "critical" moment—not to rest there and thereby mutilate this thought on the dimension of subjectivity, but to assimilate the valid themes of the philosophy of existence as they are expressed in the rationalist perspective of Fichte.

II. MARXISM: A REVOLUTION IN PHILOSOPHY

The Three Sources

> Marx is the legitimate successor of the best that was created by humanity in the 19th century in the shape of German philosophy, English political economy and French Socialism.
>
> — LENIN[1]

The break between Marx and the Young Hegelians became apparent by the end of 1843. Marx's article on "The Jewish Question" had already foreshadowed this. Again, the basic idea of the article was, as in the *Critique of Hegel's Philosophy of Right,* an analysis of bourgeois society and the political state, and the divided role of man as egoistic individual and abstract citizen. But the analysis had led into practical questions about how to assure the emancipation of man. Marx's answer was directly opposite to that of the Young Hegelians, and especially of Bruno Bauer, who claimed that in order to liberate man it would be sufficient to dissipate religious illusions and to change the political order. For Marx, true emancipation would have to be not only religious but political and social as well:

"Political emancipation is the reduction of man, on the one hand, to being a member of bourgeois society, an egoistic and independent individual and, on the other, to being a citizen, an ethical person.

"Human emancipation is achieved only when man has recognized and organized his own forces as social forces and therefore no longer estranges social force from himself in the form of political force."[2]

In thus posing the abolition of private property as an essential precondition, Marx advanced from bourgeois democracy to communism. But if he had decided on a new goal, he had not yet defined the means for reaching it. At this stage, it was still possible to end up in Utopia if the real forces capable of realizing communism were not understood.

In this respect, the rupture with the Young Hegelians was even more radical. From 1840 on, the Young Hegelians had one by one lost their literary jobs; in the face of the repressive violence of the state, pure theory had proven itself powerless. In Germany, it was not even possible to practice journalism. Bruno Bauer and his friends therefore turned away from the absurd "reality" and exalted the individual consciousness as the sacred, inviolable refuge for criticism. This attitude led them into an individualistic anarchism expressed in its most radical terms (and at the same time the least offensive) in *The Ego and His Own*,[3] the work of Stirner, one of the ancestors of existentialism.

Marx and some of the Young Hegelians (Ruge and Hess, particularly) were to choose another path. The material power of the state had been able to prevail because philosophy, remaining isolated among intellectuals, had not been able to answer violence with violence. The imperative task from now on was for philosophy to go to the masses. Marx drew this conclusion explicitly (early in 1844): "Material force must be overthrown by material force; but theory also becomes a material force as soon as it has gripped the masses."[4]

But for theory to grip the masses, it was essential that it first enter into their problems; it was essential that it should not remain utopian but that it should express the people's deepest aspirations. "Theory is fulfilled in a people only insofar as it is the fulfillment of the needs of that people. . . . It is not enough for thought to strive for realization, reality must itself strive towards thought."[5]

The radical negation of property—a necessary condition for man's emancipation—is, in some way, embodied in a specific class: "When the proletariat demands the negation of private property, it is only establishing as a principle for society what society has already established as a principle for the proletariat—which the latter, for some reason, already personifies as the negative result of society."[6]

The logical conclusion follows: "As philosophy finds its *material* weapon in the proletariat, so the proletariat finds its *spiritual* weapon in philosophy. . . . Philosophy cannot be made a reality without the abolition of the proletariat, the proletariat cannot be abolished without philosophy being made a reality."[7]

To make progress in this direction, what still remained was the necessity to communicate with the people. Marx had to publish abroad to get by the Prussian censor and repression, just as in the preceding century the French Encyclopedists had to publish their works in Amsterdam or London.

It was also essential to learn the deepest aspirations of the proletariat from its most conscious and active members, in order to achieve the fusion between the most advanced theory and the most advanced practice.

Marx was fully aware that the radical metamorphosis of philosophy demanded a change in class and class perspective which alone would make possible the entrance into another world. He wrote to Ruge (May 1843): "The bourgeois world constitutes the brutal world, the dehumanized world. . . . Let the dead bury the dead and mourn for them. The thing to be desired, however, is to be the first to enter alive into a new life—that must be our destination."

Marx had no doubt as to where he could discover the most advanced revolutionary practice; it was Paris. He named his revue *Deutsche-Französishe Jahrbücher* (Franco-Prussian Annals), announcing that it concerns teaching the Germans to "speak French," that is, to act in a revolutionary manner. The *Contribution to the Critique of Hegel's Philosophy of Right* ended: "When all the inner requisites are fulfilled, the *day of German resurrection* will be proclaimed by the crowing of the cock of Gaul."[8]

Thus, Paris seemed to be the very heart of the revolutionary movement. Engels wrote:

"France alone contains Paris, the city where civilization has attained its highest expression, where all the strands of European history converge, and from which, from time to time, electrical discharges emanate that shake the world. This city whose population combines in itself, as no other people, a passion for enjoyment and for historical initiatives; this city whose inhabitants know how to live like the most refined Epicurians of Athens, and to die like the most intrepid Spartans."[9]

This lyrical passage helps one to understand the enthusiasm with which Marx, in 1844, went to live in the rue Vaneau and to edit the *Franco-Prussian Annals*.

It was in Paris that young Marx became a Marxist.

It was there that he perceived clearly the historical law of the

class struggle and the necessity for a proletarian revolution in order
to achieve communism. But also, and above all, he ceased giving
communism a "philosophical foundation," in favor of giving it a
historical foundation—that of a science which does not seek truth
in speculative concepts but instead seeks verification in experiential
and militant practice.

The *Economic and Philosophic Manuscripts of 1844*, in their
complexity and their ambiguity, enable us, in a way, to enter the
laboratory of Marx's thought, in which there still existed, side by
side, the tenacious remnants of Hegelian philosophical speculation
and the scientific imperatives of economics and history.

In the *Manuscripts of 1844*, for the first time three principal
sources of Marxism flowed together: German philosophy, English
political economy and French socialism.

The entire work is dominated by a single idea, that of the alienation of labor and of its conquest by communism. The theme of
alienation is here developed in all its dimensions—religious, political
and economic—not without some speculative flaws but already on
the way to "reconversion." After the *Manuscripts*, this category of
alienation was to lose its philosophical universality—still colored by
speculation—to become more humble perhaps but more scientifically
effective, with a specific concept in each discipline, for example, the
"fetishism of the commodity" in political economy.

What was Marx going to find at Paris in the way of sources?

In the first place, the experience of the great social revolution,
begun in 1789 and ending in 1830. Marx studied the French Revolution, in men and in books, at its very source. He even dreamed of
writing a history of the Convention. He gave himself over to a pas-
sionate reading of the French historians of the Restoration—Augustin Thierry, Mignet, Thiers, Guizot—who, having studied the struggles of the French bourgeoisie against the feudalism of the Middle
Ages (so as to understand the liberal exigencies of the bourgeoisie
of their own time) were able to discern the essential role of the class
struggle in history. Marx rendered decided homage to these historians, recognizing the validity of their discovery of the class struggle:

"No credit is due to me for discovering the existence of classes
in modern society, nor yet the struggle between them. Long before
me, bourgeois historians had described the historical development of

this class struggle, and bourgeois economists the economic anatomy of the classes. What I did that was new was to prove (1) that the *existence of classes* is only bound up with *particular, historic phases in the development of production*; (2) that the class struggle necessarily leads to the *dictatorship of the proletariat*; (3) that this dictatorship itself only constitutes the transition to the *abolition of all classes* and to a *classless society*."[10]

Above all, his sojourn at Paris meant the assimilation of a revolutionary experience, of battles waged for half a century under the leadership of the bourgeoisie, and for some years now (since the uprisings of 1831–34 and 1839) the battles waged by the proletariat on its own account, already with class consciousness and consciousness of communist and socialist doctrines, in which were mingled such diverse influences as those of Cabet, Theodore Dézamy, Blanqui, Proudhon.

In Paris, Marx entered into relationships with German revolutionary artisans and with secret French societies. Certain police reports indicate his participation in meetings of revolutionary proletarians at the Trône Gate, Vincennes Court.

Marx became aware at this time of the human qualities of these militants. "One must be acquainted with the studiousness, the craving for knowledge, the moral energy and the unceasing urge for development of the French and English workers to be able to form an idea of the *human* nobleness of that movement."[11]

After the Congress of Vienna, secret societies against the reactionary policies of the Holy Alliance had proliferated throughout Europe. The *Carbonari** adhered to the Jacobin ideal, and Blanquist societies were the French form of "Carbonariism." Marx rejected the conspiratorial concept of small agitational groups, but in the communists he respected the radical criticism of the existing state of things and the will to forcibly overturn it. Since the French Revolution, from Babeuf (whom Marx called the founder of the first active communist party) to Blanqui (whom Marx considered "the head and heart of the proletarian party in France"[12]), the tradition of violent revolution persisted. The people could liberate themselves only by an uprising.

* An Italian revolutionary group organized around 1811 to establish a united republican Italy.—*Ed.*

Marx also spent time with the Parisian socialists and read their works. Although he felt that they harbored illusions in their belief in the possibility of transforming bourgeois society by gradual reforms and their hope of obtaining concessions from the ruling class by the force of arguments alone, he thought their critique of bourgeois society was a useful contribution. He met Proudhon and Louis Blanc, Heine and Herwegh, Bakunin and Pierre Leroux.

And, above all, he met Engels and cemented a friendship with him that was to last all their lives.

The convergence of their paths was a remarkable thing.

Engels, like Marx, had come to communism from classical German philosophy, particularly that of Hegel. Son of an industrialist, his sojourn in England in his father's spinning mills, had a significance for him comparable to that of Marx's living in Paris. Engels, in a country economically much more advanced than his own, had not only taken cognizance of the inhumanity of the capitalist system, of the poverty and degradation it imposed on workers, but also knew the magnitude of the working-class struggle manifested at that time in the Chartist movement. He had already denounced, in his *Letters From Wuppertal*,[13] the exploitation of the proprietors Barmen and Elberfeld. In his book, *The Condition of the Working-Class in England*, he directed a powerful indictment against this capitalism, the most advanced of its epoch. He saw in the Chartist movement, which gave a political form to class demands, the hope of a liberating revolution:

"While I was in Manchester, it was tangibly brought home to me that the economic facts . . . are . . . a decisive historical force; that they form the basis of the origination of the present-day class antagonisms; that these class antagonisms, in the countries where they have become fully developed, thanks to large-scale industry . . . are in their turn the basis of the formation of political parties and of party struggles, and thus of all political history."[14]

Thus, for Engels, as for Marx, it is the experience of working-class struggles and the participation in these struggles, the change of class and class perspective, that make possible the transition from bourgeois democratic radicalism to communism, as well as the transition from philosophical communism, with its still speculative foundation, to historical, scientific communism. This common experience they translated into an axiom in *The German Ideology*: "The existence of revolutionary ideas in a particular period presupposes the existence of a revolutionary class."[15]

Engel's first contribution to the *Franco-Prussian Annals* and to the development of scientific socialism was an "Outline of a Critique of Political Economy," which Marx described as a "germinal sketch." In it, Engels asserted that the categories of political economy are only various aspects of private property, whose contradictions inevitably engender crises and social revolution.[16]

Marx, for his part, in 1844 devoured the works of the economists —Jean-Baptiste Say, Frédéric Skarbek, Destutt de Tracy, Boisguilbert, and, in their French translations, the works of the great English economists—Adam Smith, Ricardo, MacCulloch, James Mill.

From the teaching of the classical economists, he derived the underlying idea of the decisive role of labor. In labor, man objectifies his own creative power. Commodities and their value are only crystalized human labor. But in the light of experience and socialist doctrine, Marx became conscious, in opposition to both Hegel and the bourgeois economists, that what rendered the world created by men hostile and alien to men was not their objectification but the fact that in a regime dominated by the division of labor and private ownership of the means of production, men are objectified in an inhuman fashion. Their labor is the labor of the alienated. Private ownership arises from this alienation of labor.

Because of this alienation, just as, in Feuerbach, on the religious plane, all that is ascribed-to God emanates from man, on the economic and social plane, the more capital accumulates, the more the worker is humanly impoverished.

Having thus arrived at these three great sources—German philosophy, English political economy, French socialism—Marx undertook in his *Manuscripts of 1844* to prove the point of his investigations. The keystone of his thought is thus the notion of the alienation of labor toward which these three sources converge.

The Alienation of Labor

> Religious estrangement as such occurs only in the realm
> of *consciousness*, of man's inner life, but economic estrange-
> ment is that of *real life*; its transcendence therefore em-
> braces both aspects.
>
> — MARX[1]

The problem of alienation, so far as Marx was concerned, is the
problem of the relationship between human activity and the objects
and institutions it has created. Four principal sources for this concept
of alienation can be discerned:

1. *Economic source:* Alienation, to the economist, is the transfer
of a piece of property to another person. In a mercantile society,
the most prevalent form of alienation is the sale.

2. *Legal source:* For theoreticians of natural rights, the term alienation designates the loss of primordial freedom, its transfer to society
by the social contract. It is in this sense that Rousseau uses the word
in *The Social Contract.*

3. *Philosophical source:* For Fichte, alienation is the act by which
the subject is posited before the object. The object, the non-ego in its
totality, is an alienation from the mind, from the ego.

4. *Theological source:* In the sense of religious faith, alienation
expresses the creation of the world by God. This notion in the religious tradition is allied to that of "procession" as well as to that of
"the Fall."

Marx borrowed from Hegel and Feuerbach the concept of alienation but in his hands it went through a profound metamorphosis.

For Hegel, it was the mind's no longer recognizing what it had
created by its own labor and of having to look upon its own product
as an alien entity. This conception is, like Fichte's, typically idealist;
it follows the inevitable course of idealism, according to which mind
precedes nature and engenders it as a moment in its development.
The problem that Hegel poses is that of all theologians: "The spirit
itself must be created in order to create something other than itself."
From this point of view, nature itself, matter in general, is a   form

of alienation: "It is the alienation of self-consciousness which establishes thinghood."[2]

For Feuerbach, alienation had assumed an already materialist meaning. First, the origin of alienation is no longer to be found in the absolute spirit (that is to say, God), but, on the contrary, in man. Applying the concept of alienation to religious criticism, Feuerbach considered that man, "alienating" his own qualities and ridding them of all limitations, projects them outside himself and attributes them to God. (For example, human love, carried to absolute perfection, becomes an attribute of God.) God is only an illusory projection of the essence of man which has become estranged from man and dominates him.

As we have seen, Marx, who applied to the criticism of the state and of politics the method that Feuerbach applied solely to God and religion, did not take Feuerbach to task for this materialist inversion of Hegelian thought; but he did take exception to his having proceeded like a metaphysician in having substituted for the "absolute spirit" an eternal "human nature": "Feuerbach's error was not in having expressed this fact (alienation) but of having idealized it and rendered it independent instead of interpreting it as the product of a specific and surpassable period of historical development."

In correcting this error, Marx returned to Hegel's underlying ideas of man as his own creator, and of *becoming*, of history, of the dialectics of this creation. From the outset, in his chapter, "Critique of the Hegelian Dialectic and Philosophy as a Whole," Marx cut through to the essentials, to the central theme of his chapters on master and slave, and on culture:

"The outstanding achievement of Hegel's *Phenomenology* and of its final outcome, the dialectic of negativity as the moving and generating principle, is thus first that Hegel conceives the self-creation of man as a process, conceives objectification as loss of the object, as alienation and as transcendence of this alienation; that he thus grasps the essence of *labor* and comprehends objective man—true, because real man—as the outcome of man's *own labor*."[3]

It is remarkable that what Marx appreciated most in Hegel was precisely the "Fichtean" aspect of his thought.

All history is this continuous creation of man by man in his dialectical development. With "the negation of the negation . . . (Hegel) has only found the *abstract, logical, speculative* expression for the movement of history."[4]

This prime discovery of Hegel should not lead us to overlooking its limitations.

The first limitation is that "the only labor which Hegel knows and recognizes is mental labor," and not concrete, material labor, i.e., the real activity of men by means of which they form and transform nature, society and their own existence.

The second limitation is that "Hegel's standpoint is that of modern political economy. He grasps *labor* as the *essence* of man . . . he sees only the positive, not the negative, side of labor. Labor is man's *coming-to-be for himself* within *alienation*, or as *alienated* man."[5]

Here we have the kernel of all the contradictions of both the Hegelian philosophy and of classic economics. It cannot be clarified from the viewpoint of the bourgeoisie. The solution of this philosophical and economic problem can only be understood from the viewpoint of another class, i.e., the proletariat.

Why is this true?

Marx writes that "Hegel's standpoint is that of modern political economy" (that is, of bourgeois economics, notably that of Adam Smith and Ricardo). He also says—and this is the same idea in a different form—"The philosopher (himself an abstract form of estranged man) sets himself up as the *measuring rod* of the estranged world,"[6] and again, "Political economy has merely formulated the laws of estranged labor."[7]

Marx carried forward in parallel fashion the critique of English political economy and of German classical philosophy, that of Hegel, both of which have the characteristic of moving on the *inside of alienation*. Now, this common character is a class character; the nature of bourgeois society is to be alienated; the bourgeois viewpoint is that of alienation. That is why "the solution of theoretical riddles is the task of practice."[8]

Why is the viewpoint of the bourgeoisie necessarily that of alienation?

Marx discerned the source of this alienation in classical economy. The bourgeois theory of economics is only a formulation of appearances as they seem to the capitalist. "Political Economy sees only what is *apparent*."[9] "Nevertheless even the best spokesmen of classi-

cal economy remain more or less in the grip of the world of illusion
which their criticism had dissolved, as cannot be otherwise from a
bourgeois standpoint."[10] As to what this appearance consists of, Marx
tells us: "The appearance only of the relations of production mirrors
itself in the brain of the capitalist."[11] Marx gives us two striking
examples of this: Adam Smith's confusion of "constant and variable
capital" and "fixed and circulating capital," as well as that of
Ricardo—"Ricardo confuses *value* with *cost price*."[12] The illusion
that lies at the base of this error is characteristic of capitalist conditions. Marx defines it thus:

"It is . . . understandable why bourgeois Political Economy in-
stinctively clung to Adam Smith's confusion . . . and repeated it
parrotlike, without criticism, from generation to generation for a
century. The part of capital laid out for wages is no longer in the
least distinguished by bourgeois Political Economy from the part of
capital laid out for raw materials. . . . Thereby the basis for an
understanding of the real movement of capitalist production, and
hence of capitalist exploitation, is buried at one stroke."[13]

In the calculations of the employer, there is indeed no difference
between these subdivisions under cost price: *wages paid* or *raw
materials purchased*. "The capital-values advanced for production in
the form of both means of production and means of subsistence reappear here equally in the value of the product. Thus the transformation of the capitalist process of production into a complete mystery
is happily accomplished and the origin of the surplus-value existing
in the product is entirely withdrawn from view.

"Furthermore this brings to completion the fetishism peculiar to
bourgeois Political Economy, the fetishism which metamorphoses
the social, economic character impressed on things in the process of
social production into a natural character stemming from the material nature of those things."[14]

Thus labor is not differentiated from any other commodity. In
bourgeois political economy, as well as in the calculations of the
employer, labor appears only in the form in which it is regarded in
the capitalist system—not as the creative activity of man but as an
activity whose destiny it is to provide money. "Political economy
conceives the social order of men, or their human essence in activity,
their human relations as species-man to a truly human life, only in

the form of exchange and traffic. . . . Political economy regards the alienated form of social relations as the essential, original form— one that corresponds to the destiny of man."[15]

This could hardly be otherwise, unless we leave behind the conditions so characteristic of the bourgeois order, on the inside of which these conditions seem to be eternal. The illusion is inescapable unless we posit ourselves outside this class and adopt another class viewpoint, that of a class to whom the bourgeois regime is not eternal nor "natural," but transient; other regimes have existed in which labor had another significance, and other systems will come into existence in which labor will have still another significance.

The illusion was shared by Hegel, for the same class reasons, and transposed by him onto the philosophical plane; Hegel regarded the historical form which the alienation of labor assumes under capitalist conditions as the only and eternal form of the objectification of man's labor, although this objectification under other social conditions might very well not be alienated.

"Political economy starts with the fact of private property, but it does not explain it to us."[16] Thus, starting from empirical "givens," beyond which it is forbidden to rise, it is also forbidden to discover beyond what are regarded as "facts" or "things" the human relations that give rise to them and which account for them. Bourgeois political economy is condemned to positivism, to the establishment of definitive laws alone as the unchanging relations between phenomena.*

The Marxist theory of alienation is not only an exposure of the illusions of positivism, but also a method for the critique of positivism.

Thanks to the class viewpoint Marx adopted, by means of which he posited himself *outside* the capitalist system, he escapes illusions as to alienation. His method consists in seeking, beyond the supposed "data" of experience, the human relations hidden beneath the "appearance" of things. He applies the same method to the critique of Hegelian idealism. The alienation of the philosopher has the same class roots as the alienation of the economist.

The division of labor, class domination and exploitation have

* Later, in the chapter devoted to political economy, we will see how Marx advanced beyond this positivist conception of science.

played a determining role in the genesis of idealist mystification. From the moment when a division of manual and of intellectual labor is instituted, "consciousness can really flatter itself that it is something other than the consciousness of existing practice, that it is *really* conceiving something without conceiving something *real*."[17]

Such is the social root of idealism.

In all class societies, the separation between directive thought and material production creates the illusion not alone of the independence of thought, moving above material reality and practical action, but also of the primacy of thought. In a class which is no longer in direct contact with things, and which acts on the world by means of the symbols of thought, of language, in planning for labor and directing production, thought is the captive of the illusion that it is the supreme and directive power of the world.

Here also the parallelism between philosophy and political economy is striking. Appearances, born of class experience, superimpose themselves as "final reality." Just as, in a commodity economy, the most abstract but also the most universal expression of the commodity, money, becomes "men's estranged, alienating and self-disposing *species nature*. Money is the alienated *ability of mankind*"[18] and the "divine power that moves all society." Just as in bourgeois society, and in the abstract conception of thought developed within it, reason is found to be the most perfect expression—as motivating force of the entire universe, of nature and of history—so in the system of Hegelian logic "the philosophic mind is nothing but the estranged mind of the world thinking within its self-estrangement—i.e., comprehending itself abstractly. *Logic* (is) the mind's *coin of the real . . . alienated thinking*."[19]

Hence the significance of Marx's critique. No longer does it posit itself *inside* thought; no longer is it concerned with the idea of the nature of the world, while leaving it as it is, but with changing the world that engenders such illusions. In a profound sense, "the solution of theoretical enigmas is a task for praxis."

It is precisely this that constitutes the true "Copernican revolution" which Marx brought about in philosophy.

This Copernican revolution was possible only by means of a change in class viewpoint. Marxism is, in the first place, the philosophy of labor because it is the philosophy of workers, for whom nature is not a creation or alienation from the mind but the very substance of labor.

When one reflects on the world as experienced in daily activity by the worker (and not in ideological speculation alone), problems are posed in materialist terms:

"These communist workers employed, for instance, in the Manchester and Lyons workshops, do not believe that '*pure thinking*' will be able to argue away their industrial masters and their own practical debasement. . . . They know that property, capital, money, wage-labor and the like are no idle figments of the brain but . . . very objective sources of their self-estrangement, and that they must be abolished in a practical, objective way for man to become man, not only in thinking, in consciousness, but in . . . life."[20]

Thus the illusion that a modification in thinking is enough to turn the world upside down vanishes, as well as the belief in the priority of thought. "For the practical materialist, i.e., the communist, it is a question of revolutionizing the existing world, of practically attacking and changing existing things."[21]

From the moment that it was understood that philosophical illusions arise from the contradictions of the existing world, it was evident that these illusions could not be dissipated by isolated philosophical criticism but only by the actual reversal of the social order that gave birth to them.

The worker is not susceptible to symbols alone, but also to things. His point of view is that of practice and not of alienation.*

Hence, by considering things from the viewpoint of the working class (and no longer that of the bourgeoisie), the philosopher is enabled to pass from ideal to real struggles.

Only thus can the "upside-down" world of bourgeois reality and bourgeois thought be put back on its feet.

Alienation is not only a spiritual phenomenon; it has its objective base in the actual living conditions of the worker.

---

* Moreover, this does not at all exclude the fact that the individual worker may himself be a victim of the dominant class ideology under which he lives, and subject to the illusions arising from alienation. Consciously or not, he is always a victim of alienation; self-consciousness liberates him not from alienation but from the illusions it engenders.

In the *Manuscripts of 1844*, Marx singles out three essential aspects of labor's alienation:

1. *Alienation from the product of labor.* With the division of labor, when a product enters by sale into the exchange cycle, it leaves its producer, it becomes a commodity, i.e., it obeys laws alien to those of its creation—the impersonal laws of the market.

The alienation of labor is a specific instance of the general alienation of the sale. It is the sale of labor power, turned into a commodity and, like it, impersonal and anonymous.

When man, the creator, the laborer, with the birth of private ownership of the means of production, no longer owns these means of production, an organic link is broken between the conscious ends man sets for himself in his work and the means he employs to attain his ends. Hence the creator finds himself separated from the product of his labor, which no longer belongs to him but to the owner of the means of production, i.e., slave master, or feudal lord, or capitalist boss. His labor is thus no longer the fulfillment of his own goals, his personal projects; it fulfills the goals of someone else. Man in his work ceases to be a man, i.e., a human being who determines his own ends, and becomes a means, a moment in the objective process of production, a *means* for producing commodities and surplus value.

"The laws of political economy express the estrangement of the worker in his object thus: The more the worker produces, the less he has to consume; the more values he creates, the more unworthy he becomes . . . labor produces for the rich wonderful things—but for the worker it produces privation. . . . It replaces labor by machines, but it throws a section of the workers back to a barbarous type of labor and turns the other workers into machines."[22] Here alienation is dispossession.

2. *Alienation from the act of labor.* In all systems of private ownership of the means of production, the worker is not only estranged from the product of his labor, but from the very *act* of his labor. His boss not only dictates the aims but also the means and methods of his work. His movements and tempos are dictated from without, in accordance with the place assigned the laborer as one of the cogs in the gears of production. They are predetermined, designed in a vacuum, in an entirely dehumanized form and to

rhythms of tools and machines that often become hallucinating, and all this with the intent of making the laborer, as Marx puts it, "the flesh-and-blood appendage to a steel machine." Here alienation is depersonalization.

3. *Alienation from species-life.* The totality of the means of production existing at a given historical epoch, the totality of scientific and technical resources of the given culture and the forces they represent—all these are the fruit of the labor and thought of all preceding generations. When a man works, his actiivty partakes of all previous humanity; his work is the expression of the species-life of man, of all the creations accumulated by the human race. Now, when the means of production are private property, all this patrimony in which the creative work of all past humanity is embodied— humanity insofar as it is "species-man," as Marx says, is in the hands of certain individuals who thus control all the contributions accumulated by millenia of human labor and genius.

Hence private property is the supreme form of alienation. "Social power has turned into the private power of the few," Marx was to say in *Capital.* Capital is the alienated power of humanity raising itself above men like an alien and inhuman power. Alienation here is dehumanization.

The true *being* of man, his creative acts (his creative acts historically accumulated) are crystallized in *having.* "The less you *are,* the more you *have,* the more the alienation of your life increases, the more you accumulate from your alienated being."* Such is the "morality" of bourgeois society.

The living labor of the worker, is crystallized into commodities, in the hands of the owner of the means of production, dead labor accumulated in the form of capital, of *having*—and thereafter it is alien to the *being* who produced it, superior to him and ruling him, making him serve a faceless, soulless law.

This relation between dead and living labor, between *being* and *having,* is the profound law of capitalist society and of its development. The more *having* increases in the hands of the capitalist, the more the *being* of the worker, who is the author of it, is im-

* See further the chapter on "Surplus Value and the Pauperization of the Working Class."

poverished. It is this that Marx proves in *Capital*, under the name of *the general law of capitalist accumulation.*

Thenceforward the relations between men are metamorphosed into relations between things. In virtue of the laws of competition and of the market, where only things and their value as commodities are compared, and where the fate of men is subordinated to this confrontation of things, men, their labors, their enterprises, their mutual relations become incidental to the objective development of things.

Under the nonhuman laws of *having*, alienated man loses his *being*, his essence, which is the self-conscious pursuit of ends that he realizes in his work. He has become an object.

This alienation evolves at all levels of life, and at all levels it dehumanizes man and fragments society.

On the economic plane, it is what Marx called "the fetishism of the commodity." In the jungle of the greeds of capitalist competition, we are often witness to the victory of some great devouring and despotic organization.

On the political plane, it is the mystification of the state, in which the so-called equality of rights is the hypocritical mask for the inequality that in fact exists between possessors and nonpossessors.

Freedom then becomes a deceptive myth in a society where money reduces all those who do not possess it to the slavery of selling themselves or of selling their labor power.

On the spiritual plane, it is a world of divided men. Indeed, from the moment when, by alienation, the project ceases to be a real aspect of real creation, it is no longer an aspect in the development of my activity but an illusory contribution made to a reality which escapes me, to a universe that mutilates me.

Thought, caught in the gears of alienation, is no longer what it is in its essence, but only a means to fabricate new means. Or else, if it attempts to escape from these gears, to identify with the real world, it hides in the illusory universe of "other-worldliness" with all its dreams and Utopias.

Alienation is the opposite of creation. That is why the alienation of labor, if it is not the sole alienation, is the root of all others. It is this that corrupts, at its very source, all creative work, that is, the essence of man.

As Marx points out in many formulations, alienation is born out of the private ownership of the means of production. It will disappear, therefore, when private ownership disappears.

Such is the cornerstone of the Marxist method summed up in a passage of the *Manuscripts of 1844:*

"*Communism* as the *positive* transcendence of *private property*, as *human self-estrangement*, and therefore as the real *appropriation of the human essence* by and for man; communism, therefore, as the complete return of man to himself as a *social* (i.e., human) being —a return become conscious, and accomplished within the entire wealth of previous development."[23]

In order to transcend alienation, it is not enough, as Hegel and Feuerbach held, to grasp alienation; it is necessary in the first place to transform the world which engenders it, i.e., the system based on private ownership of the means of production. To transcend alienation is no longer, therefore, the affair of the solitary philosophical critic, but of the class struggle.

The proletariat takes over philosophy's ambitions.

This historic change-over is possible because, with the complete victory of capitalism in the middle of the 19th century, alienation took on a universal character. Everything entered into the cycle of exchange, and all value was degraded to commodity value.

Now, in such a universe, the working class, by the very nature of its position, is drastically excluded from the ownership of the means of production; it has nothing of its own but its labor power.

In contradistinction to all other social classes, it bespeaks, says Marx, "a solitary human title," for it is reduced to the bare existence of man, to its most profound essence—which is precisely labor, the act of transforming nature, the act of creation. But at the same time the working class is stripped of the properly human attributes of its work, since it can do nothing with its labor power other than to sell it to the owner of the means of production, to alienate it to an alien power.

The difference between the working class and all other social classes is radical. For example, a poor peasant, or a petty artisan or shopkeeper, even if his condition is actually more poverty-stricken than that of the laborer, has some inherent claim to the means of production that he still possesses and that possess him, be it his plot of ground or his shop.

To be sure these claims come to him from without. He is alienated from his property. His conduct is in some degree influenced by this *having*, while the struggle of the proletariat is basically the simple necessity of *being*.

Since labor power, in fact, enables him to live—only if he succeeds in selling it to the owner of the means of production—all the possibilities of his *being* are linked to the class struggle against capital.

For him man can only *be* by breaking the iron laws of *having*. This is what one might call, in the language of early philosophy, the "ontological" meaning of the revolutionary demands of the proletariat.

It is in this profound sense that the working class is the only revolutionary class to the very end. Indivisibly its class struggle challenges the entire social order and signifies the destiny of man—of all men.

Communism is not a generalization of *having*, inside alienation, in the form of primitive, crude "sharing," such as was proposed by Sylvain Maréchal, for example, in France.

Communism, as Marx emphasized strongly in the *Manuscripts of 1844*, is not a generalization of *having*, inside the alienation of man, but the realization of the *being* of man, of all man, and the destruction of the alienating structures of class society. This alone would make possible the only genuine liberation and the only potentially limitless expansion of each man, including the former exploiters, who also have been alienated by the possession of *having*, just as workers have been alienated from the *having* of which they were dispossessed.

For Marx the road to freedom and to true morality was to participate with all his strength in the class struggle of the proletariat, whose class objectives merged with the liberation of all men.

Practice and the "Reconversion" of Speculative Concepts

> The philosophers have *interpreted* the world in various
> ways; the point however is to *change* it.
> — MARX[1]

At the stage reached by young Marx's thinking in the *Manuscripts of 1844*, he was not yet wholly liberated from speculative
philosophy. The critique of bourgeois society and the conception of
communism still retain a speculative basis; present society, as well
as the future, were judged with reference to a certain philosophical
conception of man. Bourgeois society is not consonant with the
"true" nature of man, with his "essence." Communism is to be the
"true resurrection of nature."[2] The task of the revolutionist is also
colored by this speculative foundation—to overcome the contradiction between reality and the essence of man while "realizing humanism" through communism. The social revolution and communism
are not yet apprehended scientifically, as a historical moment in the
development of humanity.

The theory of alienation and its transcendence still convey a
teleological and speculative character.

To arrive at scientific socialism, a genuine "reconversion" of
these philosophical concepts became necessary. Marx is all the more
conscious of this necessity since certain of his companions among
the Young Hegelians—especially Moses Hess—had oriented themselves toward a purely moralistic and utopian conception, that of
"true socialism," which Marx vigorously denounced.

Returning to the "humanism" of Feuerbach, Hess and then Karl
Grün substituted for real men and their class antagonisms, man in
general, the abstraction of man; and while indulging in a critical
sermon on the dehumanization of man in bourgeois society, they
extolled "true socialism," which was not to be realized by class
struggle and the social revolution but by reforms obtained as a
result of popular education. This jumble of speculation, morality,

Utopia and reformism had a class significance. It was no longer the proletariat who would bring about communism. Instead of the real revolution, "true socialism," wrote Marx, "is German philosophy disguised as socialism."

To do away with this "philosophical communism," it was not enough to grant first place to "praxis" after having given it to "alienation."

"Praxis" does not afford an escape hatch for idealism nor for speculation, if one conceives it, as Marx did in the *Manuscripts of 1844*, as the unity of alienation and its transcendence, and not clearly as labor and as class struggle. If it concerned the "self-creation" of man alone, in a sense still close to Hegel's, the "philosophy of praxis" was only a variation of German idealism, which, since Kant and Fichte, had had the merit of putting the accent on "the active side of cognition." The variation consists of replacing knowledge by action, of replacing the conscious subject by the active subject, without, however, abandoning the fundamental axiom of idealism: No object without subject.

In the *Manuscripts of 1844*, there was held out (and this is not the smallest reason for their complexity and ambiguity) the bait of a "reconversion" of the central concepts of alienation and of praxis, of an effort to rid them of their speculative origins. The social revolution is presented at one and the same time as arising from the contradiction between bourgeois reality and the "true human essence" (speculative foundation) and from the development of private property itself (historical and scientific foundation).

The "reconversion" of the concepts of alienation, of total man,* of communism, was to be achieved when the necessity for revolution appeared clearly and simply (independent of all speculation on the "true essence" of man) as a historical necessity arising from the

---

* Compare, for example, the conception of the "total man" in the *Manuscripts of 1844* with that in *Capital*, in which Marx defined it thus: "Modern Industry, indeed, compels society, under penalty of death, to replace the detail-worker of to-day, crippled by life-long repetition of one and the same trivial operation, and thus reduced to the mere fragment of a man, by the fully developed individual, fit for a variety of labours, ready to face any change of production, and to whom the different social functions he performs, are but so many modes of giving free scope to his own natural and acquired powers." (*Capital*, Vol. 1, N.Y., 1967, p. 488.)

contradiction between the nature of the productive forces and the relations of production. Only then would we transcend the stage of a philosophy of history based on a speculative conception of the essence of man and dominated by the external finality of a metaphysical "sense" of history.

How, according to Marx, do this transcendence and this "reconversion" come about?

The three principal streams of Marxist thought converge in the notions of practice and alienation. From Kant to Fichte and Hegel, German philosophy had adduced the role of human initiative—not only the active side of knowledge, but the self-creative character of man.

English political economy, from Adam Smith to Ricardo, gave this creative activity, this practice, a concrete meaning, that of labor, producer of all value, by transforming and humanizing nature, society itself being essentially a community of labor.

French socialism, especially that of Saint-Simon, developed the idea that society is "in activity," i.e., that it is the collective organism of labor in which the unity of material and intellectual production are expressed.

Another idea is borrowed from French communism, the idea that this activity is related to a specific class, the bourgeosie at the time of the French Revolution and the proletariat thereafter. If the proletariat had not previously fought with a clear consciousness of its own historical mission, at least since the rebellion of the silk-weavers of Lyons, it had been fighting with class objectives and slogans.

The speculative conception of alienation was not to be surmounted by Marx until he adopted the class viewpoint of the proletariat; the practice which surmounts alienation, revolutionary practice, i.e., that of one class, the proletariat.

This practice involves at one and the same time labor, since the communist revolution is only possible at a certain stage in the development of the productive forces; and by the class struggle, since it demands a change in the relations of production. Thenceforward, in the thinking of Marx, alienation was not man's division and laceration of himself but society's division and class antagonisms; and the conquest of alienation became more and more explicitly the concrete revolutionary struggle of the proletariat.

The expression "alienation" itself is to be less and less frequently used (without actually being abandoned). To the degree that concrete historical analysis is substituted for speculation, a scientific content will be given to the alienation of labor; the theory of value and surplus value constitutes the supersession of the theory of alienated labor, its reconversion. The abandonment, however, if only partial, of the word "alienation" (describing a condition of man) has as corollary the growing usage of the term "fetishism" (describing the structures engendering alienation).

In *The German Ideology*, Marx demonstrates that he has developed a new content in a terminology still borrowed from German philosophy; the notion of alienation serves to clarify for the philosophers by speaking to them in their own language the contradiction between the productive forces and the relations of production —and the class struggle that arises from them.

Practice, the point of departure and the goal of Marxist philosophy, is defined as social activity, as activity for the transformation of the world, uniting all forms of labor and struggle: technology, economic production, scientific experiment and research, revolutionary struggle and artistic creation.

From now on we are to see clearly of what the Copernican revolution in philosophy realized by Marx consisted: the transition from speculation to practice. "Where speculation ends—in real life—there real, positive science begins: the representation of the practical activity, of the practical process of development of men. . . . When reality is depicted, philosophy as an independent branch of activity loses its medium of existence."[3]

This demystified conception of practice led to the discovery of historical materialism, toward which all Marx's philosophical investigations converged, and which were to give a scientific foundation to his economic theory and his militant practice.

Historical Materialism

It is not the consciousness of men that determines their existence, but, on the contrary, their social existence determines their consciousness.

— MARX[1]

The world of man is the work of man. This guiding idea of German philosophy, and especially of Fichte, found its demystified, scientific and revolutionary expression in historical materialism. The first systematic study of "practice" in all its historical dimensions was made by Marx and Engels in *The German Ideology* (1846). It concerned a decision "to work out together the contrast between our view and the idealism of German philosophy, in fact to settle our accounts with our former philosophic conscience."[2]

This "settling of accounts" had begun the preceding year with *The Holy Family*, in which they laid down the opinion, in opposition to the Young Helegians, who were still bogged down in pure criticism, that "ideas cannot lead us beyond the old order of things; they can only lead us beyond *ideas* about the old order of things. In fact, ideas cannot realize anything. To realize ideas, men are needed, men who put practical forces into play. . . . Criticism does not create anything; the worker creates everything . . . the worker creates even man."[3] In *The German Ideology*, Marx and Engels take up this theme again: It is not criticism but the revolution that is the active force of history and of culture.

German philosophical criticism had hitherto limited itself to religious criticism, thereby struggling solely against the illusions of consciousness and not against the actual order of the world. Their concepts would lead not to changing the world but to leaving it as it was, changing only the idea they had created about it.

The first problem is to determine the interconnection between ideas and the world. The revolution wrought by Marx in philosophy expressed itself in a great inversion from speculation to practice. "In direct contrast to German philosophy which descends from heaven to earth, here we ascend from earth to heaven."[4] That is, we do not begin with the consciousness and the thinking of men to explain their life, but from their existence and their real practice, to render an account of their consciousness and their thought. Consciousness is taking cognizance of what exists and how one acts. "Consciousness can never be anything else than conscious existence."[5]

The central theme of historical materialism is this: "Men make their own history, but they do not make it just as they please; they do not make it under circumstances chosen by themselves, but under circumstances directly encountered, given and transmitted from the past."[6]

Human history is qualitatively different from biological evolution but it is rooted in it.

Man, as animal, has needs which both unite and oppose him to nature. But, unlike animals, who adapt themselves simply to nature, man transforms it by his labor. Human history begins with the first tool, the first production of the means for satisfying needs. Thus, human environment is not a pre-existent, *given* nature but a nature always to some degree transformed, humanized. It is less, for example, geography that determines history than history that determines geography. The relation of man with nature is an active bond. As long as men exist, Marx emphasized, the history of nature and the history of men will condition each other reciprocally. The state of the productive forces, of industry and exchange, therefore, is the first necessary element in understanding the history of man.

But in satisfying his needs and creating technical means for satisfying them, man creates new needs. This creation of ever new needs distinguishes man from all other animal species. While an animal's needs remain relatively stationary, man's needs extend illimitably. He tends to produce more than what he immediately needs. In transforming nature, he transforms himself and refines his senses so that they become capable of encompassing all that preceding generations have created. All past civilization and culture have contributed to his understanding. In the act of his labor, his creation, all humanity is present: "An animal forms things in accordance with the standard and the need of the species to which it belongs, whilst man knows how to produce in accordance with the standard of every species, and knows how to apply everywhere the inherent standard to the object. Man therefore also forms things in accordance with the laws of beauty. . . . The object of labor is, therefore, the *objection of man's species life.*"[7]

After the satisfaction of needs by labor and the creation of new needs, the third characteristic element of human history is the institution of social relations between men. The conquest, the mastery, over nature requires the division of labor. The degree of development of the productive forces is expressed in the degree of complexity of the division of labor. Separation of the city and country, separation of industrial and mercantile labor within the city, separation of manual and mental labor, delineate the progress of this division of labor. The existence of social classes is linked to the diverse phases of this historical development of production.

What defines a social class is, first of all, the position it occupies in a given system of social production, its role in the social organization of labor, and, more precisely, its relation to the means of production. What defines the proletariat, for example, is, first, the fact that it does not own the means of production. From that fact flows its function in society: It is the producer of surplus value for the profit of the capitalists, i.e., the owners of the means of production. The third element in the definition of the proletariat as a class (in addition to these two objective elements, i.e., the nonpossession of the means of production, and the production of surplus value) is the "subjective" element, i.e., the consciousness of the appurtenances of class, the comprehension of the historical task incumbent on it —class struggle, the conquest of political power by the dictatorship of the proletariat, and the communist transformation of society. This grasp of its historical mission transforms the class "in itself" to the class "for itself."

Thus history, as *The Communist Manifesto* was soon to proclaim, is the history of the class struggle: up to now all emancipations in history have had as foundation limited productive forces whose production, insufficient for all of society, renders development possible only if one class satisfies its needs at the expense of others. Therefore society up to now always developed in the framework of an opposition—in ancient times, that between free men and slaves; in the Middle Ages, between the lords and their serfs; in modern times, between the bourgeoisie and the proletariat.

The dialectic of these antagonisms is the motive force of history. The fundamental law of historical development is the law of the necessary correspondence between the state of the productive forces and the relations of production. It is the scientific expression of what Marx up to now has called alienation: Social power, i.e., the productive power, multiplied tenfold, that arises from the division of labor, appears to individuals as an alien power, and each revolution is an attempt to overcome it, i.e., to establish between men the social relations corresponding to the development of these productive forces. "This contradiction between the productive forces and the form of intercourse . . . necessarily on each occasion bursts out in a revolution, taking on at the same time various subsidiary forms . . . collisions of various classes, contradiction of consciousness, battle of ideas, etc., political conflict, etc."[8]

Thus the collisions of history have their origin in the contradiction between the state of the productive forces and the form of the relations of production.

To illustrate this major discovery, Marx and Engels, in *The German Ideology*, in a striking resumé, strove to indicate the turning points in history and to define in broad strokes the principal stages of its development.

They outlined a schema of successive systems of property—primitive commune, slave, feudal, capitalist and communist societies.

It would be futile to be dogmatic about this schema, of which Engels himself wrote forty years later that it proved "only how incomplete our knowledge of economic history was at that time."[9]

Furthermore, in *The German Ideology*, soon after this exposition of stages, Marx and Engels added that "empirical observation must in each separate instance bring out empirically, and without any mystification or speculation the connection of the social and political structure with production,"[10] and passing from the structural to the dynamic study, apropos of "the synthesis of the results of historical development," they added: "Viewed apart from real history, these abstractions have in themselves no value whatsoever. They can only serve to facilitate the arrangement of historical material, to indicate the sequence of its separate strata. But they by no means afford a recipe or schema, as does philosophy, for neatly trimming the epochs of history."[11]

On this precise point, Marx gave an example of his scientific research and deepening theoretical grasp, free of dogmatism, in his notes of 1857–58 dealing with forms of property preceding capitalist production, which gave a much more complex and subtle picture than that given in *The German Ideology*, for example, in the analysis of "the Asian mode of production."

Marx notes that the Asian mode of production, which is one of the forms of transition from a classless to a class society, presents a contradictory character, i.e., although property remains communal, it is manifested in specific forms of exploitation of man by man, and of a despotic state.

This mode of production cannot be reduced to that of the primitive commune nor to slave rule nor to feudalism. It developed in many Asian, African, Pre-Colombian societies. Marx describes its functioning in India in *Capital*; he developed the study further in his 1858 text entitled, *Pre-Capitalist Economic Formations* which was not published until 1939.[12]

Historical and ethnographic researches since then have proven the correctness and the fruitfulness of this conception of Marxism.

After a long discussion in Leningrad in 1931 on the "Asian method of production," Maxism found itself diverted from the fruitful hypothesis that there may be modes of production which escape the rigid scheme of historical evolution in which it is maintained that it must always and forever pass through the five stages: primitive commune, slavery, feudalism, capitalism and socialism. In the exposition that Stalin gave of this schema in *Dialectical and Historical Materialism*,[13] it took the form of a veritable "philosophy of history," i.e., a metaphysical speculation submitting the development of history to a kind of external necessity, a vain effort to force it at all costs to conform to the concept. This, incidentally, is the very definition of "speculation," a method that could not have been more alien to Marx's thinking.

On this path, the observer is reduced to the kind of manipulation of the stubborn disciples of Ptolemy who, before Copernicus, multiplied on their charts of the heavens the "epicycles," i.e., the orbits of stars that resisted their hypothesis and always appeared as aberrations. It would be vain for the historian to confine himself to the "five stages." If he studies Hindu or Inca society, or certain African societies, with the intent of arbitrarily classifying these phenomena under the heading "slavery" or "feudalism," it would be as if the history of all peoples could be reduced to a typical line of development that runs straight from ancient Greece to "Western" capitalism.

In his letter of March 8, 1881, to Vera Zasulich, Marx gives a good example of concrete analysis—the very antithesis of speculation —when he points out that the transition from the communal farm to private property can come about in various ways: "Two solutions are *a priori* possible, but obviously altogether different historical conditions are necessary for one or the other."[14]

Another example of the scientific application of Marxism was adduced by Lenin when he refuted the conceptions of the Populists on the economic development of Russia—not on the basis of an abstract schema of historical evolution, but on the basis of a concrete analysis of the Russian economy.

This criticism of Stalin's dogmatic approach by no means constitutes a "revision" of Marxism; on the contrary, it is a restitution of the scientific spirit as Marx conceived it.

In a fifth aspect of their research, Marx and Engels, in *The German Ideology*, traced the first lineaments of the theory of the state. In his *Critique of Hegel's Philosophy of Right* and in "The Jewish Question," Marx had arrived at the conclusion that it is not the state that conditions and regulates bourgeois society, but bourgeois society that conditions and regulates the state. He had also analyzed political alienation and the illusions engendered by it, for example, the illusory thesis that in the state the collective interest assumes a form independent of specific interests. He established that all political struggles within the state—struggles between democracy, aristocracy and monarchy—are only illusory forms under cover of which the class struggles goes on. He shows how each class attempts to take possession of political power while masking its class interests under the pretext of expressing the general interest. The import of "rights" is "always supplied by class conditions," and Marx thus defines the state: "The state is the form by which the individuals of one ruling class assert their common interests." In the specific case of the bourgeoisie, the state "is nothing more than the form of organization which the bourgeois necessarily adopt both for internal and external purposes, for the mutual guarantee of their property and interests."[15]

Finally, consciousness itself is a social product. Men produce their philosophical, political, religious, esthetic ideas as they produce their means of subsistence and their social relations. A threefold corollary emerges from this conception: First, dominant ideas are those of the ruling class; then, "the existence of revolutionary ideas in a particular period presupposes the existence of a revolutionary class";[16] and finally—and this is what distinguishes Marxism from the sociologism of Durkheim, simultaneously idealistic and mechanistic—there is the reaction of the effect on the cause, the interaction of consciousness and the conditions from which it stems.

The "reconversion" of fundamental Marxist concepts is achieved in the perspective of historical materialism: "Communism is for us not . . . an *ideal* to which reality will have to adjust itself. We call communism the *real* movement which abolishes the present state of things. The conditions of this movement result from the premises now in existence."[17]

The necessity for the communist revolution is not only a particular case for the application of the law of necessary correspondence between the relations of production and the state of the productive forces. This revolution is necessary because the actual level of technical progress and of economic organization, the relations of production, the capitalist system of property, have become obstacles to the development of the productive forces; and to the degree that production has become socialized, the private form of appropriation is an anachronism generating catastrophe.

The technical possibilities of a world organization of needs, resources and labor exist and, by the same token, the abolition of classes is from now on possible.

The very notion of "total man," despite its stemming from speculative philosophy, assumes concrete historical meaning. "In revolutionary activity self-change coincides with change in conditions." Thus the new man is forged by modification of circumstances. If it is clear that the "real intellectual wealth of the individual depends entirely on the wealth of his real connections,"[18] the control of social power, the "disalienation" that results from the correspondence between the state of the productive forces and productive relations, terminates the situation that separates the individual from society, that renders alien to the individual all the riches and all the power of the accumulated creation of humanity. "Only in community with others has each individual the means of cultivating his gifts in all directions; only in the community, therefore, is personal freedom possible,"[19] that is, freedom in the full human sense of the word. Not the worthless caprice of accident or negation, but the real power of acquiring for itself the culture and the power of humanity, past and present—the power, indeed, to create humanity itself, to bring, thanks to the immanence of all humanity in each man, his creative contribution to the future of all. Communism, wrote Marx, creates the conditions that do not make it possible for every man to be a Raphael, "but that anyone in whom there is a potential Raphael should be able to develop without hindrance."[20]

The "total man," in this concrete historical perspective, is not only man freed of alienation but man who partakes of universal life.

"The abolition of private property and of the division of labour is itself the union of individuals on the basis created by modern productive forces and world intercourse.

"With communist society, the only society in which the original and free development of individuals ceases to be a mere phrase, this development is determined precisely by the connection of individuals, a connection which consists partly in the economic prerequisites and partly in the necessary solidarity of the free development of all, and, finally, in the universal character of the activity of individuals on the basis of the existing productive forces."[21]

Total man really grows when, in the classless society, the life of the individual and the life of society are no longer in opposition to each other.

Historical materialism, enables us, therefore, to escape from empiricism, from a purely accidental history, and from the idealist and theological speculations of the "philosophers of history."

Thus, historical methodology is at the opposite pole from all dogmatism.

From the standpoint of structural analysis, Marx and Engels themselves corrected determinist, antidialectical extremes. True, some such formulations still persisted in *The German Ideology* and *The Poverty of Philosophy*. Marx, after having formulated the principle of the base, wrote: "In acquiring new productive forces men change their mode of production; and in changing their mode of production . . . they change all their social relations." He illustrated this, however, in the following schematic and mechanistic way: "The handmill gives you society with the feudal lord; the steam-mill, society with the industrial capitalist."[22]

Similarly, in *The German Ideology*, after having stated the principle of the base—"It is not consciousness that determines life, but life that determines consciousness"—he added this commentary: "Morality, religion, metaphysics, all the rest of ideology and their corresponding forms of consciousness, thus no longer retain the semblance of independence. They have no history, no development; but men, developing their material production and their material intercourse, alter, along with this their real existence, their thinking and the products of their thinking."[23]

Formulations that led to interpretations of a summary, mechanistic character were explicitly criticised and later corrected by Marx and Engels.

In a letter to Joseph Bloch, September 21, 1890, Engels wrote: "Marx and I are ourselves partly to blame for the fact that younger writers sometimes lay more stress on the economic side than is due it. We had to emphasize this main principle in opposition to our adversaries, who denied it, and we had not always the time, the place or the opportunity to allow the other elements involved in the interaction to come into their rights. But when it was a case of presenting a section of history, that is, of a practical application, the thing was different and there no error was possible."[24]

The Eighteenth Brumaire of Louis Bonaparte furnished a prime illustration of historical analysis presented in all its dialectical complexity.

In that which concerned the forms of consciousness, as well as in that which concerned the state, correcting the formulation "they lose all semblance of independence," Engels, in a letter to Conrad Schmidt (October 27, 1890) referred to their "relative independence."[25] Marx, in his *Contribution to the Critique of Political Economy*, underlining the "relative autonomy" of the superstructure, wrote: "But the difficulty is not in grasping the idea that Greek art and epos are bound up with certain forms of social development. It rather lies in understanding why they still constitute with us a source of esthetic enjoyments and in certain respects prevail as the standard and model beyond attainment."[26]

After having thus shown how certain values survive beyond the historical conditions that gave rise to them, Marx offers a striking example of time-lag between the base and the superstructure, in the attempt to eliminate mechanistic interpretations. In the fourth volume of *Capital* (*Theories of Surplus Value*) he insists that relations between art and the given structure of society are far from simple. "If this is left out of account," he wrote, "it opens the way to the illusion of the French in the eighteenth century which has been so beautifully satirised by Lessing. Because we are further ahead than the ancients in mechanics, etc., why shouldn't we be able to make an epic too? And the *Henriade** in place of the *Iliad*![27]

From the standpoint of dynamic analysis, we have already seen how Marx corrected and "dialecticized" the "schema" of the "five stages" (in *The German Ideology*). He shows how the transition from one economic and social formation to another, far from happening automatically, requires the convergence of many internal and external conditions and by no means excludes the possibility of stagnation, of decadence, indeed, of regression.

It is hence no more possible to "deduce" the stages than to "deduce the superstructure from the base." As Engels wrote, "our conception of history is, above all, a guide to study, not a lever for construction after the manner of the Hegelians."[28]

This complex, historical dialectic, because it enjoins us not to reduce everything to economics or to deduce everything from economics, because it does not relegate everything—as do many vulgarizers or superficial critics—to "economic determinism," does not consign history to lawless chance. What it eliminates is the conception prevalent in "philosophies of history" that submits history to mystical and abstract external necessity. The discovery of the laws of internal necessity requires a patient and minute study of all the evidence and not the projection of an *a priori* scheme. And this study is to be made over and over *hic et nunc* (here and now) in each specific case.

* Epic poem of Voltaire on the French King Henri IV, 1723.—*ed.*

On this point, too, there is a complete reversal of the Hegelian method. One cannot define the nature and the meaning of Marxist materialism without defining the exact nature and meaning of this "reversal" of Hegelianism.

Marx's Materialism

> The chief defect of all hitherto existing materialism—that of Feuerbach included—is that the object, reality, sensuousness, is conceived only in the form of the *object* or *contemplation* but not as *human sensuous activity, practice,* not subjectively.
>
> — MARX[1]

The radical shift in philosophy effected by Marx in his elaboration of the concept of "practice" makes it possible to describe this reversal. Marx did not reverse the Hegelian *system*, as Feuerbach did; he rejected it.

He rejected the system. This means that he rejected idealism but that he did not confine himself to Feuerbach's formulation; he did not replace idealist ontology with materialist ontology, nor metaphysics by anthropology, nor religion by another religion christened "humanism" or the religion of man.

Marxism is not naturalized Hegelianism, which contents itself with saying "matter" where Hegel says "spirit," nor does it endow matter with immutable dialectical laws such as Hegel attributed to spirit. Marxism is not speculative materialism dogmatically posited in existence and claiming that it exists "in itself" definitively, taking on itself the prerogative of legislating on the absolute, in the name of a speculative dialectics of the Hegelian type.

To explain Marxist materialism without starting from practice is to explain it in a nondialectical manner and to return to a dogmatic, pre-Marxist conception of philosophy.

There is a radical difference between Marxist materialism and, for example, French materialism of the 18th century. Marx recognized the critical value of French materialism as against feudal absolutism, theology and metaphysics, but it is worth noting that the

influence of this philosophy was brought to bear on him primarily
by Hegel and Feuerbach. It is true that he preferred Diderot as a
writer of prose, and that he held to the materialist "line"—from
Democritus to Diderot to Feuerbach—which maintained the major
thesis of the priority of matter over consciousess. But the great philosophical source of Marxism is classic German philosophy—that of
Kant, of Fichte, of Hegel, and even of Feuerbach, even though
Marx and Engels often said that Feuerbach was infinitely poorer
than Hegel.

When, in *The Holy Family*, Marx made a summary of the history
of French materialism, he put the accent, above all, on the *practical*
merits of materialism, on the moral and political consequences which
linked it directly to socialism and communism: "If man is shaped
by his surroundings, his surroundings must be made human."[2] On
this point he quotes Helvetius and Holbach at length.

From the theoretical standpoint, French materialism beginning with
Descartes, was the struggle against religion and metaphysics in the
interests of the development of the sciences of nature.

To this materialism Marx adduced two objections.

First, considering it in the form presented by mechanistic science, pre-Marxist materialism reveals a very threadbare conception
of matter as being nothing more than an abstract phantom, obedient
only to the laws of mechanics; after Bacon, "in its further development materialism became *one-sided*. . . . Sensuousness lost its bloom
and became the abstract sensuousness of the *geometrician*. Physical
motion was sacrificed to the *mechanical* or *mathematical*."[3]

Finally, and above all, it professes to posit itself inside things
instead of starting from the *practical activity of men:* "The chief
defect of all hitherto existing materialism—that of Feuerbach included—is that the object, reality, sensuousness, is conceived only
in the form of the *object* or *contemplation* but not as *human sensuous
activity, practice*, not subjectively. Thus it happened that the *active*
side, in opposition to materialism, was developed by idealism—but
only abstractly, since, of course, idealism does not know real sensous
activity as such."[4]

Eighteenth century French materialism—that of Holbach, Helvetius, La Mettrie—succumbed to a double illusion: the scientist
illusion that consists of projecting onto nature, as if they constituted

its ultimate essence, scientific laws actually known only at one given moment in the development of the sciences of nature. Hence the concept of matter is impoverished to the point of reduction to the fleshless skeleton of geometry or mechanics, while every great *scientific* discovery enriches the *philosophical* concept of matter—as Engels points out in *Ludwig Feuerbach* when he flays "the shallow vulgarized form in which the materialism of the eighteenth century continues to exist today."[5]

The second, more basic, illusion, of which the first is only a corollary, is the *dogmatic* illusion which professes to make an abstraction of practice, of the activity of knowledge, and, consequently, of its historical and historically relative character, in order to ground themselves, as do the empiricists, in so-called "given facts," as if a *fact* was not precisely something that had been *created*, constructed by the skill and brains of men, transforming nature by their work over many millenia.

All materialism that does not start by comprehending this "active" side of knowledge, this "humanization" of actual nature, and professes to speak of things while making an abstraction of man, is pre-critical materialism. One of the major merits of Marxist materialism is that it does not treat materialism as if Kant, Fichte and Hegel had never existed.

Marx writes, in a formulation that can be misunderstood only if one arbitrarily separates it from its context: "We see how consistent naturalism or humanism distinguishes itself both from idealism and materialism, constituting at the same time the unifying truth of both. We see also how only naturalism is capable of comprehending the act of world history."[6]

This is by no means, as some have interpreted it, an attempt to compromise or a synthesis between materialism and idealism, nor the so-called "transcendence" of one by the other.

The materialism previously existing, from Democritus to Gassendi, and from La Mettrie to Feuerbach, in professing to escape the jurisdiction of practice while failing to understand what was its source or its criterion, posited an abstract nature with no connection to man, his practice and his conscious activity.

Idealism, from Kant to Fichte to Hegel, while setting up the intermediate moment between the inception of knowledge and its goal, i.e., of the activity of knowledge, professed to include everything in the subject and to isolate its activity, while neglecting to start from that which is practiced or that which verifies practice.

Marx surmounted this double abstraction not by abandoning materialism, but by integrating into materialism (considered in terms of human practice) all the "active side" hitherto developed only abstractly by idealism alone.

Thus, his was the only conception of the world to connect "the beginning and the end" without abstracting, as did the older materialists, nature in its bare existence—as if we could know it other than through our cognition, our practice, our techniques and our concepts, always historically provisional and relative. Nor does Marx abstract, as do the idealists, the subjective moment of cognition or of "praxis," the subject in its pure subjectivity, unintelligibly deploying in the void an activity which would give birth to the world and about which they are able to tell us nothing of how it works, how it meets obstacles, nor how it is verified. Lenin summed up this stage of Marx's thinking thus: "The 'first beginning' is forgotten and distorted by idealism. *Dialectical* materialism alone *linked* the 'beginning' with the continuation and the end."[7]

Thus Marxist materialism is based on two essential theses, which contribute an original solution to the problem of the relation of the subject and object: The thesis of the humanization of nature, showing that knowledge and control of nature cannot abstract the subject from "praxis"; and the thesis of the primacy of matter, proving that if what la Palisse said was true, i.e., the object cannot be *known* without a subject, it is an absurdity to say that it cannot *exist* without it.

The humanization of nature is an experiential truth. Marx took exception to Feuerbach's materialism for not "understanding sensuousness as practical activity." "He does not see," he said, "how the sensuous world around him is not a thing *given* direct from all eternity, ever the same, but the product of industry and of the state of society, and, indeed, in the sense that it is a *historical product*, the result of the activity of a whole succession of generations."[8] Feuerbach, like all previous materialists, "never manages to conceive the sensuous world as the total, living sensuous activity of the individuals composing it . . . with him materialism and history diverge completely."[9]

Because the world we live in is a world of products and institutions—the accomplishment of man—it is rich in human meanings; it is not only a fabric of causal laws; it is fraught with purpose and meaning. The projects and planning of human generations for millenia are crystallized in things. The "celebrated 'unity of man with nature' has always existed in industry."[10] "The history of *industry* and the established *objective* existence of industry are the *open book of man's essential powers,* the exposure to the senses of human *psychology. . . . Industry* is the *actual,* historical relationship of nature, and therefore of natural science, to man. . . . The nature which develops in human history—the genesis of human society—is man's *real* nature. . . . History itself is a *real* part of *natural history*—of nature developing into man."[11]

Hence Marxist materialism gives us the key to the problem of phenomenology by working out a concrete method for going back from the constituted object to activity, to the subject in process of being constituted; a materialist method enabling us to grasp again the "meanings" of things and the "intentions" of men—and their interconnections. The grasp of "meaning" is at one and the same time the grasp, through historical analysis, of the purposive operations of creative, productive man and the ideational reproduction of the diverse moments of the creation of products or of institutions in their origins and systematic interconnections.

This appropriation of the object by cognition may easily engender the idealist illusion to which Hegel and Husserl succumbed. Marx took the mechanism apart:

"The concrete is concrete because it is a combination of many objects with different destinations, i.e., a unity of diverse elements. In our thought, it therefore appears as a process of synthesis, as a result and not as a starting point, although it is the real starting point. . . . By the former method the complete conception passes into an abstract definition; by the latter, the abstract definitions lead to the reproduction of the concrete subject in the course of reasoning. . . . Hegel fell into the error, therefore, of considering the real as the result of . . . thought, while the method of advancing from the abstract to the concrete is but a way of thinking by which the concrete is grasped and is reproduced in our minds as concrete. It is by no means, however, the process which itself generates the concrete."[12]

When one sees in consciousness nothing but the productive activity of hypotheses and concepts, ignoring the starting point, the obstacles encountered and the verification in practice, it is a thinking process which ends by confounding the scientific reproduction of the real with genuine production, in which the object would be entirely the work of the subject. This is the principal epistemological root of idealism; it is an illusion that constantly recurs, even in the greatest rationalists, from Fichte to Hegel and from Husserl to Bachelard.

Marx did not yield to this temptation. After having demonstrated that the practical and intellectual activity, the labor, the unceasing material creations of man had *humanized* nature, and that "nature too, taken abstractly, for itself—nature fixed in isolation from man— is nothing for him,"[13] Marx did not make the "fatal leap" of the idealist who still believes he can jump over his shadow. To recognize that we *know* nature only by the activity it brings to bear on us and by the activity that we bring to bear on it, is by no means to deny that it *exists* outside of us, independently of us, before and after us.

"The properties of a thing," wrote Marx in *Capital*, "are not the result of its relations to other things, but only manifest themselves in such relations."[14]

The fact that the properties of a thing appear only in relation to other things by no means explains why, through the relation with the same object chosen as point of reference (our body, for example, with its sense organs and its own activity), one thing appears to be different from another. This is true on even the simplest level: If one pebble is red and the other white, I must look for the cause of this difference in the difference of structure and composition that these things possess "in themselves," i.e., independently of the fact that I am looking at them. This is true at the level of the most sophisticated science as well: There exists a reciprocal action between the measuring instrument, the microscope, and the micro-organism; I cannot grasp the micro-organism except by means of the measuring instruments, and in a unilateral and partial manner, by perturbing its behavior. This does not signify by any means that the micro-object is generated by the measuring instrument; if we can *know nothing* without the measuring instrument, can we deduce from this that *nothing exists* outside of it, without preventing ourselves from understanding that such instruments can scan things and assign measurements to them?

Hence, after having emphasized that the nature "of our days" is interpenetrated throughout with humanity, and that man is no longer surrounded ("except perhaps in some Australian atolls of recent formation") by anything but the products and institutions of a "natural" environment which are the creation of man, Marx adds, "Of course, in all this the priority of external nature remains unassailed, and all this has no application to the original men produced by spontaneous generation,"[15] that is, of nature's characteristic evolution independent of all external intervention.

Marx recalls that—unless one repudiates what all science, geology, paleontology, evolution have established in the face of all creationist, theological or idealistic speculation—matter existed before consciousness, and the earth before the human species. "The creation of the earth has received a mightly blow from geogeny, i.e., from the science which presents the formation of the earth, the further development of the earth, as a process, as a self-generation. Many-sided generation is the only practical refutation of the theory of creation."[16]

To the question: "Who begot the first man and nature as a whole?" Marx answered, in *Manuscripts of 1844*:

"Your question is itself a product of abstraction. Ask yourself how you arrived at that question. When you ask about the creation of nature and man, you are abstracting, in so doing, from man and nature. You postulate them as *nonexistent* and yet you want me to prove them to you as *existing*. Now I say to you: Give up your abstraction and you will also give up your question . . . for as soon as you think and ask, your *abstraction* from the existence of nature and man has no meaning."[17]*

All questions on being emanate from a being; it is therefore contradictory, in the question itself, to imply the nonexistence of this

---

* It is noteworthy that Marx here transposes and reverses Fichte's argument on the ego. The parallelism is too striking—even in the choice of terms—to overlook. On the consciousness, Fichte wrote, "We imagine a certain condition and we ask: What was the ego previously, i.e., what is the substratum of consciousness? But then, without knowing it, we add through thought the absolute subject who perceives this substratum, that is, precisely the thing of which we profess we have made an abstraction; consequently, we contradict ourselves. We cannot think of anything without adding that through thought our Ego is conscious of itself; we can never make an abstraction of our own self-consciousness. Thus we have no answer to give to all the questions about the nature of precedence, because we cease to posit such questions after we understand ourselves." (Fichte, *Grundlage*, I, pp. 97–98.)

being. The concept of nothingness can only be held by a being and is an abstraction from a being whom one must imagine empty of all content.

To grasp the absurdity of this question, this senseless formulation of a "creation" that would be a transition from nothingness to being, is the essential role of materialism.

In the pages of the famous *Holy Family*, Marx takes apart idealism's machinery of speculative illusion. Starting with realities like apples, pears, strawberries, almonds, we form the concept "fruit." Then we declare that the apple, pear, the almond, are simple modes of existence of "fruit," which is their "essence." "It is as hard to produce real fruits from the abstract idea 'fruit,' as it is easy to produce the abstract idea from real fruits. Indeed it is impossible to arrive at the *opposite* of an abstraction without *relinquishing* the abstraction."[18]

Thus philosophy lends a mysterious property to its abstraction, a vital activity comparable to the creative power of God himself. From that moment on, the concept evolves out of itself, and in order to pass from the abstract to the concept, one interpolates on the way— as moments in the development of the concept—everything necessary to this construction by borrowing elements from the real. "In the speculative way of thinking, this operation is called comprehending the *substance* as the *subject,* as an *inner process* . . . and that comprehension constitutes the essential character of *Hegel's* method."[19] We are still left in the same confusion about the *re*production and the production of the object in which idealism turns things upside down and makes them walk on their heads.

Marx recognized in Feuerbach's materialism the merit of having put Hegel's system back on its feet, i.e., of having restored the true order of things by putting an end to speculative alienation: "Feuerbach's great achievement is . . . the establishment of *true materialism* and of *real science* . . . his opposing to the negation of the negation, which claims to be the absolute positive, the self-supporting positive, positively based on itself."[20]

The abstraction of the concept was the first negation (and the first alienation) from the concrete. The concrete produced from the concept (in reality, "*re*produced") was the negation of the negation. Materialism was established in the complete actuality of real nature, which is no more an alienation from the mind and its negation than man is an alienation from God. "The opposite of being (of being in general as Logic looks upon it)," wrote Feuerbach, "is not nothingness but sensuous and concrete being."[21] Atheism is not a negation of religion; it is actual reality, a simple affirmation of the recognition of man and of nature, without any alien addition or mystification.

Feuerbach had thus "paved the way to the materialist outlook on the world, an outlook which is *not without premises,* but which empirically observes the actual material premises as such and for that reason is, for the first time, actually a critical outlook on the world."[22]

"Man is directly a natural being . . . he is an active, natural being,"[23] with his needs, his desires and, external to him, the objects of his needs and desires, just like animals in these respects. "That is why as a natural man he is an objective man who suffers," and he acts, labors to overcome this suffering and to satisfy his needs.

"Whenever real, corporeal *man,* man with his feet firmly on the solid ground, man exhaling and inhaling all the forces of nature, *establishes* his real, objective *essential powers* as alien objects by his externalization, it is not the *act of positing* which is the subject in this process: it is the subjectivity of *objective* essential powers, whose action, therefore, must also be something *objective.* An objective being acts objectively, and he would not act objectively if the objective did not reside in the very nature of his being. He creates or establishes only *objects, because* he is established by objects—because at bottom he is nature. In the act of establishing, therefore, this objective being does not fall from his state of 'pure activity' into a *creating of the object*; on the contrary, his *objective* product only confirms his *objective* activity, establishing his activity as the activity of an objective, natural being."[24]

The materialism which is attained after having put Hegelian idealism back on its feet is not a "revealed" materialism. It is not a "postulate" in the sense of an arbitrary choice of a perspective of thought and action. Practice helps to raise it above its hypothetical character. It is the necessary precondition for the rationality of thought and for responsibility of action. A materialism of this type, which seeks no other verification than that of practice and practice alone, which seeks in practice and practice alone its "letters of credit," could not be put in doubt by practice, since it is the very condition of all real practice.

With Hegel, thought starts from immutable principles.

It ends in an accomplished, final totality.

It develops in an absolutely autonomous fashion, independent of exterior reality, without deriving any enrichment from reality, which the concept observes but which is not the concept.

Now, thought that is neither dogmatic nor speculative cannot start with immutable principles nor from eternal, crystal-clear intuitions (as, for instance, the "simple natures" of Descartes), nor from sensuous "givens," ready-made like those of the French empiricists of the 18th century. In these two instances, we remain on the inside of consciousness. Practice alone enables us to emerge from this sphere.

Marx's reversal discards both the idealism and the speculation. Human practice, even if it has today created an almost entirely "humanized" world where everything seems to be a product or an institution, nevertheless cannot account for its genesis nor its growth without recognizing materialism as the antecedent condition.

First, human practice *cannot account for its genesis*. The world does not begin with human sensibility (the postulate of earlier idealism), but then it does not begin with human practice either. Human history is preceded by biological evolution. Practice, therefore, cannot account for itself and for its origin without ruling out idealism.

Neither can it *account for its development* without ruling out idealism. The thing upon which human practice acts upon itself cannot be Kant's "unknowable-thing-in-itself." The thing-in-itself, yes, in that it exists independently of our practice and anterior to it—but unknowable, no.

That is, its structure is not just random; if it were, its resistance to certain scientific hypotheses and the verification of other hypotheses would be inexplicable.

Hence practice cannot account for its development, for its success or failure, without discarding agnosticism, pragmatism, and all the other attempts at the third way in philosophy, whether positivist or phenomenological.

How can materialism define matter?

When the materialist defines the philosophical concept of matter by saying, "matter is that which exists independently of us, which, in acting upon us, produces our sensations," the idealist or the positivist brandishes the argument of Fichte (who was indeed a formidable antagonist to Kant), asserting that this "matter" or this "thing-in-itself" is a pure metaphysical entity and therefore plays an absolutely superfluous role. To define matter as a homogeneous, formless substratum of the glittering diversity of concrete phenomena, would be to drive materialism into a corner.

Indeed, of what good would it be to affirm the existence of a thing-in-itself, distinct from my hallucinations or dreams or my conceptual or mathematical fantasies, if this thing in itself were unknowable and undifferentiated, as Kant believed? The futile phantom would be of no use to us, and Fichte was right to use his ammunition against it. It would also be as incomprehensible to draw from this abstract "matter" all of its apparent wealth as it would be to generate this wealth from combining the act with intelligence, in the manner of idealism. Engels put it well in *Anti-Dühring*[25]: "Matter, as such, is a pure creation of thought and of pure abstraction. We make abstraction of the qualitative differences of things by embracing them insofar as they exist corporeally under the concept of matter."

This was a reversion to a remarkable thesis of Feuerbach's: "Matter is light, electricity, air, water, fire, earth, plants. One cannot think of matter as something formless or congealed. Being without quality is a chimera, a ghost!"[26] From this vital and rich conception of matter, dialectics takes its meaning.

Marx's Dialectics

For Hegel, contradiction is a moment in totality.
For Marx, totality is a moment in contradiction.

Is it true that for Marx there is no dialectics in the absence of man—his thought, his action? Is dialectics for Marx only the relationship between subject and object, or the relationship between objects as well? In other words, was dialectics, applied to things, the product of an alienation by which the mind projects its own motion on to things, dialecticizes the real under the illusion of speaking of nature when it is only speaking of itself?

This, in truth, is a problem that existed before Marxism. In his *History of Philosophy*, Hegel made this complaint about Kant: "Transcendental idealism lets the contradiction remain, only it is not being in itself that is thus contradictory, for the contradiction has its source in our thought alone." And he grows ironic on the subject: "Kant shows here too much tenderness for things! It would be a pity, he thinks, if they contradicted themselves."[1]

Actually, thought was constrained to discover dialectics and to have recourse to it only in order to reconcile certain aspects of nature, resistant to another logic, with rationality. Dialectics is an effort to rationalize some complex aspects of the real: motion, contradiction, totality.

Hence, by its very nature, dialectics, far from hobbling thought, fundamentally opens up new aspects of the real.

English materialism and the French materialism of the 18th century assigned dialectics to a subordinate role, since their conception of matter was threadbare and abstract. "The first and most important of the inherent qualities of *matter*," wrote Marx, "is *motion*, not only *mechanical* and *mathematical* motion, but still more, *impulse, vital life-spirit, tension*—or, to use Jacob Bohme's expression, 'the throes of matter.' "[2]

Dialectics is the method of investigation that enables us to reconcile with rational thought the development and the contradictions that are its motive power. Hence dialectics cannot, in the materialist perspective of Marx, remain where Hegel left it. Marx did not so much preserve the Hegelian method, he *reversed* it. Here again, it is the primacy of practice that is the key to the inversion.

In the idealist, theological perspective of the Hegelian system all reality was subsumed in consciousness. This was a backward step from Fichte. This perspective held that: (1) the concept is, in the final analysis, the stuff of the world; (2) the system of concepts that constitutes the world is a completed whole, a totality; (3) dialectics, dominated precisely by this category of totality is—on the inside of the system—the study of the laws that connect each moment to the whole (the finite to the infinite, as Hegel put it).

Reversing the *system* therefore consisted of substituting for this dogmatic and theological idealism, a dogmatic and, in the end, theological materialism which would posit a finished system of dialectical laws in a finished nature.

Reversing the *method* was to go far beyond this. Marx broke with Hegelian dogmatism in passing from idealism to materialism by the path of practice. Because of the very fact that practice applies to the real world, that it starts from the real world and tries to account for it—and not to superimpose itself *a priori* on the world—dialectics is necessarily always wide open and incompleted. It could hardly profess an "accomplished" philosophy in a world that was never accomplished.

To reverse "the cage of the Hegelian idea," as Marx said, was not enough. To reverse it was still to remain inside it. Materialism made it possible to get out of it, i.e., not only to reverse it, but to smash it and emerge into the real world where reality is continuously generated. (At that epoch particularly, with the rise of the working-class movement and its struggles—Chartism in England, the rebellion of the silk-weavers of Lyons in France and the revolt of the Silesian weavers in Germany—all of which did not enter into the "completed totality" of the Hegelian idea.)

History was not finished. The regime, insofar as it was a regime, must be destroyed and rejected.

What then remained of the Hegelian method? For Hegel had put his method at the service of the regime. He had confined it there, forbidding it to break through its bars.

Dialectics, for Hegel, was dominated by the category of totality.

For Hegel, totality, the absolute, did not exist outside of this moment and could not act upon it as an external motor. In the theological transposition with which Hegel invested his system, God —present in every moment—died every moment, too. God's death is simultaneously God's eternal life. God is death, and by this death he affirms his presence and his life at every moment. Such is the central vision of the Hegelian philosophy.[3] The development of the absolute on the inside of time implies the transcendence of each moment. Thus each moment is identified with the absolute and reveals it insofar as it expresses its necessary determination, and denies it insofar as it presumes to be sufficient unto itself. This original relation, irreducible to classical logic, is dialectics.

The relation between totality and contradication are, for Hegel, only one specific case of this fundamental relation.

Totality, for a finite being, is lived as contradiction, or rather— to avoid the language of subjectivity—totality breaks up into contradiction.

The immanent presence of totality in each finite being, that immanent presence which is the source of its evolution, its death, its transcendence, is manifested as contradiction.

Dialectics is primarily a logic of relationship: Relationship, even in its most elementary form, i.e., that of identity to difference, is already dialectical.

In establishing this dialectical unity, this contradictory, living, concrete totality, at the heart of which identity and difference are only moments abstracted by external reflection, Hegel somehow posited thought at the moving heart of things: Identity did not exist in things but only in the thought which confronts identity with difference and diversity; actually, each of these terms exists only through its opposite and not through itself.

That which is simply otherness in external reflection and in abstract thought is, in actual reality, contradiction. The two terms (identity and difference) which, on the level of outer semblance, were simply different, are at the same time in an indissoluble relation, i.e., each is reflected in the other, each excludes the other and at the same time implicates it, and this is the internal source of its motion.

Contradiction is, in each finite being, in each specific being, its living soul, since this being is only a definite expression of the totality; the contradiction which sets each finite being into motion is only the definitive expression of totality in this particular being.

For Hegel the world is a totality and truth is the reconstruction of this whole. Hence, all real relationship is contradiction; each part is defined only by the form in which it is real, i.e., in its relation to the whole. Each thing is all that it is not, because all else is its condition—that by means of which it becomes necessary.

This reciprocal conditioning of things generates their characteristics—weight or color, for example. Not only is it impossible to *conceive* of an absolutely isolated thing, cut off from all connection to anything—but such a thing just cannot be. Everything in nature, as in thought, requires the existence of a thing other than itself, of something that it is not, of its opposite, which is its necessary correlative.

Dialectics is a logic of conflict. This complex relation of each with all that it is not, this contradictory relation with the whole, which marks its limits, is defined as conflict. Things, by limiting each other mutually, by putting limits to their respective growth, are found in the relation of confrontation, at times even of antagonism. Hence each finite reality finds itself contained, or rather driven back into its limitations, by another reality, by the sum-total of other realities that keep it from being the whole. Quantum physics, on its present level of development, furnishes a striking illustration with respect to matter itself in this aspect of the Hegelian dialectic.

Dialectics is a logic of motion. In this world of opposing forces, motion is a corollary of universal interdependence. If everything holds still, everything moves. Hegel showed that rest is an abstraction which is nowhere absolute rest, but only relatively stable equilibrium, and that consequently it is false to posit the question of how beings originally immobile were set in motion. The true problem is to explain, starting from the reality of motion, the appearance of rest.

Motion alone is real, while rest is only an abstraction. All scientific developments since Hegel, from nuclear physics to astrophysics, have confirmed this point of view. In the eye which might contract in a few instants by hundreds of thousandths, mountains can rise up like waves and, like them, recede. Only the grossness of my vision prevents me from seeing, beyond the illusory immobility of my table, the swarming of the atoms that compose it.

Thus Hegel eliminated both the mechanism—in which motion was external to things regarded as independent of one another and consequently motionless—and the deism which results, because if movement is not inside things and identical to them, if rest is first, it would be necessary to have recourse to the "original fillip" to set the universe going.

Dialectics is a logic of life. It is the moving aggregate of the internal relations of an organic totality in the process of development.

The finality of things is precisely the motion that they contain within themselves, the tendency, arising from the contradiction between their finite nature and that which transports them beyond themselves toward the infinite. As Lenin said, in his commentary on Hegel's *Science of Logic*, the nature of a finite being is to move toward its end.[4]

Formal logic left consciousness on the outside of things. Hegel's logic expresses the highest requirement of reason: to make the total reality of nature and of history transparent to reason; to make being in its rationality come alive for us.

To discover in our own reason the reason of things, ideally to reproduce and rebuild so as to perceive the internal necessity of that which sensuous perception presents as a poorly connected aggregate of empirical facts and events—this is the objective of all science which does not confine itself to positivism, of all philosophy which does not bog down in irrationality.

To be sure, if one retains from Hegelian thought only the closed system to which it tends and not the living method that animates it, contradictions and their universal presence in nature, history and thought take on a theological character.

To Hegel, contradiction and totality are both opposed and interconnected, like the finite and the infinite, i.e., totality from the viewpoint of the infinite is contradiction from the viewpoint of the finite. Totality is lived as contradiction by the finite being. Or again: Contradiction is the central category of the Helegian *method*; totality is the central category of the Hegelian *system*.

Out of this comes the diversity of ways in which the Hegelian heritage is utilized; one can retain unilaterally either totality or contradiction as essential to dialectics, depending on the definition given of each of them—for example, whether one substitutes the gestalt conception of totality or the Kierkegaardian conception of contradiction for Hegelian thought.

If it is indisputable that Hegel's dialectics, with its fundamental categories of totality and contradiction, has a universal significance encompassing nature, history and thought, it is no less certain that a theological conception of the world characterizes his thinking, in the first place, because of the fact that contradiction is only a moment in totality. It is totality en route, in a sense militant but not yet triumphant.

At each moment totality takes in all *becoming*; its presence, active from the beginning, is felt in each individual being as his own goad; his insufficiency as a finite being is the driving force of his development. But this incompleteness exists only with reference to totality. Furthermore, Hegel says unequivocally: "Going to the bottom of things, one finds all growth embodied in the seed." Hence totality pre-exists at moments of development and provides the bases for them; contradiction is only the small change of totality.

Thus the Hegelian conception of totality implies: (1) the existence of a world and history already complete; (2) the consciousness of this completeness, without which the circularity necessary to absolute knowledge is not realized. For this double condition, reality may indeed be perfectly transparent to reason, since basically it is identical with reason.

In terms of his *Logic*, Hegel tries to lead us into dealing only with the creative act of a world in process of self-creation.

This creative act immanent in all beings that we encompass in the absolute idea is comparable to the genesis of a work of art. In esthetic creation, there is freedom of choice in materials and content, and this creative freedom is identified with the internal necessity of the work to be created. Religion similarly affords, on the plane of myth, an image of dialectical genesis: The universal subject is like God, creator of the heavens and of earth and of becoming, which is contradictory to his Incarnation.

But this double esthetic and religious analogy does not help us to understand anything but the speculative form of the Helegian system.

Is the dialectical method indissociable from this idealist and speculative system, and from these esthetic and theological analogies?

For Marx, the materialist reversal of Hegelian philosophy and the transition from speculation to science enabled him to work out a dialectical method related to the valid method of science, which does not limit itself to positivism nor to the search for *constant* interconnections between phenomena, but which seeks the internal and necessary relations between them.

The development of the sciences has by now imposed recourse to dialectics in the study of nature and history. The existence of the dialectics of nature and history by no means implies Hegel's theological postulate of pre-existent thought immanent in nature and history, i.e., the postulate of a logic anterior to nature. To speak of the dialectics of nature is simply to recognize that the structure of matter is such that only the dialectical method can cope with it.

Dialectics is not an *a priori* scheme that one may use like armor-plate over things, or that one can superimpose on them, or that one can force them into like a Procrustean bed. This kind of speculative conception was Hegel's; in the theological postulates of his system, he had reversed the real order of things. The sciences of his time— filling the breach with the mechanistics of the Cartesians and of the 18th century with the astronomical hypotheses of Kant and Laplace, the geology of Hutton and Lyell, the predictions of transformism of Diderot and Lamarck, the biological organicism of Goethe—had furnished him with the experimental elements from which he had discovered some of the great laws of dialectics. Hegel codified and systematized these laws which testified to the marvelous resurgence of the scientific spirit. He transformed it into a kind of completed balance-sheet of the history of thought. In this he was the victim of an illusion comparable to that of Kant: From Aristotle's logic, Euclid's geometry, and Newton's physics, Kant had presumed to define once and for all time the *a priori* forms of sensuousness and intelligence. Hegel also confused what was a new stage in the scientific conception of the world with an eternal structure of nature, history and thought.

For Marx, the materialist reversal was not basically his awareness that Hegel, after Kant, had inverted the real order of things and that, as a result, he had failed to put dialectics back on its feet. The nature of Marx's materialism, as opposed to idealism and speculation, is to renounce the vain pretension of modeling things on our concepts but instead, more modestly, to model our concepts on things. What this means, in the first place, is that no concept is eternal and definitive, that philosophy cannot take the form of a closed system, that the list of dialectical categories cannot be a closed list.

This dialectical method, in its materialist—that is, open—interpretation, thus shatters the dogmatic system.

This history of the sciences shows how, under the impetus of experiment and practice, our still inadequate concepts will continue to be shattered.

The reversal of Hegelian, indeed all idealism, the metamorphosis of speculative and dogmatic dialectics into a method of experimental research and discovery, calls for an inversion of perspective, positing not totality but contradiction on the first level. To Hegel, totality was self-limiting and this was what gave rise to contradiction. For Marx, on the other hand, it is the development of the contradiction, the transcendence of the negation into the negation of the negation that engenders new totalities; it is not the universal that has primacy and is self-limiting, but the particular that necessarily transcends itself, since it does not carry within it the conditions of its existence. Dialectics is at one and the same time the insufficiency of being and the summons to thought.

For Hegel, contradiction is a moment in totality.

For Marx, totality is a moment in contradiction.

Hence it is not true that dialectics may be a kind of anthropomorphic projection onto nature of models valid only inside human history, human consciousness and practice.

Materiality is not only negation, limitation, resistance with respect to the activity of the intelligence or of human practice. For negation is not just any sort of thing, anonymous, abstract, always self-identical.

The "in-itself" answers *no* to such a hypothesis—and at times also *yes*. The negative response has a practical character. It is a sort of acceptance: Nature obeys, lets itself be controlled. In acting on this hypothesis, I have power over nature. It is true that these hypotheses are self-destructive and that no single one of them could therefore claim to reveal an ultimate structure of being. But each dead hypothesis, because it has lived, has left us a legacy of a new power over nature. This power survives the old hypothesis, and the new one is the inheritor of the hypothesis it has replaced. These powers are cumulative and my activities today in utilizing these powers to control nature delineate at least a rough sketch of its structure, more and more precisely known.

We cannot content ourselves with affirming the bare existence of primordial nature. If it manifests itself as resistance, as limitation, it is also acquiescent—which presupposes that it has a structure and that consciousness, by means of hypothesis, trial and error, models its contours on things whose motion and rhythm it espouses, for better or for worse.

Are this motion and rhythm dialectical?

The history of the sciences alone can answer. It is a fact that the requirements of the object have rendered unusable schematized techniques and outworn logic. From physics to biology, the sciences of nature have not ceased to exercise a growing pressure over our habits of thought, to the point of forcing us at a certain level to abandon traditional logic.

It has obliged investigators to have recourse to other models than those which obey the laws of traditional logic and the principles of mechanics.

Now, if a hypothesis of structure is verified, if it is proven to be valid, if its enables us to control things, how is it possible to conceive that there is no actual relation between the structure that has been conceived and the "thing-in-itself?"

How could dialectical thinking enable us to understand a being that would not be like it to any degree?

That is why Marx himself suggests the existence of dialectical relationships in nature. When he analyzes, for example, the production of surplus value and the origin of the capitalist system, he comments: "Here, as in natural science, is shown the correctness of the law discovered by Hegel (in his *Logic*), that merely quantitative differences beyond a certain point pass into qualitative changes."[5] In a footnote on this point, he makes reference to chemical phenomena. It is not accidental that the comparison was made at a moment when Engels was studying the dialectics of nature in various sciences. Marx, who followed his work closely and agreed with it (as can be unmistakably seen in the correspondence of 1873–74), insists on the dialectical character of the phenomena of nature and history. "You will also see from the conclusion of my Chapter III, where the transformation of the handicraft-master into a capitalist —as a result of purely *quantitative* changes—is touched upon, that *in the text* I refer to the law Hegel discovered, of *purely quantitative changes turning into qualitative changes*, as holding good alike in history and natural science."[6]

Does this mean that the recognition of the dialectics of nature implies an arbitrary extrapolation and a misapprehension of the specificity of stages and levels? By no means. If it is true that the laws of nature and the laws of thought belong to one and the same universe, it is not necessary to represent the former as a "thingified" projection of the latter. To do so would be to put forward a theological or, at the least, Hegelian conception, positing the existence of an absolute spirit within nature.

To say that there is a dialectics of nature is not to claim to know in advance and *ne varietur* (definitively) the fundamental laws of the development of nature; on the contrary, under the irresistible impetus of scientific discovery it is no longer to see, in Aristotelean logic nor in the principles of mechanics, anything but a specfic case at the inside of a much more general dialectics, taking into account the new aspects of nature discovered by various sciences.

There exists no closed, completed, definitive list of the laws of dialectics. The laws known at present constitute a provisional balance sheet of our knowledge; social practice and scientific experiment alone enable us to expand it further.

To say that a dialectics of nature exists is to say that the structure and motion of reality are such that only dialectic thought renders phenomena intelligible and controllable.

That is why the dialectics of nature, when it is not interpreted in a mystical, anti-Marxist manner, far from jeopardizing the freedom of men, is an instrument for their liberation.

Dialectics and Freedom

Freedom is the conquest of alienation.

The dialectics of nature does not weigh heavily on human freedom like some doom; human freedom does not have to fit itself into a rut already hollowed out by nature.

The recognition of dialectical laws outside man and his history does not make human history a mere appendix to a much vaster history—that of nature.

Nature has a history. Man also. The fact that all science tends to become historical and discovers laws of development, the fact of the historical unity of knowledge, by no means precludes the irreducibility of the sectors under study, the specificity of the stages. At each stage, specific forms of motion are manifested and dialectics takes on a specific form.

From nature to man, there is at one and the same time both continuity and discontinuity.

If there were only continuity, it would partake of mechanistic materialism.

If there were only discontinuity, it would partake of spiritualism.

For Marx, there was both continuity and discontinuity. Man is part of nature. But human history obeys specific laws. To adduce only one example: Alienation and its transcendence do not exist and are not conceivable except on a human level of development.

Man cannot reduce himself to the aggregate of his circumstances. One could hardly deduce his existence as a mechanical resultant from this aggregate. Historical materialism sanctions neither reduction nor deduction.

Reduction of the higher to the lower form is a definition of mechanistic materialism alone. The nature of dialectics and the materialism it animates is to teach us precisely that the whole is different from the sum of its parts, and this is true at each stage.

The fundamental idea that it is men who make their own history in a social environment which conditions them, as Engels stressed again toward the end of his life, cannot be confounded with the idea that in history there are only epiphenomena of economics—"the economic position produces an automatic effect"[1]—a conception of vulgar, mechanistic materialism at the opposite pole from the dialectic.

Internal necessity cannot be manifested except through an infinitude of chances, which are, in history, the only form of the existence of necessity. History, wrote Marx, "would . . . be of a very mystical nature if accidents played no part."[2]

Thus Marx amplified the tradition of the great German humanism that based the real power of man and his freedom on the recognition of necessity. Goethe, inspired by Hegel's "strategem of reason" gave the broadest expression of this: "The web of life is woven of necessity and chance. Man's reason stands between them and governs both, treating necessity as the foundation of its being and at the same time guiding the operation of chance to its own advantage, for man only deserves to be called a god of this earth, as long as in the exercise of his reason he stands firm and immovable."[3]

Necessity in human history assumes, according to Marx, two basic forms: that of external necessity, expressed in alienation; that of internal necessity, expressed in the struggle for the conquest of alienation.

In the alienated world, where, in great part, external necessity prevails, man tends to be only a link in the chain of things and events; human history, as Marx writes, tends to become similar to natural history.

This sort of necessity demands, for example, the development of capitalism, of a regime in which by reason of the alienation arising from private ownership of the means of production, the dominion of things, man is the *object* of history.

When, on the other hand, Marx spoke of the necessity for the inevitable advent of socialism, this is a far more profound necessity. It no longer concerns the *external* necessity of the development of a system from which man, regarded as a thing, is alienated, but an *internal* necessity in which man constitutes part of the *givens* of the problem: The victory of socialism will not come by itself, as a kind of necessity inherent in things—as if the working class were carried forward by the sole force of the inertia of the mechanisms of capital. This kind of mechanistic determinism has always led to reformism, to the idea of a gradual and automatic evolvement of socialism within capitalism.

Dialectical necessity in the revolutionary negation is therefore the very opposite of mechanistic necessity. The latter is effectuated without me; the former requires my participation. One teaches passivity and resignation; the other leads to mastery of its own power and to historical initiative.

External necessity properly understood delineates a range of possibilities; it definitely excludes certain possibilities, i.e., the return of capitalism to feudalism is, for example, precluded, as well as the return of monopoly capitalism to liberal capitalism. But it does not demand a choice; to say that the advent of socialism is necessary at the present stage of capitalism, does not mean that it will be established no matter what we may do. It means that the contradictions of capitalism are of such a nature that they can be resolved only by the suppression of the capitalist ownership of the means of production and the transition to socialism. But if we are not conscious of this necessity, or if we neglect the tasks that this consciousness imposes upon us, or if, having this consciousness and assuming this task, we multiply the errors of strategy and tactics, contradiction could continue to be unresolved, and this could lead to a decline in history marked by the convulsions and catastrophes inevitably generated by unresolved contradiction—crises, wars, and so on.

How does the transition from external to internal necessity operate? The first stage is that in which man, utterly alienated, is transformed into a thing or an animal; the second is that of history subjected to a fully conscious human goal. These are two extreme cases, in their idealized form. In reality there are many gradations of freedom between these extremes, of the effective intervention of man in the unfolding of history—from the jungle described by Marx, in which human projects cancel each other out, or from which ensue mechanical results that no one desires, to a classless society evolving according to conscious plan by means of the collective efforts of all men.

In the transition from one to the other, the role of consciousness, the subjective factor, grows more important. Man, formerly the *object* of history becomes the *subject*.

How is this transition to working-class consciousness effected?

The necessity that leads a worker to struggle against the capitalist system is not an external necessity; it is not endured passively by him as if were a force of history. Nor is it the necessity of "animal instinct," nor of "spontaneity"—spontaneity is only the recording of external necessity, a passive reflection of the immediate objective situation. The worker, accepting the prevailing ideas, as Marx notes, the ideas of the ruling class, can still seek immediate advantages by simply adapting himself to the existing social system; can become a stool-pigeon for his employer, or attempt to "set himself up on his own" to escape his condition, or practice class collaboration, or simply accept his condition with resignation as foreordained necessity or providential exigency. Here we have many variants of the acceptance of the immediate appearances of the system and its ideological justifications—accommodation, evasion, collaboration, resignation.

The workers' consciouness can also reflect the immediate situation not by passive adaptation but by rebellious reaction. This is also a matter of degree. Engels, in *The Condition of the Working-Class in England*, has traced the stages from the legal and even criminal actions of individuals, such as the destruction of machines, to the collective struggle for wages, in strikes and union organizations. The transformation of the workers' situation plays a major role in the transition from blind rebellion to organized forms of class struggle. The advance of industrial concentration, above all, creates the objective conditions favorable to the growing awareness of a definite solidarity among workers. But if one limits oneself to the existing state of the relations between employer and workers, it is impossible to rise above a certain level of consciousness, i.e., economic struggle and union organization.

To advance to a truly revolutionary struggle, in which the goal is not only to secure the best conditions for the sale of labor power but also to create a system where labor power is no longer sold as a commodity, one must arrive at a new, decisive level of consciousness. Here one takes one's stand on a position broader than that of of the immediate struggle between workers and employers, in order to take into account—as Marx does in *The Communist Manifesto*—the totality of the historical movement that gives meaning to the present struggles of the working class, makes it the inheritor and continuator of all man's struggles throughout history, opening up before him the perspective of a classless, unalienated society.

The task of bringing this consciousness to the working class—as we shall see more fully in discussing Marx's politics—is incumbent on the party of the working class, the indispensable instrument of its liberation. In the party, the fusing of the working class movement with scientific socialism, i.e., the consciousness of this historical movement by the only force really capable of extirpating, along with the private ownership of the means of production, capitalism's universal alienation of man, constitutes a decisive step in the conquest of freedom.

This transition from the class "in itself" to the class "for itself" is allied, in Spinoza, to the transition from consciousness of the "first order" to consciousness of the "third order," which alone opens the way to freedom.

For Marx, as for Hegel, freedom is the transcendence of alienation. But if, for Hegel and Feuerbach, this transcendence takes place in the individual consciousness, for Marx it requires a real transformation of the world—not only of the idea that we ourselves create about it. In Marx, as we have seen, alienation is not only self-alienation but that of social reality, of the reality of classes and their antagonism. Hence, the problem of freedom is not only individual but historic and social—a class problem—closely related to the revolutionary tasks of the proletariat.

Marx, in *The German Ideology*, shows us that up to the present time individual freedom exists only for individuals belonging to the ruling class.

All conceptions of freedom reflect the class position of those who profess it; each ruling class interprets as freedom the continuance of its class privileges. "A Yankee comes to England, where he is prevented by a Justice of the Peace from flogging his slave, and he exclaims indignantly: 'Do you call this a land of liberty, where a man can't larrup his nigger?'"[4]

For the bourgeoisie, freedom is the maintenance of "free enterprise"; for the proletariat, freedom is the elimination of this system.

The ruling classes always call the abolition of their class privileges tyranny and the destruction of freedom.

Long before, Montesquieu had clearly discerned the class interpretation of freedom and the fraud of abstraction:

"In politics this word freedom to a great extent only means what the orators and poets make it mean. Strictly, the word only expresses a relationship, and cannot serve to differentiate between various kinds of government, since a people's state implies the freedom of the poor and weak and the servitude of the rich and powerful, and monarchy means the freedom of the powerful and the servitude of the humble. . . . Thus, in a civil war, when it is said that one fights for freedom, this is not so: The people fight for domination over the powerful, and the powerful fight for domination over the people."[5]

Each class identifies freedom with the defense of its class interests. As the concentration of capital and the monopoly privileges of capital become the prerogative of a more and more miniscule minority, the abolition of these privileges gives freedom to the greatest number of people.

The road to freedom passes through the dictatorship of the proletariat.

Communism is identified with the advent of true freedom. It ends alienation and the illusions that alienation engenders.

It is characteristic that the bourgeoisie should identify freedom with accident and irrationality. This is consistent with the very nature of the capitalist system. As Marx said, "In competition, personality itself is a matter of chance, while chance is personality."[6]

The law of bourgeois society is anarchy, the individualistic law of the jungle, i.e., that which assures the enslavement and the crushing of the dispossessed, for whom "democratic" allusions are only a synonym for servitude in fact. Marx describes "the man, no longer bound to other men even by the *semblance* of common ties . . . the universal struggle of man against man, individual against individual. In the same way *civil society* as a whole is this war among themselves of all those individuals no longer isolated from the others by anything else but their *individuality*. . . . The contradiction between the *democratic representative state* and *civil society* is the perfection of the *classic* contradiction between public *commonwealth* and *slavedom*. In the modern world each one is *at the same time* a member of slavedom and of the public common-wealth. Precisely the *slavery of civil society* is in *appearance* the greatest *freedom* because it is in appearance the perfect *independence* of the individual. . . . In reality, this is the perfection of his slavery and his inhumanity."[7]

The individual sees the semblance of legal right, while the real drama of privilege unfolds somewhere behind his back.

Marx gives many concrete examples of this.

First, that of the capitalist market: "The sphere of competition . . . considered in each individual case, is dominated by chance; where, then, the inner law, which prevails in these accidents and regulates them, is only visible when these accidents are grouped together in large numbers, where it remains, therefore, invisible and unintelligible to the individual agents in production."[8] Every seller and every buyer thinks himself free; yet all are in the service, willy-nilly, of the law of value. And what can be said when the seller is seller of his own labor power! He may have the illusion of being free; he is not like the slave bound to a particular master or like the serf bound to the soil; he is "free" to sell himself to whomever he wishes, but he is bound to sell himself to someone, and if his "commodity" finds no takers, he and his family are still free to die of hunger in the iron jaws of this strange system of freedom.

Under the regime of alienation, everything that embodies the power and wealth accumulated by all the past generations of hu-manity has taken on the form of things and institutions—all the way from money to the state—separated from man and dominating him.

By its very nature, the classless society of communism puts an end to this opposition between individual and society by reintegrating with the individual man the hitherto exteriorized, alienated social forces, by rendering all the forces of society "interior" for the individual.

Freedom, according to Marx, does not lie in individualism, denial, negation, precarious and always hazardous withdrawal. The individual man is free when all humanity lives in him, all the past which is his culture, all his present reality, which is universal co-operation.

Thus no man achieves freedom by himself. No man is free in an enslaved society.

This is the permanent lesson of materialism which once made Helvetius remark: "Ethics is but a frivolous science, if one does not mix it with politics and legislation."[9]

Every conception of freedom which professes to be valid according to its own precepts without coping with the concrete conditions of alienation can only sow illusions. Marx adduced the example of Christianity and the dividing of man as the foundation of its traditional teaching, which carries over into ethics as the kind of dichotomy characteristic of alienation: "The only reason why Christianity wanted to free us from the domination of the flesh was because it regarded our flesh, our desires as something foreign to ourselves; it wanted to free us from determination by nature only because it regarded our own nature as not belonging to us. . . . If I myself am not nature . . . all determination by nature . . . seems to me a determination by something foreign . . . *heteronomy as opposed to autonomy of the spirit.*"[10]

That is why Marx was to write: "The Christian ideal of freedom, i.e., . . . the illusion of freedom."[11]

This is applicable not only to Christianity but to all conceptions of freedom which are not rooted in history and mankind's struggles, which claim to bestow freedom on man without giving all men the power to master nature and their social relations.

Freedom, said Marx, equals real power.[12]

Socialism is the advent of a society that destroys all material obstacles, and especially those which are economic and social, to the integration of all humanity into each man. Freedom without illusion is the potentiality for all men to have access to the sum-total of human culture, to participate fully in the consciously organized, common tasks of all men and in the wealth and power so produced— and then to develop their full creative powers with no limitation other than their own capacities or talents.

Freedom, "the all-around development of the individual will only cease to be conceived as an ideal . . . when the impact of the world which stimulates the real development of the abilities of the individual comes under the control of the individuals themselves, as the communists desire."[13]

Marx was to define in *Capital* the economic and social foundation of this concrete humanism: Communism is a "community of free individuals, carrying on their work with the means of production in common, in which the labour-power of all the different individuals is consciously applied as the combined labour-power of the community."[14]

Does this mean that with the achievement of the classless society under communism history will have come to an end? Certainly not. What comes to an end with the capitalist system is the brutal prehistory of mankind. "The bourgeois relations of production are the last antagonistic form of the social process of production. . . . This social formation constitutes, therefore, the closing chapter of the prehistoric stage of human society."[15].

Communism is the beginning of properly human history; it is not made up of the carnivorous conflicts of the jungle, of class struggle and war. "Just as knowledge is unable to reach a perfected termination in a perfect, ideal condition of humanity, so is history unable to do so."[16]

This society will no longer have need as the only motivating force.

"In fact, the realm of freedom actually begins only where labor which is determined by necessity and mundane considerations ceases; thus in the very nature of things it lies beyond the sphere of actual material production. Just as the savage must wrestle with Nature to satisfy his wants, to maintain and reproduce life, so must civilized man, and he must do so in all social formations and under all possible modes of production. With his development this realm of physical necessity expands as a result of his wants; but, at the same time, the forces of production which satisfy these wants also increase. Freedom in this field can only consist in socialized man, the associated producers, rationally regulating their interchange with Nature, bringing it under their common control, instead of being ruled by it as by the blind forces of Nature; and achieving this with the least expenditure of energy and under conditions most favorable to, and worthy of, their human nature. But it nonetheless still remains a realm of necessity. Beyond it begins that development of human energy which . . . can blossom forth only with this realm of necessity as its basis."[17]

Marx adds that the basic prerequisite for this expansion is the shortening of the working day, because the gauge of wealth will no longer be working time; it will be leisure.

Is it possible to say the living soul of dialectics is contradiction as the only "forward drive?" What will history become when the class struggle is no longer its driving force?

Contradictions will not be abolished, but these will not be the antagonistic contradictions between men.

Then the infinite dialectics of history will fully unfold.

In the first place, man's conquest of nature will persist. In the endless laboratories of that triple infinity—the microscopic, the large and the complex—man has the perspective of exertions without end: in the realm of microphysics and the disintegration of matter; in the realm of the cosmos; in the realm of more and more new chemical syntheses such as those of chlorophyl and of life. To master the elements, to change climates, to achieve better controls in biology than those our own century has achieved over inert matter—these are among the vistas that open before us. From these researchers and these discoveries in science, we contemplate unlimited powers: the chilling thoughts of those who go so far as to touch upon the death of man and the human species, envisaging, for example, the thermic death of the universe; the first advance of man into the infinite which opens the perspectives of cosmic migrations. And if the power to split the atom from now on makes the annihilation of life on earth possible, might not the social uses of atomic energy, the utilization of the internal energy of matter, enable a united humanity to concentrate its powers in such a manner that it might be able to change the orbit of the earth, as has been accomplished with artificial satellites?

Then, beyond the violent dialectics of our history, or rather, of our prehistory, the classless communist society will for the first time create the real conditions for a dialectic of dialogue—that of criticism and self-criticism, of which Socrates and Plato first dreamed. Then will arise uniquely human cooperation in the discovery of the truth between minds possessing all the previous culture of mankind, with none of the trickery of the spurious "democracy" of class systems warping the free and equal confrontation of highly individualized—because highly socialized—intellects in perfect reciprocity.

Finally, this creation will have the character of esthetic creation, i.e., a creation, in the first place, that is not constrained by any other need than the specifically human need for creation and self-creation. But, it might be said, if the base of society will no longer change, how according to the theses of historical materialism will superstructures, and especially the creations of the mind, be able to develop? Summing up in *Capital* the basic idea of historical materialism, Marx wrote: "Technology discloses man's mode of dealing with Nature, the process of production by which he sustains his life, and thereby also lays bare the mode of formation of his social relations, and of the mental conceptions that flow from them."[18]

From the two elements that constitute the base of all society, the first, the productive forces, will be more mobile than ever; and the second, social relations, can hardly fail to be transformed in terms of this expansion without, however, once again becoming antagonistic and generating rationalizing ideologies. Besides, as we have seen, Marx never drew a straight line of causality between the base and the superstructure. On the contrary, he recognized in the latter a relative autonomy and a specific range: Art, music, painting, poetry are not the outcome nor the passive reflection of the base from which they spring; they participate actively in the creation of a new aspect of humanity. No doubt, this creation will no longer have agony as its inspiration. Men will remember that Dante also wrote of paradise, and that his poem inspired the dances in Botticelli's "Springtime." Why cannot man create without the spur of need and anguish, when the Christians themselves conceived a God whose creation was not by an inevitable generation, but was rather a free gift of love? Marxist materialism, faithful to its Fichtean and Faustian early inspiration, is the creator of a world inhabited by untroubled gods, whose creation inaugurates a dialectics opening on infinity.

III. MARX AND POLITICAL ECONOMY

Marx's *Capital* bears the subtitle, "A Critique of Political Economy." This "critique" is different from that of Kant, but, like it, constitutes a real "Copernican revolution" in political economy as well as in philosophy. The economic revolution is as profound as the philosophical one and employs a similar methodology.

In political economy, as in philosophy, Marxist criticism has the following characteristics in common with Kantian criticism: It deals with similar principles of consciousness; it considers "phenomena," sense impressions in order to determine their nature and to explain their origin; it is concerned with the essential role of man's activity, of his "practice."

It differs from Kantian criticism in that even while integrating the discoveries in Hegel's *Phenomenology of Mind* and his *Science of Logic*, Marx is aware (as was Hegel) of the impossibility of separating method from content, of making, in advance of consciousness, a critique of all consciousness (as if one wanted to learn to swim without going near the water); he realized that the formal conditions of consciousness cannot be isolated from matter and the development of consciousness. Still less can man's activity, his historical and social practice, be isolated from his products and his institutions. Like Hegel, Marx created what one would today call a "model," enabling one to take cognizance of sense impressions, of their internal structure, their genesis and their law of evolution. But there was this difference from Hegel: Marx does not confound this "conceptual" reproduction of the concrete with the creation of the world by the consciousness.

It is not an easy matter to sum up the living and constantly meaningful teachings of Marx. Nevertheless we must attempt to extract those fundamental discoveries and advances that enable us today to raise political economy to the level of a true science,

111

capable of creating a synthesized view of contemporary economic structures, of their laws of development, and the perspectives open to them.

Marx's Method in *Capital*

If Marx did not leave behind him a *"Logic,"* he did leave the *logic* of *Capital*.
— Lenin[1]

The objective of all science is the passage from the simple, apparent motion of phenomena to their real, internal motion. Political economy did not become a genuine science until it accomplished this transition. Marx very precisely expounded the meaning of this Copernican revolution. On the subject of competition, he wrote: "A scientific analysis of competition is not possible, before we have a conception of the inner nature of capital, just as the apparent motions of the heavenly bodies are not intelligible to any but him, who is acquainted with their real motions."[2]

Marx's task was to build political economy into a true science, i.e., to penetrate the true, inner totality of the relations of production in bourgeois society, in opposition to vulgar economy, which limited itself to external appearances.

It is a characteristic of vulgar economy to confine itself to recording facts as they are given in immediate experience, empirically, and then to establish the relationships between them. This was the way in which astronomy before Copernicus functioned: It observed the apparent motion of the stars, the sun, the planets and other heavenly bodies, which seemed in fact to be gravitating around the earth, and then merely multiplied the "epicycles" in Ptolemy's system.

The economist who restricts himself to plotting the graphs of prices, the variations in crises, the mechanisms of operations, even if he uses the most refined mathematical procedures and the most modern econometric methods, remains the prisoner of appearances.

In political economy, the positivist reluctance to advance beyond appearances has a definite class bearing, for in this domain appearances are a function of the class viewpoint of the observer.

"The point of view of the petty bourgeoisie and the vulgar economist . . . results from the fact that in their minds it is always the phenomenal form of relations which is reflected, and not their internal connection."[3]

In a general way, the bourgeois class viewpoint leads it to follow only the vicissitudes of the circulation of capital. In the sphere of the *circulation* of capital, everything is invariably a commodity, while in the sphere of *production*, everything is the creation of value. In the first instance, political economy is concerned only with "things" and their relations; in the second, it discovers in human relationships the very origin of appearances, products, institutions and things. Passing from the first to the second point of view, and proceeding from there to account for appearances themselves is the great inversion realized by Marx—putting political economy back on its feet, as he had already done with philosophy. "Capital is not a thing, but rather a definite social production relation."[4]

To better understand the nature and the importance of this reversal, let us start from immediate appearances as do vulgar economists and capitalists, whose illusions the economist accepts as matters of fact and not as a point of departure for further investigation.

In the accounting of an enterprise, all expenditures as well as all receipts are reduced to a common denominator. For example, what is spent to purchase raw materials or machines is not *qualitatively* differentiated from what is spent to pay labor. In both cases it is regarded as a certain *quantity of invested capital;* in the apparent composition of the cost of production, no difference is seen between constant and variable capital.[5]

Out of this arise the principal illusions generated by the capitalist system and later decodified by capitalist political economy. The capitalist deducts his profit in terms of the aggregate of invested capital, and daily experience teaches him that profit originates on the market, in the sphere of circulation, that it comes from profitable sales, that his prices depend on supply and demand, and so on.

"The capitalist cost of the commodity is measured by the expenditure of *capital*, while the actual cost of the commodity is measured

by the expenditure of *labour*. . . . The cost-price of a commodity is
by no means simply a category which exists only in capitalist book-
keeping. The individualisation of this portion of value is continually
manifest in practice in the actual production of the commodity,
because it has ever to be reconverted from its commodity-form by
way of the process of circulation into the form of productive capital,
so that the cost-price of the commodity always must repurchase the
elements of production consumed in its manufacture."[6]

How does this reversal take place? How is the optical illusion
created by which, as in virtually all the sciences, as Marx noted,
things are often manifested in phenomena in reverse?

Direct experience in the capitalist system shows that capitals of
equal size which put equal quantities of living labor to work will
yield equal profit. That is the *appearance* of things. Now, from the
theory of value—previously put forward by Adam Smith and
Ricardo, and taken over and developed by Marx—it follows that
only the capital which puts the same quantity of labor power to
work should yield the same quantity of surplus value, and consequently, profit. That is the *substance*.

The substance is expressed in phenomenal forms which contradict
it. "The value of labour-power being given, and its degree of
exploitation being equal—vary directly as the amounts of the variable
constituents of these capitals, i.e., as their constituents transformed
into living labour-power. This law clearly contradicts all experience
based on appearance. . . . Vulgar economy . . . sticks to appearances
in opposition to the law which regulates and explains them."[7]

It is the same for the majority of economic realities. Surplus
value as such *does not appear directly*; it appears under phenomenal
forms: industrial or commercial profit, the rate of interest, dividends,
etc.

Value no longer appears directly but under the phenomenal form
of prices. There, too, one would have to start with the substance to
account for appearances which mask or even contradict it: "The
exchange, or sale, of commodities at their value is the rational state
of affairs, i.e., the natural law of their equilibrium. It is this law
that explains the deviations, and not vice versa, the deviations that
explain the law."[8]

Whatever the example cited, Marx considered that to pass from appearances to essential reality in political economy is to pass from phenomena of circulation, observable on the surface, to the realm of the creation of wealth, where its true nature, its genesis and its development are explained.

Marx emphasizes in many passages this concern with discovering the "inside" of phenomena: "The various forms of capital, as evolved in this book, thus approach step by step the form which they assume on the surface of society, in the action of different capitals upon one another, in competition, and in the ordinary consciousness of the agents of production themselves."[9]

On the other hand, he insisted on the necessity of beginning with the fundamentals of things before coming to the surface to reintegrate the elements of concrete totality, one by one: "We leave aside the manner in which the interrelations, due to the world-market, its conjunctures, movements of market-prices, periods of credit, industrial and commercial cycles, alternations of prosperity and crisis, appear to them as overwhelming natural laws that irresistibly enforce their will over them, and confront them as blind necessity. We leave this aside because the actual movement of competition belongs beyond our scope, and we need present only the inner organization of the capitalist mode of production, in its ideal average, as it were."[10]

Advancing beyond the vulgar economists like Jean-Baptiste Say or Bastiat, who accepted capitalist illusions as direct and eternal data and evolved apologetic systems for them, Marx goes back to the sources of bourgeois political economy, to the great English classics—who were the first to attempt to transcend appearance and to seek the secret of appearance in production.

English political economy, since William Petty, considered that the substance of wealth is *work*. Benjamin Franklin was to formulate what Marx called "the fundamental law of modern political economy." "Trade in general," wrote Franklin, "being nothing else but the exchange of labour for labour, the value of all things is . . . the most justly measured by labour."[11] To be sure, he is referring to labor in the form in which it is manifested in capitalist society, i.e., the labor that produces commodities, the labor whose end is the alienation of its product on the free market.

Adam Smith expressed this law in its most general form: "Labor

is the real measure of the exchangeable value of all commodities."[12]
He considered all society on the model of the capitalist enterprises
of his time, i.e., large-scale manufacture in which the division of
labor increases labor productivity.

Ricardo, too, starts with this conception of society—a totality of
labor. From the very first chapter of his *Principles of Political
Economy and Taxation*, he asserts: "The value of a commodity, or
the quantity of any other commodity for which it will exchange,
depends on the relative quantity of labour which is necessary for
its production, and not on the greater or less compensation which is
paid for that labour."[13]

Ricardo also emphasized the social character of labor and production; he formulated the law of labor value, and he took note of the
difference between the wages actually paid and the quantity of labor,
that is, he recognized the existence of surplus value.

It is true that Ricardo stated, without explaining it, the difference between the amount of labor supplied by the laborer and
the wages paid him. He does not answer the question: "Why is not
wage labor, like other commodities, paid for according to its value?"
Marx explains why Ricardo could not answer this: Posed in this
form, the question is unanswerable because labor as such is placed in
opposition to commodities—a certain quantity of living labor for a
certain quantity of already realized labor.[14] There is in fact no
common measure between creative living labor and labor already
realized in the form of product or object. Marx was to show that
law of value applies not to labor but to the value of the labor power
of the worker (that is, the value of the totality of the means necessary for his subsistence).

Nonetheless, Ricardo's conception of society already seemed dangerous to his contemporaries; the totality in which there are only
men working collectively and exchanging the products of their labor,
constituted an organism in which any individual or group which
appropriated a portion of the common production under a claim
other than that of labor was an unprincipled parasite. This theory,
which had been a weapon for the ascendant bourgeoisie, could be
turned against it by other social groups. As early as 1848, Carey, an
apologist for capitalism, denounced Ricardo as "the father of communism." He wrote: "Mr. Ricardo's system is one of discords. . . .

It tends to the production of hostility between classes and nations.
. . . His book is the true manual of the demagogue, who seeks
power by means of agrarianism, war and plunder."[15]

Ricardo is nonetheless a grand bourgeois who did not seek to
undermine the principles of capitalism in the English Parliament
where he sat, nor in his works. He considered capitalism a "natural"
and eternal mode of production, despite the contradictions he found
in it.

This is clearly apparent in his theory of wages. "The natural
price of labour is that price which is necessary to enable the laborers,
one with another, to subsist and to perpetuate their race, without
either increase or dimunition."[16] He even sees that "labor value"
is determined by the subsistence which is necessary traditionally in
a given society to maintain and reproduce the workers. But just
at the point where he comes close to making the crucial discovery
later made by Marx, i.e., that wages are determined by the cost
of production of labor power, Ricardo sees only that this law
results from the transformation of labor into a commodity, from its
fetishization into an object, i.e., from the very principle of the
capitalist system which reduces everything to the common denominator of commodity value. He attributes this phenonomenon to what
is actually only a secondary effect of the system—the competition
of the workers and the law of supply and demand. From the viewpoint of his own doctrine this is inconsequential. His ambition had
been to reduce all economic categories to labor value, and to achieve
the merit of putting himself at the standpoint of production; now
he passes over to the point of view of distribution and circulation
to account for wages. He places in juxtaposition a profound analysis
and a superficial description. "He should have spoken of labour
power," wrote Marx, "instead of speaking of labour. Had he done so,
however, capital would also have been revealed as the material conditions of labour confronting the labourer as a power that had become independent of him. And capital would at once have been
revealed as *a definite social relationship*. As it is, for Ricardo it is
only distinguished as 'accumulated labour' from 'immediate labour'."[17]

Now, there is a difference in nature, a radical opposition, between
living labor (that cannot be separated from the active subject, from
the laborer) and dead labor, the labor accumulated in the form of

commodities, alienated labor (which can be appropriated by other men, accumulated and transformed into a means of exploitation and oppression). In a society where the means of production (the land, the tools of labor) are common property in the hands of each laborer, equivalence is the rule of exchange. On the other hand, when the land and tools of production are monopolized by one class and turned into *capital* for that class, other revenues than those of labor appear, such as profit or rent.

This confusion vitiated Ricardo's doctrine.

He defined profit as the surplus of the value of the commodity over wages; rent as the surplus over wages and profit. And he formulated a very general law that emphasized the contradictions between wages and profit and between profit and rent: With the development of society and the increase in population, rent increases, real wages do not change, profit diminishes.

This law, in another betrayal of his first principle, was not deduced from his theory of value, but from an absolutely accidental circumstance in connection with his theory. He adopted the so-called "law of population" of Malthus and the conception of differential rent resulting from it. Malthus, an ideologist in the service of the East India Company,* which financed his education, sought in this so-called natural law for a rationalization which would exonerate the capitalist system of responsibility for the bloody orgies that had marked its advent. Starting from the arbitrary and absolutely untenable postulate that population would increase in geometrical progression, while the means of subsistence would increase in arithmetical progression, Malthus proclaimed that if lands were of unequal fertility, the capital invested in them would yield unequal profits. This difference between the normal rate of profit on mediocre land and the greater rate on more productive land constitutes a rent profitable to the owners of the more fertile lands. Ricardo, incorporating this thesis into his theory of value, deduced from it that in agriculture the price of commodities is determined by the labor expended under the least favorable conditions, on the most mediocre lots of land. The growth in the population which makes it necessary to exploit even

* In 1805, Malthus was appointed Professor of History and Political Economy at the East India Company's Haileybury College.

the most stubborn land results in an increase in rent and consequently an increase in nominal wages (real wages remaining constant, since with a higher nominal wage the worker buys a quantity of commodities that Ricardo assumes as fixed once and for all). The increase in nominal wages, therefore, lowers profit, since, according to Ricardo, wages and profit are in inverse relationship.

Ricardo's theory has the threefold merit of clearly enunciating the law of labor value, of baring the antagonism between labor and capital, and of showing that differential rent is a revenue that is not only valueless for the development of capitalism but is brought about by a worsening in the conditions of its development.*

His weakness was to attach his demonstration to Malthus's absurd thesis. Toward the end of his life he was already moving toward a "law of population" no longer defined as a law of nature, an eternal law, but as a historical law, generated by the structure of society itself and developing to its present stage.

In Chapter XXXI of his *Principles,* which created consternation among his successors—from MacCulloch to Böhm-Bawerk—Ricardo wrote with the "scientific impartiality" and "love of truth" that Marx valued in him: "The class of labourers also, I thought, was equally benefited by the use of machinery, as they would have the means of buying more commodities with the same money wages, and I thought that no reduction of wages would take place, because the capitalist would have the power of demanding and employing the same quantity of labour as before, although he might be under the necessity of employing it in the production of a new, or at any rate of a different commodity. . . . I am convinced, that the substitution of machinery for human labour, is often very injurious to the interests of the class of labourers."[18]

He went further in a letter to MacCulloch: "I said that a manufacturer disposing of floating capital could employ many men. If it is profitable for him to replace this floating capital by constant capital of the same value, this would inevitably be followed by the dismissal of some of the workers, since constant capital cannot employ all the

* Ricardo's theory of rent has a class meaning: It is directed against the agrarians. It has supplied a great number of theoretical arguments to the partisans of "free-exchange" in the countryside, which was to result in the law of June 25, 1846, abolishing the right to tax grains (the "Corn Laws").

labor it must replace. I vow that this truth seemed to me as exact as any theorem of geometry, and I am simply stupefied to have gone so long without noticing it." Ricardo was at that time on the way to a "law of population" deriving from the law of the capitalist system itself, which had enabled him to put a base under his entire theory. The displacement of the laborer by the machine results in the formation of a reserve army of unemployed, pressure on wages, and growing antagonism between the laborer and the capitalist.

What then is the principle which explains the inconsistency and the weakness of Ricardo's classical work?

Ricardo, like Adam Smith, regarded labor solely in the form it assumes in bourgeois society—embodied in a commodity—and he considered this state as natural and eternal.

Thence there was no distinction to be made between live and dead, accumulated labor, i.e., between labor, properly speaking, and capital; relations between them would exist only on the plane of circulation (where they are in fact interchangeable) and not on the plane of production (where they oppose each other radically). Money, which is their common denominator, in such a perspective, is no longer anything but a means of circulation. Even when Ricardo studies the relationship of men and of classes, he defines them on the level of the distribution of wealth and not on the deeper level of production.

Ricardo discovered one of the essential laws of the development of capitalist society—the law of the tendency of the rate of profit to fall—but he explains it by the increase in the value of agricultural products stemming from Malthus's so-called "law of population": "Profits tend naturally to fall since, in the development of society and of wealth, the increase of necessary subsistence demands ever increasing labor." On this, Marx commented: "Those economists . . . who, like Ricardo, regard the capitalist mode of production as absolute, feel at this point that it creates a barrier itself, and for this reason attribute the barrier to Nature (in the theory of rent), not to production."[19]

Marx was to show, on the other hand, that the law of the tendency of the rate of profit to fall did not result from fortuitous circumstances, alien to the capitalist system, but, on the contrary, from the essence of this regime, which involves an increase in constant capital (tools and machinery) and a relative diminution of variable capital (capital used to purchase labor power, alone capable of creating surplus value).

A discovery of this nature leads to the further idea that capitalism bears within itself the law of its own destruction. "What worries Ricardo," wrote Marx, "is the fact that the rate of profit, the stimulating principle of capitalist production, the fundamental premise and driving force of accumulation, should be endangered by the development of production itself. . . . It comes to the surface here in a purely economic way—i.e., from the bourgeois point of view, within the limitations of capitalist understanding, from the standpoint of capitalist production itself—that it has its barrier, that it is relative, that it is not an absolute, but only a historical mode of production corresponding to a definite limited epoch in the development of the material requirements of production."[20]

Finally, one of the last results of Ricardo's initial error was the inability to account for capitalist crises. He said at one and the same time that "profit appeared simultaneously as a condition for and as an impetus to accumulation" and that capitalist production involves the satisfaction of needs.

Is capitalist production driven by profit or by the impetus of satisfying needs? Ricardo credits both motivations, and in both cases, in order to defend the unlimited potentiality for growth of capitalist production, he is not able to foresee the profound contradictions inherent in the system. The cycle of periodic crises began in 1825; Ricardo died in 1823. His doctrine is that of the unbounded development of capitalism.

The failure of classical political economy to account for crises was destined to bring about a crisis in political economy itself.

The economist-apologists for capitalism, in order to deny the depth of its contradictions, had to renounce the pioneers who sought the key to economic phenomena and their essence in production. The apologists had to take refuge in the timid positivism of vulgar economics.

Marx was to extend classical political economy by putting it back on its feet. The reversal would be comprised of three basic aspects:

(1) The application of *historical materialism* to the solution of

the problems of political economy, which also permits the discovery of the relative and provisional nature of the capitalist mode of production;

(2) The analysis of the *alienation of labor and of the fetishism of the commodity*, which permits the discovery, beyond the mere appearance of the circulation of things, of the essential reality of the human relations of production;

(3) The discovery of the contradictory character of these relations and the internal *dialectics* of their development, which permits the transcendence of all forms of empiricism or positivism in economic investigations.

1. HISTORICAL MATERIALISM AND POLITICAL ECONOMY

What characterizes bourgeois political economy, wrote Marx, is that "the capitalist regime is looked upon as the absolutely final form of social production, instead of a passing historical phase of its evolution."[21]

Marx was to demonstrate that the economic categories—labor, exchange, commodity, value, money, market, profit, wages, and so on—are historical categories, and that the social relations of which they are the expression form an organic whole bearing within themselves the contradictions that engage it in unceasing development.

"The categories of bourgeois economy consist of . . . forms of thought expressing with social validity the conditions and relations of a definite, historically determined mode of production, viz., the production of commodities. The whole mystery of commodities, all the magic and necromancy that surrounds the products of labour as long as they take the form of commodities, vanishes therefore, so soon as we come to other forms of production."[22]

Applying this historical method, Marx resolved the problem posed by Ricardo of the difference between the quantity of labor supplied and the wages paid—the crucial problem of surplus value.

As long as men produce only just enough of the means of subsistence to keep alive, an objective base for the continued and organized exploitation of the labor of others would not exist; the product of labor is barely equal to the cost of maintaining labor. It is only with the first great technical advances (for instance, those that made possible the transition from the life of nomad hunters to that of settled farmers) that labor's productivity is considerably increased and that the fight to appropriate the surplus products of labor begins.

Slavery was the first form of this exploitation. Here the mode of appropriation of surplus value is very simple and obvious: The master distributes food to his slaves and appropriates for himself the entire product of their labor. For example, in the classical epoch in Greece, in the 5th and 6th century B.C., the selling price of a slave was about 180–200 drachmas. According to the testimony of Demosthenes and of Xenophon, after all maintenance expenses were paid, a slave produced on the average one obol a day, i.e., in round figures, 300 obols (or 50 drachmas) a year. After ten years of labor, each slave returned to his master 500 drachmas, that is to say, after deducting the amount invested in the original purchase price, a surplus value of 300 drachmas. Demosthenes thus calculated his father's income in his cutlery shop and in his furniture factory.[23]

Medieval serfdom equally reveals clearly the origin of surplus value. The feudal seigneur appropriated the products of the free labor that the serfs had to furnish in the form of the corvée. Then, notes Marx:

"For the very reason that personal dependence forms the ground-work of society, there is no necessity for labour and its products to assume a fantastic form different from their reality. They take the shape, in the transactions of society, of services in kind and pay-ments in kind. Here the particular and natural form of labour, and not, as in a society based on production of commodities, its general abstract form, is the immediate social form of labour."[24]

In all of these economic and social systems, surplus value is nothing but the difference between the value created by the laborer and the cost of his maintenance. All the accumulated wealth on the earth is only the aggregate product of this surplus value. When wealth, the fruit of the work and genius of all antecedent genera-tions, is the private property of individuals, groups or classes, it is the alienated power of species-man that has been seized or inherited. St. John Chrysostom once said to the rich merchants of Antioch:

"You are the receivers of stolen goods, if you are not actually the thieves of them." Proudhon, 15 centuries later, was to write "Property is theft."

But the mechanics of the appropriation of surplus value in the capitalist order is more complex and more mysterious than in all other economic and social structures.

The slave seems to have labored from morning to night for his master, while in reality he did work part of the day to reproduce his own means of subsistence, the expense of his maintenance, and to amortize the original price of his purchase.

By an illusion in reverse, the wage laborer seems to work from morning to night for himself, while in reality he works part of the day gratuitously for his employer, who has purchased his labor power at a wage much lower than the new value created by the laborer. The illusion consists in considering wages as the price of labor and not of labor power. "Hence," wrote Marx, "we may understand the decisive importance of the transformation of value and price of labour-power into the form of wages, or into the value and price of labor itself. This phenomenal form, which makes the actual relations invisible, and, indeed, shows the direct opposite of that relation, forms the basis of all the juridical notions of both labourer and capitalist, of all the mystifications of the capitalistic mode of production, of all its illusions as to liberty, of all the apologetic shifts of the vulgar economists."[25]

2. THE ALIENATION OF LABOR AND THE FETISHISM OF THE COMMODITY*

What is the specific form of the appropriation of surplus value in the capitalist system?

In a society where labor is dominated by commodity exchange, in which man does not produce for his needs or for those of the community to which he belongs but for the market, each man's labor no longer produces use values but exchange values. In the process of becoming a commodity, man's product is cut off from his relations with other men. This is true in a double sense: His labor

* See the discussion on alienation in the first part of this book.

is separated from *need*, since it is destined for an impersonal market; it is separated from *labor*, since the productive labor in the commodity is equally impersonal, homogeneous and undifferentiated, except with respect to *quantity*.

All exchange relations, Marx explains,[26] are characterized by this abstraction: There no longer remains anything but the common character of labor; it is all turned into the same human labor, at the expense of human labor power, without regard to the particular form in which this power has been expended.

It is not merely an abstraction in the mind but a real abstraction; this reduction of all individual and living labor to a common denominator, purely quantitative and faceless, is an abstraction which takes place daily in the social process of production.

This depersonalization of labor and the objectivization by which each man's work falls into this inhuman quantification result from the fundamental contradiction of capitalist society, which gives a social character to labor (in transforming the whole of society into a vast, common cooperative enterprise), while maintaining the private character of appropriation (which empowers some men to appropriate the collective labor power of mankind and then to transform this power into an authority external to, and above, the workers).

The division of labor and exchange create a solidarity among men which private ownership prevents them from realizing to the full. In a commodity society, where the productive forces have become social while the relationships of production have remained individual, human relations lose their clarity; men are no longer bound to one another directly but indirectly, by the intercession of the market, where encounters occur among the things into which their labor has been transformed. The relations between men take on the appearance of relations between objects; labor power, the property of the individual, in commodity production becomes an abstract "quantum," a thing; and *need*, the other attribute of the living human being, also turns into a quantum, a payable claim calculated in figures.

In capitalism, the fetishism of the commodity has encompassed the greatest reversal in human history: Things rule the men who have created them. Marxist "reversal" consists in putting back on their feet not political economy alone but the society itself which has generated it.

Alienated and appropriated labor in the form of capital lives its own life, inhuman and devouring, masking under deceptive appearances the reality of human relations. "Interest as such expresses precisely the existence of the conditions of labour as capital, in their social antithesis to labour, and in their transformation into personal power vis-à-vis and over labour. It represents the ownership of capital as a means of appropriating the products of the labour of others."[27]

In a society having such a structure, man gives a mystical form to the relations that link him to his own nature, to external nature, and to other men. The vulgar economists (J. P. Say, Bastiat, and any number of them) are at home in this very alienation.

Earlier, in the *Manuscripts of 1844*, Marx had pointed out that "political economy . . . carries to its logical conclusion the denial of man."[28] It considers alienated labor, in fact, in the form of a "thing," and does not see that these "things" produce wealth only because they are crystallized labor accumulated from all anterior humanity. Marx was to prove that land does not produce rent, nor does capital produce profit, and that labor produces much more than wages—specifically, profit and rent.

All the confusions of vulgar economy result from the fact that the viewpoint of the bourgeoisie and its ideologists is that of alienation. Without departing from the alienation characteristic of bourgeois social relations, it is impossible to distinguish between living labor and dead labor, accumulated in the form of capital, and to understand their deep-seated antagonism.

In classical theory, capital is labor accumulated for the continuance and expansion of production (raw materials, tools, machines, etc.). Marx shows that, on the contrary, the means of production become capital only when they are appropriated by the special privilege of an individual, a group or a class. The aggregate of commodity values become capital by reason of the fact that "as an independent social power, *i.e., as the power of a part of society it preserves itself and multiplies by exchange with direct living labour-power.*" Capital is not a thing but a social relation, and it has a historical character: "*Capital* . . . is a social relation of production. It is a *bourgeois relation of production*, a relation of production of bourgeois society." Emphasizing this double character in simple images, Marx adds: "A Negro is a Negro. Only under certain conditions does he become a slave. A cotton-spinning machine is a machine for spinning cotton. Only under certain conditions does it become *capital*. Torn away from these conditions, it is as little capital as gold by itself is money, or as sugar is the price of sugar."[29] Thus, integrating social relations and the categories that express them into the aggregate of historical conditions, instead of regarding the fetishistic categories of bourgeois economy as eternally "given," wrote Marx, we utilize the only materialist and therefore scientific method.

3. THE DIALECTICAL METHOD IN POLITICAL ECONOMY

The most profound characteristic of dialectics is that it does not isolate method from content. Hegel once criticized Kant for claiming to explore forms of cognition and making *a priori* critiques of them without touching on their content, in the manner, he said, of that scholasticist who wanted to learn to swim without going near the water. Dialecticics, for Marx, as for all materialists, embodies both the subjective aspect of thought and the objective content of what it contemplates. It is no longer, as with Hegel, a speculative procedure but a method with access to the real. Method is inseparable from content. It is not only a logic of consciousness but a logic of the real, i.e., of that which is not a concept but what the concept envisions and reconstructs ideally.

From the poems of Heraclitus to the *Phenomenology of Mind* and the *Science of Logic* of Hegel, thought and the real are grasped in their living unity, as an organic whole in constant development, with their contradictions, each form preparing its successor, in the eternal cycle of birth, development and death.

(a) This tradition of dialectical thought, whose rich heritage Marx redeemed by integrating it into the materialist conception of the world, was, in the first place, opposed to the empiricists who profess to give consciousness an absolute point of departure, a first start, a given sensuous representation, without seeing that their so-called "facts" have already been moulded from concepts nourished by previous theory and practice. In the *Contribution to the Critique of Political Economy*, Marx defined the concrete as "a process of synthesis, as a result, and not as a starting point."[30]

The empiricist theory of knowledge, one of the postulates implicit in classical political economy, led English economists (Adam Smith, for example) to regard as immediate "givens," eternal and natural, representations which were in fact those of a social class at a moment in historical development. It is noteworthy that one of the foremost theoreticians of English political economy, John Locke, was also a classical philosopher of empiricism: "Locke's analysis is all the more important," wrote Marx, "since he is the classical exponent of bourgeois society's ideas of right in opposition to the feudal, and his philosophy moreover served all subsequent English economists as the foundation for all their ideas."[31]

Locke's position was, indeed, very advanced for his time, not only from the philosophical viewpoint—in that his empiricism was a weapon against the scholastic and theological speculations of his day and cleared the way for a new conception of the world and a rational method (clearly recognized by the French philosophers of the 18th century)—but also from the viewpoint of political economy. At a time when the capitalist bourgeois form of property was far from being the sole form of property, Locke chose it as the sole authentic and natural one and, from Adam Smith to Ricardo, this great school of political economy waged a merciless theoretical struggle against the historically outdated feudal forms of property.

Nonetheless, notions of the base were borrowed, as if they were natural "givens," from what was the expression of a historical development and elaboration, notions which implicitly contained a social practice, a theory that expressed it, and the multiple illusions generated by this theory and this practice.

The so-called initial "givens" in the case of political economy, for example, are always elaborate abstractions: statistics, evidence, books, documents.

Moreover, the method of utilizing these prime assumptions consisted exclusively of formal logic grounded on the same empirical postulates. Ricardo, for example, who, no more than Locke or Adam Smith, distinguished theoretical abstraction (i.e., oversimplified hypothesis) from empirical abstraction (i.e., generic concept) when he studied facts from the standpoint of their internal connections, subsumed all logical relations under *reduction* and *deduction.* To him, what this meant was to reduce complex phenomena to their "simple" components and to *deduce* all the economic categories from one of them.

Ricardo's starting point was the definition of value by the quantity of labor time. According to him, this was a general abstract concept which encompassed the characteristics common to all the phenomena included in it. The relations between the concept of value and the concepts of money, profit, rent, wages, interest, etc., are the relation between genus and species. For all these concepts, value is what the abstract notion of "fruit" is to apples, cherries, strawberries, etc.

According to this conception, both empirical and metaphysical, of the relations between the particular and the general, one passes from the particular to the general by removing all sensuous characteristics from the concrete—as one might draw colored segments from a mosaic in order to save only the guiding veins. Money and profit are no more than particular forms of value. But in this empirical concept of abstraction and this formal conception of deduction, if it is easy to draw the general from the particular by successive subtractions, the process cannot be reversed; one cannot recreate the concrete by the addition and accumulation of abstractions. To cite only one example of the difficulties to which a method like this leads, Ricardo, after having defined profit as a particular form of value, discovers a contradiction between the general law of value and the law of the average rate of profit. No mediation permits him to pass "logically" from one to the other and to explain how, in spite of the law of value, the same quantity of capital putting different quantities of labor time to work can yield equal profits.

(b) Neither does the dialectical method admit the notion of an absolute point of departure, an original genesis from *intelligible data,* Platonic essences or rational principles of the type, for example, of Descartes' "simple natures." Dialectical epistemology is always and necessarily, as Bachelard put it, "a non-Cartesian epistemology." On the plane of the intelligible, as on the plane of the sensuous, there are never "things given," all complete. The "simple" already has a complete structure. There is no pure simplicity nor absolute genesis in any form whatsoever.

This is what the most radical reversal of the Hegelian dialectic consists in. One does not obtain a science by reversing an ideology. One does not obtain scientific dialectics by reversing speculative dialectics. In spite of Hegel's efforts to establish the circularity of knowledge, everything occurs for him in the speculative perspective of his *Logic*, as if one started with a simple, original unity of being, evolving only because of its negativity. Hegelian totality is the alienated development from original unity of being.

For Hegel the concrete is defined as totality, as an organic totality, as a resultant, and, above all, as the work of consciousness engendering the world by a auto-development of which internal contradiction is the motive power.

Marx, as a materialist, rejected the Hegelian system founded on the idea that the intellect was the creator of the world, and in reversing it, he retained the movement of thought passing from the abstract to the concrete. What did this reversal consist in? In the first place, in the materialist perspective—the method by which the mind moves from the abstract to the concrete—a consistent method of appropriating to oneself the real, of reproducing it—but not of *producing* it. Then, in the perspective of non-speculative thought, dialectics is not a law for the construction of the real, but a mode of access to it; it is, therefore, the "interminable dialectic," of which Bachelard spoke; it is posited within the movement of scientific thought that works out its concepts, rejects them, corrects them, forms new theories, refutes them, re-examines principles, institutes new ones, generalizes them, bumps into inconsistencies, and tirelessly begins the cycle of constant rectification of the body of acquired culture.

This mobility must not be confounded with that of the sceptic, nor this relativism with sophistry, for if the sciences and scientific philosophy move in this manner from bypassed theory to rectified theory, every new stage, every new negation, gives us a new grasp of the real, greater control over nature, and renders our practice more enlightened and more effective.

Through the vicissitudes of scientific development, through even the shipwrecks of discarded hypotheses, a model of reality is designed which is more and more faithful and more and more concrete.

The various sciences, particularly since the 19th century, from the analogies in physics adduced by Maxwell to the structural formulas of Kekulé in chemistry, have made increasing use of the notion of a model, and in the course of the past few years, since the investigations of Norbert Wiener, cybernetics, by greatly extending the construction of models of a new type, has suggested that here was an important method of knowledge and research.

From the materially realized model to the ideal representation, conceptual, symbolic or mathematical, this always concerns a construction which reproduces a studied reality—its structure, its functioning, its behavior, its development. This hypothetical, schematic, idealized, simplified reproduction can have the abstract character of a theory or the more concrete form of a model, but it always concerns a system of concepts, referring by analogy to a real organic whole—the concrete always remaining the objective pursued by the mind; the abstract always being a *means*. The two phases, moreover, are not consecutive, isolated from one another; they are, rather, two poles of the same organic development of thought, through its concepts reproducing phases of reality itself.

The hypothetical-deductive method is a moment in dialectic thought; it tends either to ideally analyze the whole, or to resemble it by adducing the evidence of the internal logic of the real. Whether it concerns itself with structural analysis or dynamic synthesis, the dialectical method never loses sight of the reciprocal implications of induction and deduction, of analysis and synthesis, of the abstract and the concrete. Concepts, for dialectical materialism, are neither essences in the Platonic sense of the term, nor simply threadbare abstractions from the sensuous (as with the empiricists); concepts are hypotheses to be verified in practice, and the hypothesis is always simultaneously the point of arrival and the point of departure.

Marx's *Capital* gives us an example of the application of this complex, rewarding method. It is this that led Lenin to say: "If Marx did not leave behind him a *Logic*, he did leave the *logic* of *Capital*."[32] One constantly finds in this gigantic work that it is the

construction, always incomplete but always alive, in continual development, from a model of the economic and social formations of
the capitalist system, of three constituent aspects of the method.

The first is the aspect of abstraction in which, discarding the
adventitious and the accidental, thought extracts the law of the
phenomenon in its ideal purity, by means of a simplified hypothesis.
For example, Marx, in formulating the law of labor value, effected
the same scientific advance as Sadi Carnot when he mentally constructed an ideal steam engine, practically as unworkable as any
geometrical figure. This mental construction is not, strictly speaking,
immediately verifiable by any experiment, and yet it is indispensable
in accounting for every concrete experience that apparently contradicts it. Between Marx's law of labor value and the phenomena of
prices, there is the same relation as between Carnot's model and
the actual functioning of steam engines.

The transition from the ideal model to concrete reality, therefore,
calls for a second aspect of the method: The transition from the
abstract to the concrete, by means of which one reintroduces mediations and reconstructs reality more and more concretely to take
account of appearances. "We shall see," writes Marx, "that the rate
of profit is no mystery, so soon as we know the laws of surplus-
value. If we reverse the process, we cannot comprehend either the
one or the other."[33] He says even more emphatically,"The transformation of surplus-value into profit must be deducted from the
transformation of the rate of surplus-value into the rate of profit,
not vice versa. And in fact it was the rate of profit which was the
historical point of departure. Surplus-value and rate of surplus-value
are, relatively, the invisible and unknown essence that wants in-
vestigating, while rate of profit and therefore the appearance of
surplus-value in the form of profit are revealed on the surface of
the phenomenon."[34]

It is only in terms of this reproduction that we can approach the
third aspect of the method: *verification*, i.e., the comparison between the results obtained by the transition from the abstract to the
concrete, and reality. This simple observation enables us to refute
the petty objections, empiricist or positivist in origin, of the economists who think they can achieve an easy triumph over Marxist
economy by carelessly leaping from the first to the third aspect,

omitting the intermediate steps and asserting, for example, that the price curve does not "verify" the law of value, nor the wage curve, the law of pauperization, nor the profit curve, the law of the tendency of the rate of profit to fall—as if *Capital* ended with its first volume! As if Marx, in bringing internal relations to the surface, from the constituent parts to the constituted whole, had not written, after the book on production, the book on circulation!

It is exactly as if one derided Carnot's principle by declaring it incapable of direct experimental verification, and as if one concluded from this that Carnot was an incompetent engineer.

Only in terms of the conceptual reconstruction of the organic whole of development that constitutes an economic and social formation can one grasp the phenomenon, that is, determine its position and role within the totality, the organic necessity of its appearance as only one moment in the whole.

Marx was convinced, as Descartes had been, that "the nature of things is easier to conceive when one sees them evolving little by little than when one sees them as all finished," and, like Hegel, that "the end result is nothing without its process of becoming." Thus when he passed from the commodity to money and from money to capital and thus reproduced the "genesis" of the structures of capital, Marx showed that only the analysis of the commodity enables one to comprehend the unity and the *sense* of the capitalist system of production.

Now, this analysis of the commodity brings us back to labor— from the product to production, the constituted whole to the constituent part.

If we freely utilize the vocabulary of Husserl, the resemblance is not accidental. Husserl's notions of "comprehension," of "totality," of "sense," of "constituent activity," are by no means alien to Marxism. Marx's dialectical method enables us to reconsider the basic notions of Husserlian phenomenology while demystifying them, i.e., to rediscover the living historical relation that connects these notions with the real and to give them meaning in the concrete reality of an honest investigation. But the real moment, detached from the whole, with Husserl, and even more with his followers, becomes idealism and speculation.

Constituent activity, cut off from historical and social practice, becomes that of a transcendental abstract subject, while in the materialist, historical, dialectical perspective, it is human labor—a historically determined relation, the concrete practice of social man in the course of his historical development; it is social production by a being who is a historical product, a constant development from his own activity.

The "sense" is not bestowed on things by transcendental consciousness or by an absolute, extra-historical subject. The "sense" is written into institutions and products by historical and social practice which produces these institutions and products. "Consciousness" does not project them on to things; it discovers the clue to things by bringing to life the purposes and the fossilized human projects which are historically inscribed in things. Culture is only the assimilation and constant recapitulation by man of the whole genesis of the human universe that surrounds him, of which he becomes the responsible inheritor through this consciousness, this "comprehension."

"Totality" is not an abstract category, but a living organic reality, moving with the life of thought and with the life of what thought perceives—but it is not thought. Beyond the phenomenology which, above all, conceives of totality as a structure, Marx also conceives totality as a source. In *Capital*, as in the *Contribution to the Critique of Political Economy*, Marx begins with an analysis of the commodity, both because it is the basic expression of the relations between men in the capitalist economic and social formation, and because, historically, the commodity mode of production preceded the capitalist economy itself and constituted its point of departure.

Historical order and dialectical order—that of chronology and that of logical source—are one. Engels pointed out that logical order is historical order stripped only of the disturbances of chance.

Marx himself sought constantly to discover, under the accidental and the incidental, a rhythm and structure of the internal dialectics of the relations between man and nature and the relations among men, in order that logical sources might coincide with historical sources:

"Money may exist and actually had existed in history before capital, or banks, or wage labor came into existence. With that in mind, it may be said that the more simple category can serve as an expression of the predominant relations of an undeveloped whole or of the subordinate relations of a more developed whole (relations) which had historically existed before the whole developed in the direction expressed in the more concrete category. In so far, the laws of abstract reasoning, which ascends from the most simple to the complex, correspond to the actual process of history."[35]

The logical development of simple, or complex, or general forms of the monetary form of value corresponds to the actual history of the development of production and of commodity circulation.

This is true on the next stage—that of the transition from money to capital. Marx underlined this in a letter to Engels on April 2, 1858:

"Simple money circulation does not contain the principle of self-reproduction within itself and therefore points beyond itself. Money, as the development of its determinations shows, contains within itself the demand for value which will enter into circulation, maintain itself during circulation and at the same time establish circulation—that is, for capital. This transition is historical also. The antediluvian form of capital is trade capital, which always develops money. At the same time, real capital arises from that money or merchants' capital which gains control of production."[36]

This is true for almost all the phases of the dialectics of *Capital*. From the beginning, exchange based on value, i.e., according to the amount of labor, has historically preceded exchange based on prices.[37] "Apart from the domination of prices and price movement by the law of value, it is quite appropriate to regard the values of commodities as not only theoretically but also historically *prius* to the prices of production."[38]

Still another example is the passage of absolute surplus value to relative surplus value. Historically the employer has always begun by lengthening the working day. It was only later that technical progress permitted the growth of surplus value by reducing the time necessary to produce the laborers' means of subsistence and thus augmenting the surplus labor of the worker.

But historical order must not be confused with strictly chronological order—any more than necessity with chance. Historical order, properly speaking, is generally discovered when one approaches the study of each moment at the point of its development at which it attains full maturity and classical purity.

Thus, certain apparent exceptions in the correspondence between the historical and the logical are explained. For example: "Rent cannot be understood without capital," Marx wrote, nor can capital without rent. . . . It would thus be impractical and wrong to arrange the economic categories in the order in which they were the determining factors in the course of history. Their order of sequence is, rather, determined by the relation which they bear to one another in modern bourgeois society.[39] That is why, although ground ownership and rent played a primary role before capitalism itself, it is only after the study of profit that the study of rent provides its full meaning in the context of the organic totality of capitalist society.

The position in *Capital* (Volume I) of the chapter on "Primitive Accumulation" may appear even more puzzling; while it constitutes, chronologically, the starting point, it is not treated until Chapter XXVI. Marx explained the reason for this:

"The capitalist system presupposes the complete separation of the labourers from all property in the means by which they can realize their labour. As soon as capitalist production is once on its own legs, it not only maintains this separation, but reproduces it on a continually extending scale. The process, therefore, that clears the way for the capitalist system, can be none other than the process which takes away from the labourer the possession of his means of production. . . . The so-called primitive accumulation, therefore, is nothing else than the historical process of divorcing the producer from the means of production. It appears as primitive, because it forms the prehistoric stage of capital and of the mode of production corresponding with it."[40]

Properly speaking, the history of capitalism in its internal logic, gives us the key to its prehistory: "The anatomy of the human being," Marx wrote, "is the key to the anatomy of the ape. But the intimations of a higher animal in lower ones can be understood only if the animal of the higher order is already known."[41] This discovery of the "sense" does not imply any "finality." If Marx began *Capital* with the history of primitive accumulation, capitalism would appear as the fortuitous result of a chaotic series of colonial adventures and pillages; while the bloody forays of the *conquistadors* who consummated this primitive accumulation do not fully reveal its full "sense" until the inception and development of the capitalist system is considered in its necessary existence as a form of human relations which could only be reproduced and expanded by still further separating the means of production from the workers who operate them.

It is a question, therefore, of studying the "movements of capital considered as a whole,"[42] for production, circulation, etc." are all members of one entity, different sides of one unit." Between the various elements there is reciprocal action. This applies to any organic totality.[43]

The characteristic of the dialectical method is to refrain from separating the study of structures from the study of the internal dynamics of these structures, of these organic totalities, and the contradictions which act as their motive force.

"In this method," wrote Engels, "we proceed from the first and simplest relation that historically and in fact confronts us. . . . We analyze this relation. Being a *relation* already implies . . . two sides, *related to each other*. . . . Contradictions will result which demand a solution. . . . Contradictions, too, will have developed in practice and will probably have found their solution. . . . We shall trace the nature of this solution, and shall discover that it has been brought about by the establishment of a new relation whose two opposite sides we shall now have to develop."[44]

Having arrived at this point of the working out of the materials of economic knowledge, the method is identified with the internal motion of the content. In the building, functioning and development of the "model," we will witness the ideal genesis of the capitalist system by following throughout *Capital* the real development of the basic contradictions between use value and exchange value. As Marx wrote to Engels (February 1, 1858), the moment has come in political economy to "bring a science by criticism to the point where it can be dialectically presented."[45]

After having transcended the speculative mystifications of the Hegelian dialectic and after forging an instrument of scientific research and discovery, Marx gives dialectics its scientific form. It is a form which involves the elimination of all dogmatism, of all absolute "origins," all speculative deduction, all idealist illusions as to the creation of reality by consciousness, all theological conceptions which maintain that diaectical thought is built into things, as if there was nothing more to do than to discover the pearl of divine thought ready-made in the shell that enfolds it.

Dialectics begins with practice, experience and constant rectifications, develops with practice, which re-examines principles and laws (without sacrificing the fruits of earlier discoveries), and is verified in practice, which brings renewed proof every day that the structure and evolution of the real are such that only dialectical thought can account for and permit an understanding of them.

Lenin considered that one cannot understand Marx's *Capital* perfectly—and particularly its first volume—without having completely absorbed Hegel's *Logic*. And Engels, in a letter to Conrad Schmidt (November 1, 1891), supplied this supplementary detail: "Compare the development of the commodity into capital in Marx with the development from Being to Essence in Hegel, (and) you will get quite a good parallel."[46]

We will follow this suggestion and sketch out such a comparison.

The problem of the point of origin is posited in analogous terms by Hegel and Marx: The starting point of consciousness—as it is of reality—is necessarily concrete but this concrete thing is already a complex totality, a balance sheet, and it must be broken down into its component elements with all their contradictory interconnections.

Becoming, in Hegel, is the first concrete reality, but within it being and non-being confront each other like "moments that have no existence in themselves."

It is the same with Marx so far as the commodity is concerned. It is the first concrete reality, with which he opens *Capital:* "The wealth of those societies in which the capitalist mode of production prevails presents itself as an 'immense accumulation of commodities,' its unit being a single commodity. Our investigation must therefore begin with the analysis of a commodity."[47]

But the commodity is intelligible only if it is not regarded as a raw datum, a thing, but in its internal and contradictory relations: It is both use-value and exchange-value. Here we are in the presence of this double entity which Lenin saw as the soul of dialectics. From it ensue contradictions demanding to be resolved.

What are these contradictions? A product is only a commodity because the *thing* involves relationships between two persons or two communities, interrelationships between the producer and the consumer which are no longer incorporated in one person. Here we have an example of a fact which from the very outset has caused disastrous confusion among bourgeois economists: Relationships between people appear as relationships between things; human relationships are always linked to things and appear as things.

From the moment that we have grasped "alienation" we have already broken away from empiricism or positivism which could not encompass the contradiction within things: *Things are.* From the moment when, transcending appearances and passing from the whole to its parts, Marx discovered in the commodity a condition in which men and classes were face to face, he passed from positivist descriptions to the real dialectics of human relations. Such was Marx's fundamental discovery in political economy, as well as in philosophy —the discovery of the real interrelationships between men and things and of men among themselves.

If we follow the development of the commodity economy under the pressure of the contradictions the commodity bears within itself, we see that with the generalization of exchange "the distinction becomes firmly established between the utility of an object for the purposes of consumption, and its utility for the purposes of exchange. Its use-value becomes distinguished from its exchange-value."[48] But the simple quantitative increase in the number of exchanges reveals the material and technical impossibility of attributing to any particular commodity the function of a general equivalent. This function will therefore be attributed to a special commodity, of which the characteristics (incorruptibility, divisibility, easy transport, etc.) are such that they will embody exchange value in some way. "Money is a crystal formed of necessity in exchanges, whereby different products of labor are practically equated to one another and thus by practice converted into commodities."[49]

Thus the simple quantitative accumulations of the operations of exchange have engendered a new qualitative reality: the twofold aspect of the commodity and money. The contradiction between use value and exchange value is resolved practically, historically, in social life, by creating "a *modus vivendi*, a form in which they can exist side by side,"[50] i.e., money.

The new contradictions arising out of the opposition between commodities and money create new forms of development of the monetary economy by giving rise to capital.

In primitive times money was, in effect, only the universal medium

for the circulation of commodities. But, from the moment the value
of commodities is detached and separated from commodities, is
actually even opposed to them, then, in the guise of money, there
appears a new possibility for the movement of society: "the current
of the stream of gold and silver"[51] flows on and swells; money acquires a powerful autonomy in relation to other commodities. It
becomes the synonym of all wealth and it therefore seems to be
able to increase and multiply itself. "Value . . . suddenly presents
itself as an independent substance, endowed with a motion of its
own . . . money in process, and, as such, capital."[52]

Here, too, in the transition from money to capital—as previously
in that of commodity to money—a quantitative accumulation arrives at a qualitative change: Money, in acquiring autonomy in
relation to all other commodities, acquires a new, original function
—as compared with the traditional circulation of commodities in
which the producer sold what he did not need in order to get
what he needed. Thereafter, the rupture with need is consummated,
and the *movement can be reversed:* The capitalist buys what he
does not himself need (means of production, raw materials, man-
power etc.), in order to sell and to get back what he has invested,
augmented by a profit.

With the appearance of a surplus, of "surplus value," a third type
of movement begins, no longer that of commodity nor of money
but that of capital. With it, new contradictions arise which are
destined to set the system on the road to its own destruction and
engender a new form of the historical movement of society, with
new laws of development. As Marx wrote, "the historical development of the antagonisms, immanent in a given form of production,
is the only way in which that form of production can be dissolved
and a new form established."[53]

Such is the major thesis of scientific socialism.

At this stage, what is the controlling contradiction of capital?

First, what is it that makes possible the formation of surplus
value? Unless one supposes that money itself creates money, there
must exist a particular commodity "whose use value possesses the
peculiar property of being a source of value, whose actual consumption, therefore, is itself an embodiment of labour, and, consequently, a creation of value."[54] This commodity is labor power.

Hence, capital is also discovered to be not a *thing* but a *social relationship:* the relationship between the owner of the means of production and man who does not own them and has only his labor power to sell.

Out of this splitting into antagonistic relations of what seemed to be one thing—an object, capital—a flood of contradictions ensue. The general law of accumulation, resulting in the accumulation of wealth at one pole and poverty at the other; the law of the tendency of the rate of profit to fall; crises; and, finally, the revolutionary resolution of the fundamental contradiction engendered by the private ownership of the means of production existing under economic and social forms in which labor has a collective character. "This expropriation is accomplished by the action of the immanent laws of capitalistic production itself, by the centralization of capital. . . . Along with the constantly diminishing number of the magnates of capital, who usurp and monopolize all advantages of this process of transformation, grows the mass of misery, oppression, slavery, degradation, exploitation; but with this too grows the revolt of the working-class. . . . The knell of capitalist private property sounds. The expropriators are expropriated. . . . It is the negation of negation."[55]

Before examining how the application of this dialectical method permits an end to man's alienation by its liberating, militant functioning, it remains for us to verify the scientific, nonspeculative character of dialectics. Did Marx through the use of this method achieve his goal, which was to "lay bare the economic law of motion of modern society?"

Marx's Great Discoveries and Their Significance

The fruitfulness and validity of Marx's method in political economy is capable of double verification: (1) indirect, external verification by means of comparisons with results obtained by non-Marxist economics; (2) direct, internal verification by the examination of the concrete problems that this method has been able to predict and resolve. It is obviously impossible, within the limited confines of this book, to adduce more than merely a few examples.

Bourgeois political economy, before Marx, through its most eminent representatives—from Petty to Ricardo—tended to set itself up as a science; and in considering the problems of production, to set forth a series of theoretical arguments against decadent feudalism.

Petty defined the seignorial class and the social strata attached to it as men who "do nothing at all, but eat and drink, sing, play and dance . . . study the Metaphysicks."[1] Adam Smith gave a theoretical foundation to the accusation of parasitism directed against this class and its social strata, characterizing them as "non-productive."

The adoption of the production point of view has class implications. At the stage of economic development at which the capitalist, in his turn, begins to appear as a parasite on the social organism of production, it becomes dangerous to the bourgeoisie itself to continue to uphold the point of view of production—as did the great contemporary classic economists of the period of the ascendant bourgeoisie, when the function of the capitalist played a still positive role.

A veritable historical renaissance now came about in the scientific investigation of economics. Marx was to continue, to integrate, and to transcend the work of the bourgeois classical economists, even while positing himself, as they did, at the standpoint of production. Thus this objective scientific economics, formerly a weapon against feudalism, was to become a weapon against capitalism. The vanguard of the working class found its identity in *Capital*; Engels wrote in 1886: " 'Das Kapital' is often called, on the Continent, 'the Bible of the working class.' "[2]

On the other hand, in the middle of the 19th century, after the insurrection of June 1848 in Paris, when the working class appeared as an autonomous social force that threatened class privilege, bourgeois political economy beat a craven retreat into subjective positions.

The subjective attitude in political economy consists in cutting off economic research from the study of the relations of production, and in considering that the base of economic relations is in exchange, not in production. This subjective current prolonged the tradition of what Marx called "vulgar economics" (that of Say or of Bastiat, for example).

In this empiricist, positivist perspective, they began with isolated individuals, considering society only the arithmetical aggregate of individuals. The subjective attitude of the buyer or seller passes on to the first level of importance. This general trend of thought is called "marginalism," thus defining this school by its method and not by its content, its conception of man. This school starts from a very schematic and threadbare conception of man, the kind of shallow bourgeois individualism that is expressed in the "utilitarian" psychology and ethics of Bentham: "Economic man" is a being moved solely by the incentive of seeking to obtain the maximum gain or the maximum satisfaction for himself. One of the most eminent representatives of this school, Stanley Jevons, wrote in the Preface to *The Theory of Political Economy:* "In this work I have attempted to treat Economy as a Calculus of Pleasure and Pain . . . [to render the maximum pleasure, that is the problem of economics]."[3] Similar formulas of vulgar hedonism are found in Stuart Mill or Nassau Senior.

After having posited this goal for the economy, the means and methods are those of "marginalism," tending to attach exchange value to use value by the mediation of the "marginal consumer." They start from use value (the individualist and subjective viewpoint), but they believe that it is not the intensity of need that measures value, but the last portion of unsatisfied need, the "marginal" use. Starting with this, they are able to trace the curves of equilibrium and elaborate a general theory of equilibrium—wages, prices, profits—for all economic phenomena, making them appear as the resultant of exchanges made on a footing of equality; and this because they did not begin with social production (where social classes confront each other) but with the consumption of individuals (in isolation and abstraction).

This theory, which corresponds to the period of rising capitalism, plays an apologist role by justifying capitalist structures as immune from profound contradictions.

But it could not explain crises nor imperialism.

The great crisis of 1929–33 sounded the knell of this political economy and all its variants, even when adorned, as in Walras, with a seductive mathematical trimming—but still incapable of explaining a crisis.

In 1931, under the suggestive heading: "Bankruptcy of Political Economy," the *Manchester Guardian* asserted bitterly: "We are more familiar with the electron's speed of motion than we are with the speed of circulation of money. We know more about the earth's cycle around the sun and the sun's cycle in the universe than we know about the industrial cycle."

Now, it is not only necessary to write an apologetic theory for capitalism but also to save it, in a practical sense. From being apologetic, bourgeois political economy becomes purely pragmatic: The task assigned to it is to put back on its feet a practical technique for consolidating capitalism in distress.

The "savior" at that time was Keynes, who wrote his major work in 1935: *The General Theory of Employment, Interest and Money*. Keynes is a practicioner who has had a range of experience of which no previous economic theorist could boast. In England, for 20 years, approximately ten per cent of the working class was unemployed.

Keynes does not seek to theorize but to embellish necessity pragmatically. Considering that the investments of enterprises determine the employment level (and not purchases by private individuals, who spend practically the whole of their incomes), Keynes proposed that public expenditures supplement the insolvency of private investment to prime the pump of recovery. This intervention by the state into great capitalist complexes should lead to a lessening of periodic fluctuations. The class character of this conception of income and investment is obvious. It is merely a method of palliating the difficulties of capital by raising the funds necessary for state expenditures by taxes on the whole of the nation and by inflationary practices. It does not by any means conceal the pragmatic character and the class implications of his method: He acknowledges that he deliberately chooses inflation and the resultant rise in prices because the workers resist a decrease in real wages less vigorously than one in nominal wages.

We will further examine the practical efficacy of these expedients. Let us note for the moment the general trajectory of bourgeois economics in the course of its history and the circuitous path it

follows: (1) an ascendant period—that of the great classical economists, basing themselves on a scientific, objective study of the
relations of production in their struggle against declining feudalism;
(2) an apologist period corresponding to the period of the maturity
of capitalism, characterized by an individualist, subjective conception, by a prudent retreat to positivism insofar as method was
concerned; and, (3) at the epoch of the great cracks in the
capitalist order and the rise of a socialist economic system, the
relinquishment of any ambition to create theory and exclusively the
pragmatic concern with serving the practical demands of a weakened
and jeopardized system.

At this last stage, initiated by Keynes, bourgeois political economy,
if it has had to forego any over-all view, still strives to elaborate
techniques and to formalize its research. Since the notion of a base
was a "rarity" (a heritage of marginalism), political economy was
to be defined, by Robbins,[4] for example, as "the science that studies
human behavior insofar as the relations of ends and means to
alternative practices are concerned." One finds similar definitions
in Von Mises and in the majority of contemporary economists.

One of the unexpected consequences of this evolution of political
economy was that the direct polemics against Marxism on the economic plane subsided, as bourgeois political economy moved thenceforth on another plane than Marxism, having had to abandon to
Marxism the terrain of the constitution of a science of economics,
properly speaking, and of a synthesis of totality, in order to take
refuge in the elaboration of techniques (otherwise quite useful, and,
as we shall see, perfectly integrable with Marxism—the methods of
econometry, for example).

Keynes was already content to assert that Marx's *Capital* was
"an outmoded economic manual, not only erroneous from the
economic point of view but, even more, without interest or relevance
to the modern world."[5] He explained this opinion by declaring that
the Soviet economy had no future! The master, not having been
proved by events to possess prophetic clairvoyance, was followed
by successors who have become more prudent and, to avoid a too
drastic discrediting of non-Marxist political economy by prognostications (always a dangerous pastime for authors), have sought other
arenas for the battle against Marxism. A considerable number of

economists who asserted with assurance several years ago that none of Marx's economic theses—whether on the future of capitalism or on the possibilities of socialism—were susceptible to scientific verification, today prefer, more cautiously, to carry the debate on to the terrain of ethics, and to confine themselves, on a suitably economic level, to a degree of generalizing in which class relations are effaced to the point of leaving room only for the purely technical relations characteristic of all "industrial society."

In contrast to the impotence of non-Marxist political economy to make long-term predictions on the development of the capitalist world and, even less, on the future of socialist economy, Marxist economics has received a tremendous verification on both of these levels—as much for its prognostications on capitalism as in the building of a socialist economy.

In considering some of the crucial problems of our epoch, we will underscore by a number of facts the significance of Marx's basic theses on value, surplus value and the pauperization of the working class, the tendency of the rate of profit to fall, the concentration of capital and its imperialist development. We are deliberately omitting other phenomena characteristic of our time—for example, the general crisis of capitalism or state monopoly capitalism, for the understanding of which Marx's methods constitute a working tool and an indispensable clue, but which did not exist to any degree in Marx's lifetime and on which he could not have arrived at a direct analysis.

1. LABOR VALUE

> In the creation of value, the time that is socially necessary alone counts.
>
> — MARX[6]

A very elementary review of the fundamentals of the Marxist theory of labor value is essential here in order to judge its relevance to the solution of present-day problems.

Capitalist production is commodity production. As in all economies where exchange predominates, each producer does not manufacture products designed to satisfy his own needs or those of his immediate neighbors, but rather products that he throws on the market in order to exchange them for other products which he does need. In this instance, these products are called commodities. The interrelation among the possessors of commodities are established by the market.

On the market an object can be exchanged for a greater or lesser number of other objects. The degree to which this exchange is effected defines the *value* of an object.

In what respects does this value vary? All exchange presupposes a buyer and a seller. The buyer, who is in the position of the consumer, looks upon the commodity in the light of its use for him. This is called use value. The seller, who is in the position of the producer, regards the commodity in the light of the labor it has cost. This is called exchange value.

Exchange, therefore, takes place between use and labor. Between the two terms, there exists no common measure. Use value in particular is a purely relative notion: A glass of water in a desert for a man who is dying of thirst is beyond all value. But there is a reduction to a common denominator on the market, i.e., at the point where an indefinite number of producers can furnish the same commodities, and where an indefinite number of consumers want to procure them.

Let us imagine peasants bringing produce to the village market— some of them, butter; some of them, cheese: If the price of butter is very profitable and that of cheese less so, farmers will turn their milk into butter and not into cheese for the next market. Then the price of butter will decrease and that of cheese will increase.

How can equilibrium be established? In other words, what will be the average ratio by which a certain quantity of butter can be exchanged for a certain quantity of cheese? Or again (and this amounts to the same thing), what will be the value of the two products?

It may be objected that if the price of cheese takes a leap, it is because less cheese than necessary has been produced; and if its price drops, it is because more than necessary has been produced. What this amounts to is that the value of a product is a function of supply and demand.

But on the market it cannot be precisely like this, since commodities can neither increase indefinitely (competitive producers throw enormous quantities of these commodities on the market), nor diminish indefinitely (the producers turn to the production of another sort of commodity). The market will therefore play the role of regulator, and after many fluctuations an average will be established. Which?

When the two commodities are equally profitable, the producer, obviously, will produce the one that requires the least labor. The only element common to diverse commodities is the labor required for their production.

Thus one could formulate the fundamental law of exchange: The use factor does not intrude on the market; commodities are exchanged there according to the labor their production requires. This law is valid only in the case of the "ideal market," i.e., a market where, in principle, only products which can be fabricated in unlimited quantities are exchanged. It may in fact happen that at a given moment a product may be scarce or in excess; its price will vary within certain limits, in accordance with the law of supply and demand. A reverse fluctuation will happen very rapidly, so that the average will still be determined by labor. Labor is like a magnet dominating the pendulum movements of supply and demand.

From the narrow viewpoint of the merchant, these are the variations that matter, since they threaten his woolen stockings or his strong-box, but from the viewpoint of the historian studying long-term political economics, this is not the case.

Some may still raise the objection that the "resale price" of a commodity comprises not only labor but raw materials, tools, buildings, transportation, etc. But for the supplier of each of these products the problem is posed in similar fashion, and little by little one approaches iron, coal, stone, which have no other value than the labor their extraction requires. Hence the value of a commodity is nothing but crystallized labor.

But, one might say, how does one compare the labor of a cobbler with that of an architect, or even the labor of two cobblers working, according to their individual ability, at differing rates of speed? Here, too, we have a common denominator in the market: If eight hours of the baker's labor are estimated to be more lucrative than eight hours of a metallurgist's labor, young men preparing to enter an apprenticeship in a mechanic's shop will by preference go into a bakery. And this will happen in all branches of production, all things being equal, i.e., the savings possible during the apprenticeship, the physical exertion called for, and so on.

When we recapitulate all the factors (quality of labor, length of apprenticeship, etc.) it can be seen that the spontaneous regulation of the market permits the establishment of new relationships: 1 hour of a fitter's labor will be equivalent to $1\frac{1}{2}$ hours of a weaver's labor, etc.

In other words, all concrete labor will come back to the single measurement of abstract labor. All the composite forms of labor will be reduced to simple units of labor. Composite labor is that which required skills acquired at the expense of more or less time or money. A given amount of time in composite labor produces more value than the same amount of time in simple labor. But the market links the products of composite labor and those of simple labor. Thus, spontaneously, regardless of the producers, the value of the products of composite labor is expressed in terms of definite quantities of simple labor. Finally, at a given moment, labor is accomplished by certain technical means. So much the worse for the backward-looking individual who would choose to build an automobile by himself, using artisan's techniques. His auto would bring the same price as one of equal equality that came out of a shop equipped with modern tools.

Thus we arrive—with these details and these provisos—at the following formulation of the law of value: What determines the value of a commodity is the labor time socially necessary for its production. It is the case of a worker of average ability working with average intensity with the technical instruments of production in general use at a given epoch.

Actually, value is not expressed directly by hours of social labor, the quantity of which remains, in practice, unknown, but it is expressed, in terms which relate to the medium of exchange, by another commodity containing the same quantity of socially necessary labor. The relation which is thus established between two or more commodities is the form of value. This method is not unusual in the sciences: Scientific notions are expressed only indirectly and through the medium of certain of their effects. Heat, for example, is measured only by the expansion or contraction of bodies.

When one no longer confuses, as do the empiricists and positivists, the Marxist theory of value with the study of the immediate mechanism of price; and when, starting with the essential, which in economics is posited at the level of production, and then introducing all the complex mediations which permit certain phenomena to rise to the surface—then the objections, as empty as they are time-worn, disappear. For example, the objections which involve the prices of works of art or the price of land overlook the fact that these are commodities of limited quantity, of indeed unique character, and are no longer market prices but monopoly prices. Or, again, the objection that drags on interminably in the manuals of political economy involving wine, which, in aging in wine cellars "augments its value without the mediation of additional labor." This is a strange "refutation," professing once again to go directly from the essence to the phenomenon without traversing the necessary intervening steps, i.e., the equalization of the rate of profit, the speed of circulation of capital, etc., which permits the explanation of why the price of aged wine exceeds its value, and the profit realized on it exceeds surplus value.

When all these elements are reassembled, we see that Marx's theory of labor value not only readily withstands these pitiful and everlasting snipings, but enables us to resolve a great number of questions; to understand, for example, long-term trends of prices, which do not fluctuate in a void—as anti-Marxist theories would have it—but around a solid axis whose revolutions are dictated by the progress of technology and productivity.

We will also be able to see how the theory of labor value is at the base of the theory of surplus value—which reduces profit, interest and ground rent to a single source (a problem which Ricardo could not resolve)—and to comprehend the dialectics of the accumulation of capital and the pauperization of the workers.

This theory of labor value accounts for the tendency of the average rate of profit to fall and, consequently, for the dialectics of crises and the fundamental contradiction in the capitalist order between the *social* character of production and the *private* ownership of the products of labor.

In a word, the theory of labor value alone can establish political economy as a science, give it synthesized unity and internal rationality. Thanks to this theory, it is possible to established a "model" of economic production in which capitalism and socialism would be two variants, the socialist variant alone making truly rational planning possible. Marx was thus able to anticipate, without utopianism, and to formulate the basis of socialist planning:

"If production were socialised instead of capitalistic, these products of department I [the production of instruments of production] would evidently just as regularly be redistributed as means of production to the various branches of this department, for purposes of reproduction, one portion remaining directly in that sphere of production from which it emerged as a product, another passing over to other places of production, thereby giving rise to a constant to-and-fro movement between the various places of production in this department."[7]

Emphasizing the role of the theory of labor value in the Forward to his *Theoretical and Practical Problems of Planning*, Bettelheim comments: "It is the only thing that provides us simultaneously with a unity of homogenous accounting and a unity of accounting having a human meaning."

2. SURPLUS VALUE AND THE PAUPERIZATION OF THE WORKING CLASS

> The rate of surplus value is therefore an exact expression for the degree of exploitation of labour-power by capital, or of the labourer by the capitalist.
>
> — MARX.[8]

> Along with the constantly diminishing number of the magnates of capital . . . grows the mass of misery, oppression, slavery, degradation, exploitation; but with this too grows the revolt of the working-class.
>
> — MARX.[9]

Here again is a brief review of the main characteristics of the Marxist theory of surplus value, essential for understanding the dialectics of the pauperization of the working class.

Up until the rise of capitalism, money was only the equivalent of diverse commodities whose exchange it facilitated: The owner of commodities sold what he had no use for to buy what he needed.

The capitalist, on the other hand, begins by buying what he

himself does not need (means of production, raw materials, etc.) to sell and to get back the value invested in the purchase, augmented by a profit.

The analysis of the law of value shows that the prices of commodities tend toward the level of value, i.e., toward the amount of socially necessary labor time consumed in their production.

On the average, the capitalist buys and sells merchandise at its value. In the operations of buying and selling, one of the traders may, because of the fluctuations of supply and demand, profit at the expense of a competitor, but as each capitalist is in turn buyer and seller, as he profits or loses from momentary fluctuations, these operations cannot explain the profits of the capitalist class; they can only explain the fortuitous modifications of the sharing of profits among capitalists.

Hence, profits cannot be explained by the process of circulation. Marx posed the problem in all its sharpness: "Our . . . embryo capitalist must buy his commodities at their value, must sell them at their value, and yet at the end of the process must withdraw more value from circulation than he threw into it at starting."[10]

This problem cannot be resolved unless we find a commodity on the market which has the characteristic of creating value. Now value is created by labor power. Of all the commodities appearing on the capitalist market, labor power is the only one that can work. It is therefore the only one that can be the source of value.

This commodity, labor power, like all commodities, has a value determined by the time socially necessary for its production.

The worker each day expends a certain amount of energy; to renew it, he consumes certain products (means of subsistence: lodgings, furniture, clothes, food, etc.) and he must also reproduce himself in order that this labor power may continue to be available, and must therefore have the means of sustaining his family. Finally, he needs a certain amount of training and skill which will require time for their acquisition and involve expenditures. The more qualified the worker is, the more important will be the socially necessary labor time devoted to apprenticeship.

The value of all these means of subsistence, i.e., the socially necessary labor time for production, will constitute the value of labor power.

The capitalist hiring a worker, i.e., buying the commodity "labor power," can dispose of it at will; he therefore is going to make him work. But labor power has the faculty of producing more labor than is necessary to maintain it. On the basis of recent American statistics, it can be established that on the present level of technology, and taking into account the average scale of living of present society, three hours a day would be enough to supply the worker's needs.

After having worked three hours, for example, under normal conditions, the worker with his labor will have reimbursed the capitalist for the daily expense of reproducing his labor power. But, in hiring him, the capitalist has acquired the right to use him all day, for example, eight hours. The employer, therefore, is going to appropriate the production of five hours of labor free of charge. This product is *surplus value*, i.e., the difference between the amount of labor furnished and the quantity of labor necessitated by the production of what is paid as wages. The relation between the two terms, excess time (in the example chosen, five hours)) and necessary labor (three hours) is called the *rate of surplus value*, or the *rate of exploitation*.

To create still more surplus value, the capitalist has access to a very simple device, that of prolonging the working day. Up to 1848, there was no fixed limit; thanks to the revolution of February 1848, the decree of March 2 limited the working day to 10 hours in Paris and 11 in the provinces. After the working class defeat of June 1848, the law of September 30, 1848, put the working day back to 12 hours.

Surplus value can also be augmented by increasing the intensity of labor by speed-up, a system of fines, or piece-work, the rate of which is fixed in accordance with the output of an unusually strong or competent worker.

But the prolongation of the working day and the increase in the intensity of labor more and more meet the organized resistance of the workers.

There remains still another solution for the capitalist: to decrease the labor time socially necessary for the production of labor power, that is to say, for the production of the worker's means of subsistence. This is made possible by technical progress. The surplus value derived from this method is called relative surplus value. It is this which has stimulated the advance of mechanization.

In its turn, the progress of mechanization creates masses of workers who are ousted from their jobs by the competition of machines. As Marx says: "The increase of the variable part of capital, and therefore of the number of laborers employed by it, is always connected with violent fluctuations and transitory production of surplus-population. . . . The laboring population therefore produces, along with the accumulation of capital produced by it, the means by which itself is made relatively superfluous, is turned into a relative surplus-population. . . . This is a law of population peculiar to the capitalist mode of production."[11]

Thus what Marx called an "industrial reserve army" is created, which, by competition between workers, exerts a constant pressure on wages, downward toward a level approximating the simple expense of the reproduction of labor power. Today once again the leaders of the capitalist world consider a certain amount of unemployment as normal and necessary to prevent wages from rising "excessively." In the United States, for example, a level of unemployment of four million is considered "normal" or "non-critical."

Since this labor overpopulation is a burden on the law of supply and demand in the labor market, Marx concluded: "In proportion as capital accumulates, the lot of the labourer, be his payment high or low, must grow worse. . . . This law . . . establishes an accumulation of misery, corresponding with accumulation of capital. Accumulation of wealth at one pole is, therefore, at the same time accumulation of misery, agony of toil, slavery, ignorance, brutality, mental degradation, at the opposite pole, i.e. on the side of the class that produces its own product in the form of capital."[12]

From the "absolute law" of capitalism, "the production of surplus-value,"[13] this necessary consequence follows: It is the nature of capitalist production to limit the share of the producer to what is necessary for the maintenance of his labor power.

This objective law of the development of the capitalist system is a tendential and a historical law. Hence it cannot be confused with Lassalle's "iron law," which states that the wages of workers can in no case exceed a certain rate arising from the absolute number of the population. Lassalle based this dogma on the Malthusian theory of population, while Marx insisted, in opposing these so-called "natural laws," on the historical character of the laws of population and also on the value of labor power. The sum-total of the means of subsistence necessary for the worker, and also the modes of satisfying them, depend "to a great extent on the degree of civilization of a country." It is therefore necessary to introduce into this evolution a "historical and moral element."[14]

A historical law, but also a tendential one, implying a continuous and inevitable evolution, but one that, because of a favorable combination of events, great working class struggles can temporarily hold in check; or for a period they may reverse a trend which is manifested only over the long term.

Moreover, since the law of value cannot be translated immediately and directly into figures, as a simple empirical study or in terms of short-term prices, the law of pauperization cannot be identified with the curve of real wages nor with the curve of the evolution of the value of labor power.

Out of this, two consequences arise:

(1) Pauperization cannot be linked to a pure and simple decrease in real wages. The decrease in real wages can be one of the elements in pauperization, but it is this decrease against which the "opposing factors" make their most direct fight, in the first place, trade union and political struggles.

(2) Pauperization can no longer be defined merely as a growing gap between the value of labor power and real wages. First, because, as stated above, the workers in their struggle against the owners succeed at times in imposing at least a partial recognition of their needs and, as a result, bring their real wages closer to the value of their labor power (including historical elements related to "the traditional standard of living," as Marx commented). Besides, this definition is inadequate because it bears on the worker's "labor power" alone and not on his entire individuality.

Even if real wages coincided exactly with the value of labor power and followed a historical progression (which is far from being true) and even if real wages manifested a constant advance (which is even farther from being always true), the condition of the worker would nevertheless continue to worsen in the degree that capital accumulates.

This worsening is *relative*, in the sense that in the national income the share of wages decreases and that of capital increases.

This worsening is *absolute*, in the sense that even without reference to the capitalist, obstacles to the workers' human development multiply.

Relative pauperization is very little challenged. Marx defined it in clearcut fashion: "Profit and wages remain in inverse proportion,"[15] and all the empirical data verify the tendency toward a reduction in the share accruing to wages in the product created by labor. In France, when productivity increased by 24.6 per cent (from 1954–59), real salary decreased during the same period by 10 per cent. In England, John Strachey, a systematic adversary of Marxist economics, states: "The share of wages in the total national income . . . appears to have been around 50% in Marx's day; to have declined to about 40% in the early years of the twentieth century; to have stayed about there till 1939, and then (including . . . the pay of the Forces) to have gone back to around 50% by the end of the Second World War."[16] And this in spite of the constant struggles of the wage workers.

In the United States, this tendency is perfectly apparent. According to official statistics, the share of wages in the net product ("value added") for manufacturing industry declined from 48 per cent in 1880 to 35 per cent in 1952.[17]

All the present modes of compensation based on premium wages, those of the Rowan, Halsey, Bedeaux, Emerson, Refa systems, etc., have this in common: The labor contribution grows more rapidly than wages. From the volume of values created by the worker, a constantly smaller fraction is returned to him, and surplus value increases proportionately. Thus, in the Rowan system:

> if output increases by 50%, wages increase by 33%;
> if output increases by 100%, wages increase by 50%;
> if output increases by 200%, wages increase by 60%.

The Bedeaux system in the United States generally arrives at an increase in production of 50 per cent against an increase in wages of 20 per cent.[18]

This means, as Marx wrote, that "the worker is able to be in a bearable situation only on condition that he create and strengthen the power which is hostile to him, his own enemy. . . . When the relation between labor and capital is understood, the attempts of Fourier and others toward conciliation are exposed in all their absurdity." Far from denying the possibility of a relative amelioration, Marx adds: "The quicker the working class multiplies and augments the power inimical to it—the wealth of another which lords it over that class—the more favourable will be the conditions under which it will be permitted to toil anew at the multiplication of bourgeois wealth . . . content thus to forge for itself the golden chains by which the bourgeoisie drags it in its train."[19]

Here we have the elements of a definition, not only of relative pauperization but also of absolute pauperization. The law of absolute pauperization expresses a growing alienation not only of labor, but also of the life of the laborer. Even if the proletariat succeeds in enlarging the scope of its pleasures, to the degree in which capital accumulates, the weight of this power increases—a power born out of the labor of man but now, as capital, become alien to him, ruling and exploiting him. An increasing part of the properly human life of man, of his human needs, is taken away from the worker by the operation of the capitalist system.

The law of absolute pauperization implies not only a greater insecurity of existence, but a growing separation between the historically defined needs of the working class and the means it possesses for gratifying them.

The mutilation of the working man is manifested on all levels, ranging from the physical to the intellectual and ethical.

It is translated into tragic statistics: The number of labor accidents rose in France from 619,000 in 1938 to 1,229,000 in 1958. The effects of production campaigns and the speed-up is written in the flesh and minds of men. In the Seine District, in one year, the number of mental patients doubled, rising from 10,500 in 1954 to 21,000 in 1955. For all of France, Professor Piedelièvre estimates that the number of mental patients quadrupled between 1953 and 1959.

As can be seen, the law of absolute pauperization is expressed not only in terms of wages but also in the fact that a greater part of the life of the worker is consumed by his role as a wage employee of capital. As Marx wrote in the *Manuscripts of 1844*, an "in crease of wages . . . would therefore be nothing but *better payment for the slave*, and would not win either for the worker or for labor their human status and dignity."[20]

The alienation characteristic of this impoverishment of man is, in the first place, the radical separation between labor and other dimensions of human life, the worker's loss of control not only over the product but also over the very act of his labor. There is an increase in the tempo of labor, an increasing mechanization, a lowering of standards, a nervous attrition degrading even his leisure by not affording him anything other than passive, dehumanized and commercialized distractions. For example, the sale of books listed as "books of general culture" on the domestic market in France has fallen by 4 per cent since 1955. By contrast, the sale of detective stories and "heart-throb" novels has more than doubled from 1955 to 1959.

In Paris, the amateur popular choruses which flourished in 1938 no longer exist, and the number of amateur concert societies has decreased in 20 years from 53 to 12, yielding to the passive leisure pursuits of television.

The conception of the law of absolute pauperization that rises out of the basic law of the development of capitalism, while excluding all reformism, gives a concrete, revolutionary base to an authentic humanism. The destruction of the capitalist, profit-based economy will put an end to the alienation of man and create the conditions for the expansion of the total man.

3. THE CONTRADICTIONS OF CAPITALISM AND CRISES

The real barrier of capitalist production is capital itself.
— MARX[21]

Along with the pauperization of the working class, another law of the development of capitalism, also arising from technical progress and the increase in mechanization, contributes to putting capitalism on the road to its own ruin. That is the law of the tendency of the rate of profit to fall. As Marx wrote, the "development of the social productiveness of labour expresses itself with the progress of capitalist production on the one hand in a tendency of the rate of profit to fall progressively and, on the other, in a progressive growth of the absolute mass of the appropriated surplus-value, or profit."[22]

Here again it is a matter of an internal and inevitable law of the capitalist order: Under the pressures of competition and the workers' demands, capitalist enterprise is unceasingly constrained to improve its production techniques. In capital, the share of constant capital (C), i.e., machines, grows greater; even if the share of variable capital (V), i.e., wages, remains unchanged or even decreases somewhat, the rate (r) of surplus value (sv) will necessarily increase since:

$$r \text{ equals } \frac{sv}{C+V}.$$

This is a law that even the opponents of Marxism must know. One of them writes: "As a system accumulates more and more productive plant and equipment, the rate of return on new and existing capital becomes depressed."[23]

Official statistics report facts that confirm this inevitable law. In the United States, for example, the statistics show very clearly that between 1889 and 1919 the rate of profit declined from 26.6 per cent to 16.2 per cent.[24]

To sustain the increase in the volume of profits despite the lower rate, enterprises are driven to developing their production and hence their equipment (i.e., to still more accelerate the lowering of the rate), and to exploit labor power more intensively (thus increasing pauperization). The contradiction becomes more and more striking between the development of the productive forces necessary to obtain the maximum individual profit and the relations of production, which are less and less responsive to this development.

The reduction in the cost of production and the increase in the productivity of labor necessary to business profits demand better and costlier plants. The success of enterprises in which the organic composition of capital is highest leads to the elimination of lesser and weaker competitors.

"The increased scale of industrial establishment" wrote Marx, "is the starting point for a more comprehensive organization of the collective work of many . . . for the progressive transformation of isolated processes of production, carried on by customary methods, into processes of production socially combined and scientifically arranged."[25]

This phenomenon of concentration is too obvious in industry, as well as in commerce and agriculture, for us to spend too much time on it. The history of capitalism is the history of the dispossession of the greatest number from ownership for the profit of a more and more restricted monopolistic minority.

Capitalism leads to the growing proletarianization of the middle classes who, having once been owners of capital, no longer own anything beyond their own labor power.

This evolution of the class structure in strikingly apparent in the United States; between 1880 and 1957 the ratio of wage-earners of all sorts in the gainfully employed population rose steadily from 62 per cent to 84 per cent, with a corresponding decline for entrepreneurs of all kinds (from 37 per cent to 14 per cent).[26]

These changes in class structure, as well as other data, such as the growing number of bankruptcies among the lesser companies, reflect the growth of monopoly in the major branches of industry, which is common to all big capitalist countries. The same trend toward concentration has been especially marked during recent years in agriculture, with the mass dispossession of small owners and the rise of large farm enterprises.

One can, no doubt, talk of the "new middle classes," whose standard of living on the whole corresponds to that of the old middle classes. These new middle classes arise from complex hierarchies based on large-scale enterprises and interposed between workers and employers. They include techicians, laboratory directors, sales and publicity managers, the personnel of planning bureaus, market analysts, researchers, etc. But these new middle classes are primarily distinguished from the old middle classes only by the fact that they are no longer owners of the means of production but wage workers, even if their wage level, the traditions they create for themselves, their way of life and their prejudices differentiate them, strictly speaking, from the proletariat.

Crises are among the most characteristic phenomena of capitalist economic development. We will recall the major factors in the mechanism of crises, as described by Marx.

The mass of proletarians consume a decreasing share of the growing social wealth (relative pauperization), and thus the tendency to the unlimited expansion of production collides with the limited purchasing power of the masses. "The ultimate reason for all real crises always remains the poverty and restricted consumption of the masses as opposed to the drive of capitalist production to develop the productive forces as though only the absolute consuming power of society constituted their limit."[27] Thus, crises of overproduction are produced, i.e., periods where abundance gives rise to poverty.

The cause of these crises is the inability of the mass of proletarians in a capitalist society to buy the products that a more and more powerful industry produces in ever greater quantities and ever more rapidly. In the capitalist system, production is accomplished socially in large and powerful enterprises. On the other hand, the appropriation of profits is accomplished individually—it is the act of a handful of capitalists, who are incapable of consuming all the wealth produced. The overwhelming majority of the workers, who could consume these commodities, are deprived of adequate purchasing power. Thus they produce much and consume little. This is one of the contradictions of capitalism and the permanent cause of crises. Crises arise from the contradiction between social production and capitalist appropriation. Thus the cause of crises of overproduction is rooted in the capitalist system, from which arises their cyclical character. With the exception of the periods affected by the wars of 1870, 1914 and 1939–45, these crises appeared at intervals of seven to 11 years, with a tendency toward an accelerating rhythm in their recurrence.

In *Anti-Dühring* Engels describes the phenomena of crises in this striking résumé: "Since 1825 when the first general crisis broke out, the whole industrial and commercial world, the production and exchange of all civilized peoples and of their more or less barbarian dependent people have been dislocated practically once in every ten years. Trade comes to a standstill, the markets are glutted, the products lie in great masses, unsalable, ready money disappears, credit vanishes, the factories are idle, the working masses go short of the means of subsistence because they have produced too much of them, bankruptcy follows upon bankruptcy, forced sale upon forced sale. The stagnation lasts for years, both productive forces and products are squandered and destroyed on a large scale, until the accumulated masses of commodities are at last disposed of at a more or less considerable depreciation, until production and exchange gradually begin to move again. By degrees the pace quickens; it becomes a trot; the industrial trot passes into a gallop, and the gallop in turn passes into the headlong onrush of a complete industrial, commercial, credit and speculative steeplechase, only to land again in the end, after the most breakneck jumps—in the ditch of a crash. And so on again and again."[28]

The crisis, surmounted at the cost of all these catastrophes, has one basic result: the intensification of capitalist concentration, since the crisis has brought about the disappearance of a number of enterprises.

Thus "the *real barrier* of capitalist production is *capital itself*." All the contradictions of the mode of capitalist production finally add up to a fundamental contradiction, the contradiction between the social form of production and the private form of appropriation.

In the capitalist world, where production is governed not by the satisfaction of needs but by the realization of profits, production seems to be separated from consumption, seems to live an autonomous life, to be an end in itself. Crises come periodically, in a spasmodic way, to work out the readjustment of production to the possibilities of purchasing power, *a posteriori*. Periodic crises are crises of the realization of surplus value. As Sismondi once noted, the insufficiency of the masses' purchasing power prevents the latter from buying all the products manufactured in the course of a given period. The surplus value created remains frozen as unsaleable commodities.

Hence production develops in a staccato tempo, with leaps forward and times of standstill and even of recession. The introduction of new machines, new methods of production change the net cost but the change is only noted after the thunderbolt, when the failure to sell makes it seem that too much social labor has been expended in a given sector.

It is for this reason that crises in capitalist society have a cyclic character, dependent on the rate of circulation of capital. In his *Treatise on Marxist Economy*, Mandel writes quite accurately: "The cyclic movement of capital is therefore nothing more than the mechanism by which the tendency of the average rate of profit to fall is realized. It constitutes at one and the same time the reaction of the system against this fall by the devaluation of capital in crises. Crises make possible the adjustment of the quantity of labor effectively expended in the production of commodities to the quantity of socially necessary labor, the individual value of commodities to the socially determined value, the surplus value contained in these commodities to the average rate of profit. Because capitalist production is not consciously planned and organized, these adjustments show up not *a priori* but *a posteriori*. For this reason, they cause violent shocks, the destruction of thousands of lives, of enormous volumes of value and created wealth. . . . The fluctuations in the rate of profit unmask the internal workings of the economic cycle. They explain the general meaning of the cycle as a periodic readjustment of the conditions of equilibrium of capitalist production."[29]

In order that expanding reproduction develop without explosions or crises, it would be necessary by who knows what mysterious pre-established harmony (impossible in the capitalist economy of the market) that the purchases of the commodities of consumption in relation to the means of production should be in a ratio permitting exact equilibrium. The development of production without crisis (possible only with the abolition of the capitalist system and the establishment of a social order based on need and permitting conscious planning) demands a rigorously balanced development of the two sectors. In the capitalist regime, crises are the sign of the periodic breakdown of equilibrium, followed by a ruthless rehabilitation.

Are these crises and their cyclic character still present today? Even when they do not manifest the characteristics of a cataclysm like that of 1929, these crises reappear periodically, reflecting the spasmodic nature of the development of capitalism. Even when they are partially masked by the economically pathological hypertrophy of production for war, they are evidenced in a temporary decline in production and a wave of unemployment. Such was the case with the depression in the United States in 1948–49, and again in 1957–58, when industrial production in the capitalist world as a whole also suffered a decline.

On the other hand, between the two crises, a relative rise from 1950 to 1955 arose from the impetus given by the Korean War and the resulting inflation. The *Bulletin des Sociétés financières* (June 8, 1957) stated: "One of the factors making for activity still remains armaments, which absorb a great part of industrial activity; by this token . . . it would be an economic disaster if the U.S.A. and the USSR arrived at an understanding." Moreover, this was not a pathological phenomenon nor an exceptional one, but a consequence flowing from the very nature, the very essence of the capitalist regime.

However, state monopoly capitalism makes possible the application on a vast scale of state capital expenditures, such as those recommended by Keynes to stimulate the economy. The armaments race plays a decisive role in this attempt to stimulate the economy, but this expedient is precarious and aggravates the internal contradictions of capitalism, further shrinking the buying power of the masses by heavy tariffs, taxes and the resulting inflation. This "shot-in-the arm" for the capitalist economy is as injurious and ruinous in the end for economic health as physiological dope is for the living organism.

The same comments apply to the other expedients resorted to by the big capitalist countries. Aid to the underdeveloped countries is adduced as a panacea, and in fact it could help to resolve some problems. But it is used as a temporary expedient, and it is hobbled by the fear that the rapid industrialization of these countries will turn them into competitors.

The sickness of the internal dialectics of the system and its contradictions cannot be cured—they can only be masked for greater or lesser periods by the necessarily fleeting expedients of production for war or of neo-colonialism.

The proof of the Marxist theory of crises and of its present pertinence is furnished by the economic development of the socialist countries, who have terminated the internal contradictions of capitalism and achieved rates of development incommensurable with those of the capitalist world.

After having had to recognize that the abolition of the private ownership of the means of production did not lead to economic chaos, as Keynes and the others had prognosticated; after having had to confess the practicality of "plans" which they had first characterized as Utopian; after having had to confess that, far from running out of breath when their economic equipment had achieved a certain level (as they never ceased to predict), deferring its downfall year after year, the capitalist "experts" admit that the tempo of development is accelerated and increases in geometrical proportion. Economists, technicians and policy-makers now openly express their fear of defeat in the economic competition between the two systems. It is significant that the author of *The Stages of Economic Growth: A Non-Communist Manifesto* (1960), Walt Rostow, writes: "It is not Soviet economic aid and trade that threatens us in Latin America and elsewhere; it is the attractiveness of the Communist method as a device for organizing the rapid modernization of an underdeveloped society."[30]

Special Adviser to the State Department, Chester Bowles, asserted with some bitterness in 1961: "The Soviet economy develops at a far more rapid tempo than our own. For those in America and other countries who are inclined to accept their own desires as realities and who for many years looked upon the scientific and industrial potential of the USSR with contempt, the hour of a bitter awakening has sounded."

Such, on the economic plane, is the extent of Marx's posthumous victory. He wrote in 1848 in *The Communist Manifesto:* "A specter is haunting Europe; the specter of communism." This specter, which has taken on flesh, today haunts the world; and from the theoretical as well as the practical point of view, in spite of one furious prediction after another, its enemies after half a century can boast of nothing but defeats in their battles against communism. In spite of the desperate denigrations of anti-Marxist economists, who vainly try to close their eyes, the practical experience and the massive verification of Marxism is being realized on a planetary scale.

For Marxists themselves this creates new demands.

It is no longer enough, as it was in the days when Marxism was only a hope, to popularize the guiding theses of Marxism, or to refute the sophistries of anti-Marxism. These teachings and these polemics retain their validity; indeed they are more essential than ever. But Marxism is no longer a position to be stormed or to be defended. The triumph of Marxism on the grounds of practical efficiency makes the most audacious and victorious theoretical advances possible.

The objections directed against the Marxist theses appear more and more thin-spun, a tissue made threadbare by sophistry. For example, the "technocratic" objection, according to which capitalism, as Marx described it, no longer exists; the element directing the economy no longer are the capitalists but the "managers." This disregards, in the first place, what Marx had clearly described in *Capital*, i.e., the growing role of the industrial organizer, management being more and more separated from proprietorship.[31] Moreover, this argument does not seriously challenge anything in Marx's fundamental demonstration, since "technocracy," that is, direction by technicians, exists no more in the capitalist system than it does in the socialist system. Here, as there, it is not the technicians who determine the goals, profits or real needs of the nation. In the capitalist system, the technician who functions as a technocrat by putting himself at the service of monopoly is only a manager devoting his knowledge and techniques to research and to working out the most effective *means* for obtaining the maximum profit—a basic *end* which is not determined by him.

Among the various technologies there are some which are perfectly adaptable by Marxism for use in the pursuit of other ends. These possibilities of creative development, of integration and progress (in economics, in philosophy, in other cultural realms), partially hampered in their development during the period when Stalin cast economics in a pragmatic or an apologetic role, and when it was hobbled by dogmatism and ideology of justification, today can expand in an unprecedented fashion. And this not only by the exploration of unkown realms for the building of socialism under the most diverse conditions, as well as the building of communism, but also by the utilization, in the service of socialist planning, of techniques discovered in capitalist contexts and doomed by capitalism to sterility.

The technical discoveries of enconometry, and the effort to represent an economic system in the form of a mathematical model, make possible the study of cycles in economic growth and can only find their true terrain for application in the planned economy of socialism.

Here they can offer a choice among diverse projects, assigning the correct share to each of the various sectors.

It is not only a matter of techniques, i.e., of methods which permit the posing of problems or the orientation of the economy, but also the solution of problems on the basis of objectives established by a general theory of economics, that of Marx.

It is the same with operational research, i.e., the art of preparing decisions scientifically, with a view to assuring the efficiency of practice. This logic of practical activity, whose rationality is assured, makes it possible to determine resources and means with respect to objectives defined in advance, to recommend the most effective organizational structures to rationalize the' activities of management.

The science of programming and input-output analysis (the internal accounting processes of the program), which deals with the choice of appropriate means to realize a given end—when the means are measurable and the end can be realized in varying degrees; cybernetics, which studies in abstract fashion a system of elements linked by reciprocal relations of interactions, translating into mathematical terms the relation between cause and effect and their reverse actions, determining the development of the system; perspective, as a study of the distant future, its tendencies and the factors which determine a technique of prediction, with a view to preparing future activity—all this finds in the perspective of Marxist economy (and in this perspective alone) the conditions for full expansion by putting these sciences and these techniques to work—no longer for maximum profit but in the service of man and the unlimited development of the whole man.

IV. KARL MARX AND POLITICAL STRUGGLES

"It is the ultimate aim of this work," Marx wrote in the Preface of *Capital*, "to lay bare the economic law of motion of modern society."[1]

From this law the transition from capitalism to socialism flows naturally. Marx called this "the expropriation of the expropriators." But Marx has never confused necessity and fatality. Man's action is one of the elements by which necessity is achieved. Marx defined the working class movement as "the conscious participation in the historical process that turns society upside down."[2]

From Utopia to the Class Struggle

The fundamental concept of Marxist politics, as of Marxist philosophy and economy, is the concept of class. The analyses in *Capital* have laid a scientific foundation for this concept. In conformity with the general orientation of Marxist political economy, in which the essence of economic reality must be sought at the level of production, social classes are defined by the role they play in production. From this point of view, the proletariat, for example, is defined as the class which (1) does not possess any means of production; (2) produces surplus value through the sale of its labor power; (3) has a more or less clear consciousness of its position in capitalist society and its historical mission.

In *The Communist Manifesto*, Marx gives a definition of communism which also establishes the fundamental task of the movement: "The communists fight for the attainment of the immediate aims, for the enforcement of the momentary interests of the working class; but in the movement of the present, they also represent and take care of the future of that movement."[3] Before Marx, the concept of class had been elaborated, notably by the French historians of the Restoration and the English economists, and the notion of a proletariat had been advanced by the utopians; but the proletariat was defined much more in terms of its poverty and suffering than by its struggle and its goals.

Marx, in his *Contribution to Hegel's Philosophy of Right* had characterized—still in philosophical form—the proletariat as an autonomous historical force exerting the Hegelian function of negativity in history.

In *Capital*, the definition of the proletariat was to become objective and scientific, and, along with this, the capitalist bourgeoisie was to be defined not by its wealth or its conception of the world or by any other criterion located in the economy at the level of distribution (or even at the ethical level), but by the position it occupied in production as owner of the means of production and appropriator of the surplus value of the workers.

Capital insists particularly on the two classes whose role is decisive in the development of the capitalist system. But Marx does not neglect the other social classes. In the second and third volumes of *Capital*, he analyzes not only the structure and development of the class of the landowner-receivers of rent and the specific forms of agrarian exploitation, but he also analyzes the middle classes and the distinctions, founded on objective criteria, between producers and non-producers. In *The Communist Manifesto*, Marx underlined in particular the inherent contradiction in the very nature of the middle class: "all these fight against the bourgoisie, to save from extinction their existence as fractions of the middle class. They are therefore not revolutionary, but conservative. Nay more, they are reactionary, for they try to roll back the wheel of history. If by chance they are revolutionary, they are so only in view of their impending transfer into the proletariat; they thus defend not their present, but their future interests; they desert their own standpoint to adopt that of the proletariat."[4]

The richness and complexity of the Marxist class conception is substantiated in Marx's historical works—*Class Struggles in France* and *The 18th Brumaire of Louis Bonaparte* (a model of historical analysis of classes and their relations), as well as in his studies on the Paris Commune.[5]

The essential task that Marx undertook on the plane of political theory was to determine with precision, by the functioning of objective criteria, the historical mission of the proletariat: "The question is not what this or that proletarian, or even the whole of the proletariat . . . *considers* as its aim. The question is *what the proletariat is*, and what, consequent on that *being*, it will be compelled to do."[6]

With this mission, the proletariat cannot become fully conscious on the level of economic struggle alone. It will succeed only by political consciousness and by access to a theoretical and scientific consciouness of the whole development of history. In *The Poverty of Philosophy*, Marx shows several objective factors which make possible the transition from economic to political struggle: "Large-scale industry concentrates in one place a crowd of people unknown to one another. Competition divides their interests. But the maintenance of wages, this common interest which they have against their boss, unites them in a common thought of resistance—*combination*. Thus combination always has a double aim, that of stopping competition among the workers, so that they can carry on general competition with the capitalist. If the first aim of resistance was merely the maintenance of wages, combinations, at first isolated, constitute themselves into groups as the capitalists in their turn unite for the purpose of repression, and in face of always united capital, the maintenance of the association becomes more necessary to them than that of wages. . . . In this struggle—a veritable civil war—all the elements necessary for a coming battle unite and develop. Once it has reached this point, association takes on a political character."[7]

The grasp of theoretical consciousness, indispensable for the proletariat, the consciousness of the class "in itself" becoming the class "for itself," is the result of a hard battle against the dominant ideas to which the masses are subjected in spite of themselves—the ideas of the ruling class.

This consciousness demands a permanent struggle against utopianism. It is at this point that Marx begins his political struggle; but once more, in 1877, he leads the fight when he declares: "A rotten spirit is making itself felt in our Party . . . with a whole gang of half-mature students and superwise doctors who want to give socialism a "higher ideal" orientation, that is to say, to replace its materialistic base (which demands serious objective study from anyone who tries to use it) by modern mythology with its goddesses of Justice, Freedom, Equality and Fraternity."[8]

The very development of Marxist thought, beginning with the break from utopianism, verifies the theory that "the existence of revolutionary ideas at a particular period presupposes the existence of a revolutionary class."[9]

English chartism, the working class insurrections of the silk-weavers of Lyons and of the Silesian weavers in Germany, were indices of the existence of a working class which was becoming an autonomous historical force. The scientific merit of Marx and of his conception of history is demonstrated by his awareness that these movements were not fortuitous but that they were more or less developed forms of the same historically determined struggle of the proletariat against the ruling class.

From that time on, communism could not be utopian, the illusory and sentimental creation of the ideal of a perfect society, but a consciousness of a real movement of nature, of conditions, and of the final goals of a struggle effectively led by the working class. *The German Ideology* had already given a scientific foundation to communism. It was no longer only a doctrine; it was also a movement. It was not a matter of starting from moral aspirations, nor from Hegelian speculations, nor from Feuerbachian humanism, but from objective and scientific analysis of the laws of development of history.

This new conception clashed with early conceptions of utopian and conspiratorial communism.

After the defeat of the Blanquist plot of 1839 in Paris,* the League of the Just had been dispersed. Differences arose between the refugee elements in Switzerland, who held, with Weitling, to a

---

* Louis Auguste Blanqui (1805–1881), French revolutionary and utopian communist, advocated conspiratorial methods. He was the leader of the secret society, *Société de saisons,* and organizer of the abortive insurrection of May 12, 1839.—*Ed.*

conspiratorial and utopian conception, and the refugee elements in London who, under the influence of the Chartist movement, struggled against this orientation. Marx saw in this opposition the inception of the rupture between utopian and scientific communism. In the spring of 1846, to help bring about ideological clarification, Marx set himself the task of creating committees of correspondence. In his letter of May 5, 1846, to Proudhon, he wrote: "The principal aim of our correspondence will be to put German socialists in touch with French and English socialists."

Marx knew he was leaving utopianism behind in thus linking himself with an actual movement. The correspondence, in printed or lithographed pamphlets, would be used to criticize sharply the mélange of French-English socialism and German philosophy which characterized the secret doctrine of the League; it would be used to replace this by a theoretically solid foundation—the scientific view of the economic structure of bourgeois society; and, finally, the correspondence would make clear that it was important to lay aside utopian systems and participate consciously in the historical process of the immanent social revolution.

At the beginning of 1846 Marx conducted a very lively polemic against Weitling, against what he called the "communism of artisans" and "philosophical communism." Weitling, at least, had the merit of being an enemy of reformism; he felt the emancipation of the working class could not be realized by reforms obtained in agreement with the bourgeoisie but only by working class struggle and by a social revolution directed against the bourgeoisie—a revolution that would destroy the domination of money and establish, along with social ownership, equality and fraternity among men. But this ideal and this rebellion were founded not on a scientific analysis of real historical developments but on moral exigencies, and, finally, in his book, *The Evangelist of the Poor Fisherman* (1843),Weitling defined communism as the realization of primitive Christianity.

After having refuted Hermann Kriege, friend of Weitling and propagandist of a typically bourgeois sentimental communism, Marx once again in *The Poverty of Philosophy* (1847) denounced and refuted petit-bourgeois reformism and the Proudhon type of utopian anarchism. "Property is theft," said Proudhon, and then developed from this a form of socialism expressing the utopian aspirations of the middle classes. At the end of his book, *Justice in the Revolution and the Church*, Proudhon sums up his fundamental experience: "I was 20 when I completed my studies; my father had lost his land; mortgages had devoured him. Who knows—if he had not believed in the good faith of a land bank, I might have spent all my life as a peasant and conservative."[10]

It would be difficult to better define the class standpoint from which Proudhon never departs. Son of a small ruined peasant who became a cooper after the liquidation of his land, he retained a nostalgia for his lost estate all his life. He was to define socialism as "the establishment of moderate fortunes, the universalization of the middle class." The problem of credit is central for him; the panacea for all evils to this petty bourgeois, condemned by the evolution of capitalism and the tyranny of banks, is to get loans without interest.

From this point, contradictions multiply in the work of Proudhon. Extremist formulas follow apologia for the established order.

After having proclaimed that property is theft, in his last work, *The Theory of Property*, he eulogizes property in its bourgeois form simply by predicting illusory guarantees of equilibrium. After having proclaimed "God is Evil," and after having proclaimed himself the "enemy of God," in the introduction to his book he declares that he needs the hypothesis of God, and nothing remains for him but to invoke Providence and "eternal ideas and laws." After having asserted that "the true form of government is anarchy," he accommodates himself unequivocally to the dictatorship of Napoleon III, to whom he dedicates his work.

The revolutionary phrase masks his spirit of conciliation with power: "I have preached the conciliation of classes, the symbol of the synthesis of doctrines,"[11] he writes, and he gives credence to Napoleon III's formula: "To satisfy the just demands of the proletariat without harming the acquired rights of the bourgeois class."[12]

With his mania for moralizing, he strove constantly to eliminate the "bad side," "the excesses" of capitalism, while maintaining the basic structure of the regime itself.

Marx says of Proudhon at the end of *The Poverty of Philosophy*: "He wanted to soar as man of science, above the bourgeois and the proletarians; he is merely the petty bourgeois, continually tossed back and forth between capital and labour."[13]

"Proudhon has done enormous mischief," wrote Marx, because his is a doctrine totally incapable of turning the masses to effective action. The revolutionary phrase, verbal anarchism, philosophical eclecticism that perpetuates contradiction by its inability to use the real dialectics of the class struggle—all this is the Proudhonian heritage against which a true working class, Marxist party would have to take its stand.[14]

Marx combatted not only the utopian but also the conspiratorial aspect of communist sects. In April 1850, in the *Neue Rheinische Zeitung*, Marx delivered a pitiless judgment on conspirators, whose concepts imply contempt for reality, for theory and for the masses. "Their social situation entirely conditions their character. A proletarian conspiracy naturally only assures them very limited and uncertain funds. They are therefore constantly forced to tap the till for the conspiracy. Many come into direct collision with bourgeois society and make a more or less conspicuous appearance within its jurisdiction. . . . It goes without saying that these conspirators do not stop at organizing the revolutionary proletariat. Their activity consists precisely in anticipating the revolutionary process, bringing it artifically to the breaking point, improvising revolution without the conditions of a revolution. For them, the sole condition of the revolution is the adequate organization of their conspiracy. These are alchemists of the revolution, and they share the mental disorder and the fixed ideas of alchemists of an earlier day. . . . The police tolerate their conspiracies and tolerate them only as a necessary evil. They tolerate them as centers easy to watch, where the most violent revolutionary elements of society are brought together—like the courses in revolution which have become a tool of the French government as necessary as the police themselves. Finally, they tolerate them as a bureau of recruitment for their own stool pigeons. . . . Espionage is one of the principal occupations of conspirators. It is therefore not astonishing that they so frequently make that small leap that turns a professional conspirator into a spy appointed by the police—so much the more easily since this leap is facilitated by poverty and prison, by promises and threats. From this comes the excessive growth of the system of espionage in conspiracies, where the membership sometimes select stool pigeons as leaders and place all their confidence in them."[15]

The theoretical struggle by Marx made it possible for communism to pass from utopianism to science, and from conspiracy to the class struggle.

In March 1847 Marx had joined the League of the Just. He had set himself the task of winning the vanguard of the working class to scientific socialism. One of the old directors of the League, Moll, had asked Marx to collaborate in a new theoretical orientation and in the reorganization of the League. Feeling that the coming revolution would truly determine the destiny of the world for centuries, on the eve of the great European movements of 1848, Marx believed that the most important task was to organize a genuine working class party, to give it a class program and to sharpen its tactics.

The Congress of the League opened in London on June 1, 1847, and under the influence of Marx profound transformations ensued. The change of name in itself was significant: the old League of the Just would henceforth be called "The Communist League." For the old slogan "all men are brothers" the watchword "proletarians of all countries unite" was substituted. The new bylaws testified to the seriousness of this working-class movement. The first article reads: "The goal of the League is the overthrow of the bourgeoisie, the rule of the proletariat, the abolition of the old bourgeois society based on class antagonisms, and the establishment of a classless, propertyless new society." The structure of the organization set out to eliminate the possibility of conspiratorial methods, and called for a leadership composed of members who were elected and subject to recall.[16] Convocation of a second congress was decided for December 1847, and Marx was charged with the project of preparing a program. This was *The Communist Manifesto*, written several weeks before the outbreak of the European revolution.

The essential merit of *The Communist Manifesto* was that while it embraced in a comprehensive synthesis the whole historical evolution of society, it imparted to workers a clear exposition of the historical situation of their class, its mission and its perspectives.

It was at the same time a program of long-term applicability to an entire historical epoch—the epoch of the struggle for the proletarian revolution, as well as a masterly definition of the immediate objectives of the proletariat, its concrete conditions and methods of leadership. It assigned a double task to the workers:

(1) The struggle, in alliance with the middle class, against the most reactionary classes. This united front was to last as long as the

bourgeoisie played a revolutionary role against the survivals of the feudal past. The proletariat was to sustain the bourgeoisie, to propel it forward and denounce all compromise that it might want to make with reaction.

(2) The struggle to "instill into the working class the clearest possible recognition of the hostile antagonism between bourgeoisie and proletariat, in order that the German workers may straightaway use, as so many weapons against the bourgeoisie, the social and political conditions that the bourgeoisie must necessarily introduce along with its supremacy, and in order that, after the fall of the reactionary classes in Germany, the fight against the bourgeoisie itself may immediately begin."[17] The strategy and tactics of this struggle were to vary in accordance with the level of historical evolution characteristic of each country. They were not, for example, to be the same in Germany, where the bourgeoisie was still far from being in power, as in England and France, where it ruled. The revolutions of 1848 were also to offer Marx an immense field of experience and of confirmation for this strategy and these tactics.

Strategy and Tactics

Marxist strategy and tactics are the application of a rigorous materialist, dialectical method.

Materialist, in the sense that it is not founded on a subjective conception but on an objective study of classes and their relations, scientifically defined by Marx's economic theses. *Dialectical*, in the sense that they take into account the totality of the various classes and segments of classes and their reciprocal interactions in a given society; also that they take into account the degree of development of each of the social forces at each moment; and, finally, that they take account of the relations between each society and other societies in the world (for example, in such phenomena as international cartels).

Thanks to historical materialism, Marx's methods alone were capable of scientifically organizing the class struggle of the proletariat by opening up both the close-up and the distant perspective;

by analyzing objectively at each moment the relationship of forces; and by determining the strategy and tactics of the struggle—establishing at each moment, in terms of these perspectives and in relation to these forces, the direction from which the principal blows would emanate; to determine what alliances were possible, what reserve forces were available and, finally, to define objectives and methods of work when the movement itself was in a period of advance or setback.

For some time before the 1848 revolution, and in conformity with the principles announced in *The Communist Manifesto*, Marx's objective was to avoid the isolation of the working class by uniting its movement with the democratic international movement. After the revolution of 1830, several suggestions were projected for uniting all the revolutionary organizations of Europe and thus opposing a "holy alliance" of the people to the Holy Alliance of kings. On September 27, 1847, the Democratic International Association was founded, with the participation of the Communist League; Marx had raised the objective of the development of a great democratic mass movement.

In the same spirit and with the same incentive, he took the platform at a demonstration commemorating the Insurrection of Cracow in 1848. He exalted this insurrection, which he said, had given a glorious example to Europe "by identifying the cause of nationality with the cause of democracy and with the enfranchisement of the oppressed class."

The day after the February (1848) revolution in Paris, Flocon, a member of the provisional government, invited Marx to return to France, writing him: "Tyranny has banished you; France, the free, opens to you her gates—to you and to all who fight for the Holy cause, the fraternal cause of every people."[1] Marx soon left Brussels for Paris, where, after passing the frontier, he saw the railway station decorated by the red flag along with the tricolor.

In *The Communist Manifesto*, Marx did not limit himself to depicting a scholar's fresco of historical evolution by sketching out the trajectory of the development of the capitalist system up to the moment when the economic contradictions and class struggles which it inevitably engenders would lead it to its own destruction. He also indicates the positions which the proletariat of the great European countries would have to take up in order to defend their class interests. Outside of England, where the ruling bourgeoisie had won a victory against Chartism, and Tsarist Russia, where autocracy and essentially feudal absolutism were still powerful, problems were posed in a profoundly different way in France, for example, where the middle classes rose against the ruling bourgeoisie allied to royalty; or in Germany, where the whole of the bourgeoisie, depending on both middle classes and proletariat, were opposed to the still predominantly feudal absolutist regime.

Marx had stressed in *The Communist Manifesto* that only the proletariat remained a revolutionary class to the end, since it proposed not to reform but to abolish the capitalist system. But he always took issue with the idea that all other classes formed a mere reactionary mass. In 1875, in his *Critique of the Gotha Programme*, Marx vigorously opposed Lassalle's ideas: "It is . . . nonsense to say that they (the middle class), together with the bourgeoisie, and with the feudal lords into the bargain, 'form only one reactionary mass' in relation to the working class"[2] He accorded such importance to the role of the middle class that he said of the peasants: "In Germany everything depends on the possibility of sustaining the proletarian revolution by a repetition in some form of the Peasants' War."* Tactics and strategy were to be differentiated in accordance with the level of economic and social development of the various classes. In France, where the big bourgeoisie had acceded to power and no longer sought, as in 1789, to destroy the existing economic and social regime but, on the contrary, manipulated it to its own advantage, the proleariat must sustain the petty bourgeoisie in its struggle against the big bourgeoisie. In Germany, on the other hand, where the entire bourgeoisie stood opposed to the feudal regime, it was essential to destroy the latter and to replace it with a capitalist regime—a bourgeois revolution at a much more advanced stage of economic and social development than that of the preceding English and French revolutions, since the latter had already been able to establish a prelude to a proletarian revolution.

In the light of this analysis, Marx oriented his actions in France

* The reference is to the Peasants' War of 1525 during the German Reformation, in which Thomas Münzer emerged as the revolutionary leader. See Engels, *The Peasant War in Germany*, N.Y., 1926.—*Ed.*

and Germany. Hardly had he arrived in Paris, when he had to oppose an adventurous attempt by German, Belgian, Italian and Polish immigrants to export the Paris revolution militarily by provoking revolutionary risings in all countries. On March 6, in a public demonstration, Marx came out against the formation of a German legion, 2,000 strong, which was preparing to cross the frontier. He proved that this would amount to a futile massacre of the most ardent revolutionaries.

Marx was then swimming against the current, and he had to break with the democratic club that espoused the views of the poet Herwegh and of the German Legion. The "ultra-revolutionaries" defeated Marx, the "man of reason," who, at a time when "true" revolutionaries ought to take arms, called conferences on political economy and turned workers into doctrinaires. What Marx had foreseen happened: Lamartine, an expert at provocation, had allowed this legion to be organized in Paris under the direction of Bornstadt, a secret agent in the pay of Prussia, and had at the same time seen to it that Prussian troops would be so alerted that the legion would be wiped out the moment it had cleared the bridge at Kehl.

Marx, who frequented the central club of the Society for the Rights of Man and Citizen, directed by Barbes, and had organized the German Workingman's Club (which had its meeting place at the Picarde Café, rue St. Denis), advised the workers to go back quietly, one by one, to Germany, where they should create revolutionary workers' organizations under the leadership of members of the Communist League. Marx moved to Cologne, the largest industrial center in Germany at that time, and set himself at first to establishing contacts and connections with workers' organizations which had been formed before the revolution. Under his influence, a great agitation developed in all the Rhineland. Petitions filled with thousands of signatures demanded radical reforms. The vital center of the movement was the Workingmen's Union of Cologne, at one and the same time the heart of the trade union movement, a study circle and a political club.

Marx's essential preoccupation at that time was to prevent the proletariat from being cut off from the main body of the democratic movement. For the first time in German history, the March (1848) revolution had created a parliament for all Germany. Marx did not hesitate to waive all communist propaganda that would have led to a rupture between the bourgeoisie and the proletariat in their necessary common struggle against feudal and monarchical reaction. Here, too, Marx came into conflict with the ultra-revolutionaries, Gotschalk, for example, local director of the Communist League, who supported a boycott of the elections under the pretext of refusing all compromise, all agreements—even the most temporary—with democratic groups. Marx condemned the slogan of boycott that would result in the relinquishment of all political struggle by the Left—to the advantage of reaction. He wrote in the *Neue Rhenische Zeitung:* "We do not nourish the utopian hope that a German republic, one and indivisible, may now be proclaimed, but we demand of the so-called radical and democratic parties that they do not confound the beginning of the revolutionary struggle and movement with its ultimate goal. It is not a question of the fulfillment of this or that opinion, of this or that political notion."[3] He proved that the sectarian tactics of Gotschalk had led not only to breaking the temporary alliance between the proletariat and the bourgeoisie in the struggle against absolutism, but also to isolating the most advanced workers from the great working masses.

Marx, in creating the *Neue Rhenische Zeitung*, was able to exert a profound influence on the orientation of the democratic movement. In 1884, Engels recalled the profound meaning of Marx's strategy and tactics at that time: "When we founded a great newspaper in Germany, our banner was determined as a matter of course. It could only be that of democracy, but that of a democracy which everywhere emphasized in every point the specific proletarian character which it could not yet inscribe once for all on its banner. If we did not want to do that . . . then there was nothing left for us to do but to preach Communism in a little provincial sheet and to found a tiny sect instead of a great party of action. But we had already been spoilt for the role of preachers in the wilderness; we had studied the utopians too well for that, nor was it for that we had drafted our program."[4]

When, after June 1, 1848, Marx was named editor-in-chief of the *Neue Rhenische Zeitung*, this journal became the most influential in all Germany. It was the organ of a great party of action that was to stimulate the German democratic revolution. Marx systematically avoided anything that would divide the united front of German democrats. For several months he did not deal with the specific interests and tasks of the worker in his columns; he no longer laid special stress on the distinction between proletarian and bourgeois democracy: "The proletariat must march with the great democratic army, at the extreme edge of its left wing but guarding always against breaking its connection with the main body of the army. It must be the most impetuous in attack and its combative spirit must inspire the army assaulting the 'Bastille.' Because the Bastille is not yet stormed, absolutism is not yet overthrown. As long as the Bastille remains standing, democrats will have to remain united. The proletariat has no right to isolate itself; it must, no matter how hard this may appear, reject all that would separate it from its allies."

Marx differentiated sharply between the situation in Germany and that in France. In Germany, the Bastille still remained to be stormed, and he did not hesitate to accept the necessary compromises to avoid weakening the unity of the democratic forces. In an article dated July 30, 1848, he wrote: "The most striking proof that the German revolution is only a parody of the French Revolution is this: August 4, 1789, three weeks after the storming of the Bastille, the people abolished its feudal encumbrances in a single day; on July 11, four months after the barricades of March in Germany, the feudal forces still lord it over the people."

The first objective was the achievement of the German revolution, of the bourgeois revolution, of the German 1789—and this required the close unity of all democratic forces. (On the other hand, Marx resolutely defended the insurrection of the Paris workers in the month of June.) And at the same time he denounced any hesitancy or possible betrayal of the revolution on the part of the democratic left. Parliament, composed largely of big liberal bourgeois, was above all haunted by the concern with maintaining order: It did not dare to proclaim itself sovereign, to dissolve the ancient Diet of the Empire, or to form a federal government and an army to support it. This impotent parliament of Frankfurt even went so far as to elect the Archduke Jean president of the German Empire, that is to say, it gave over its power to the princes. Under these conditions, the King of Prussia did not hesitate to put a reactionary minister in office.

Marx organized many mass demonstrations, but opposed an insurrection, which, because of Germany's lack of preparedness for a general uprising, would only have served to decapitate the movement of its most active elements. But the Prussian government intensified the repression.

A state of seige was proclaimed. This measure aroused even the most peaceable members of the middle classes against Prussian militarism. Marx then issued the order for a tax strike, a mass mobilization of all able-bodied men, the distribution of arms and the establishment of committees of public safety in defense of democracy. Then the ultra-revolutionary partisans of Gotschalk enjoined the workers not to take arms under the pretext that it was not in the interests of the working class and that they must let the absolutists and the constitutionalists fight it out among themselves. On the other hand, the communists, in pursuance of *The Communist Manifesto's* order to sustain the revolutionary movement against feudal reaction, participated in the insurrection.

When Marx appeared before the jury in Cologne,* he explained the reasons for his attitude: "We have participated in the struggle between the old feudal democracy and modern bourgeois society, between the free competitive society and the corporative society, between the society based on landed property and industrial society, between the society of religious faith and that of science."

But however much the bourgeoisie wanted to make its revolution, they delayed the development of a revolutionary situation because they feared the masses; alone, they were too weak to hold out against the feudalists. The feudalists, therefore, used the bourgeoisie against the people and then they dispensed with their services.

The German bourgeoisie showed itself incapable of making its own revolution. It could no longer be a question of uniting the proletariat and all the sections of the bourgeoisie under the banner of democracy in a common battle against absolutism and feudal reaction. The upper middle class had excluded itself from this alliance.

---

* On February 8, 1849, Marx and his associates were charged with inciting armed resistance. Marx defended the group in a long and powerful speech and the jury voted for immediate acquittal. Its foreman thanked Marx for his instructive explanation. See John Lewis, *The Life and Teaching of Karl Marx*, N.Y., 1965, pp. 122–3; and Franz Mehring, *Karl Marx*, N.Y., 1935, pp. 208–10.—*Ed.*

It was a question thenceforth of uniting the middle classes and the
proletariat in the struggle for a regime that would not abolish the
private ownership of the means of production but in which peasants,
workers and the lower middle class would obtain a maximum of concessions.

Once more, at the beginning of 1849, the leftists—and especially
Gotschalk—violently attacked Marx, who demonstrated in the *Neue
Rhenische Zeitung* that the revolution could not as yet have anything
but a bourgeois character. At a meeting of the Communist League,
September 15, 1850, Marx violently denounced their demagogy:

"The minority replaces critical observation with dogmatism, a
materialist attitude with an idealist one. It regards its own wishes
as the driving force of the revolution instead of the real facts of
the situation. Whilst we tell the workers that they must go through
15, 20, perhaps even 50 years of war and civil war, not only in
order to alter existing conditions, but even to make themselves fit
to take over political power, you tell them, on the contrary, that they
must seize political power at once or abandon all hope. Whilst we
point out how undeveloped the German proletariat still is, you
flatter the nationalism and the craft prejudices of the German artisan
in the crudest fashion, and that is naturally more popular. Just as
the Democrats made a sort of holy entity out of the word people,
you are doing the same with the word proletariat—and, as with
the Democrats, the word replaces the act with you."[5]

In opposition to pseudo-revolutionary phraseology, Marx defined
precise tactics. Without excluding the collaboration of working-class
associations and democrats, he insisted thenceforth on one essential
issue: to preserve the independence of the organization of the
working-class party.

In Paris, where the hesitations of the bourgeois liberals recalled
the indecisions of the German left parliamentarians at Frankfurt,
the "Mountain"* was shattered. A belated appeal to the masses,
June 13, 1849, had no other result than the arrest of the "Mountain"
deputies. Marx was expelled from Paris on July 19; he left the
following month for England, where he was to spend the half that

---

* Marx defines the "Mountain" as "the parliamentary champion of the democratic bourgeoisie." See *Class Struggles in France, 1848–50*, N.Y., 1964, p.
92.—*Ed.*

remained of his life. Refusing to adhere to secret societies or petty sects, he prepared for the future by working at the construction of his monumental scientific work, *Capital*. When, toward 1860, American communists proposed that he reconstitute the Communist League, he answered that he was convinced he could better serve the working class by his theoretical work than by participation in associations that no longer corresponded to the requirements of the epoch.

Marx had derived from the great political experience of the revolutions of 1848 fundamental principles of strategy and tactics for a proletarian party. In 1875 he defined these in his *Critique of the Gotha Programme*. He would not make compromises nor concessions on the plane of principle, remaining absolutely firm on doctrine. Nevertheless, a party of genuine action must know at each moment how to work with its allies, even those who were temporary and unreliable; how to develop a plan of struggle and forms of organization acceptable to all:

"Every step of real movement is more important than a dozen programmes. If, therefore, it was not possible—and the conditions of the time did not permit it—to go *beyond* the Eisenach programme,* one should simply have concluded an agreement for action against the common enemy. But by drawing up a programme of principles (instead of postponing this until it has been prepared for by a considerable period of common activity) one sets up before the whole world a landmark by which the level of the party movement is measured. The Lassallean leaders came because circumstances forced them to come. If they had been told from the beginning that there would be no bargaining about principles, they would have *had* to be content with a programme of action or a plan of organization for common action"[6]

* The program of the Social Democratic Workers' Party of Germany, led by Wilhelm Liebknecht and August Bebel, which was drawn up at its congress in Eisenach, Saxony, in August 1869. The Lassalleans, organized as the All-German Workers' League, was nicknamed by Marx the "Royal Prussian Socialists," because they would rely on the Prussian state for improvements in the economic conditions of the workers. The Gotha program, severely criticized by Marx, was adopted at the joint congress of both parties at Gotha, May 25, 1875.—*Ed.*

The State

In the General Rules of the International Working Men's Association (the First International, organized in 1864), Marx had inscribed this fundamental formula: "The conquest of political power becomes the great duty of the proletariat!"[1]

This conviction grew out of the analysis of the state begun in the writings of his youth in which he had already defined the state as a form of alienation. In his writings of 1843 and in the *Manuscripts of 1844*, as in "The Jewish Question," the state was defined as a power emanating from society and existing above it in increasing estrangement—as Engels was to emphasize in *The Origins of the Family, Private Property and the State*.[2]

The state, in its bourgeois democratic form, adds to its actual alienation an ideological alienation, comprised of democratic illusions. In Marx's essay, "The Jewish Question" (1843), and in his *Critique of Hegel's Philosophy of Right*, he set out the limits of the political emancipation expressed by the Declaration of the Rights of Man and the class meaning of the radical abstract separation between "civil society" (with its economic relations of property and the relations of exploitation and domination that arise from it), and the political sphere (with its abstract political equality). "All the assumptions of this individualistic life continue to subsist in civil society outside the political sphere but as properties of bourgeois society."[3]

Marx stressed three essential aspects of bourgeois democracy:

(1) Political emancipation, with all the illusions that its abstraction engenders, has a class character; it expresses the profound needs of the development of capitalist economy and of bourgeois society.

(2) Political emancipation, however unsatisfactory it may be, constitutes a significant advance over the feudal system, in spite of the fact that it permits under the abstraction that citizens have equal rights all the inequalities which result from class relations under capitalism.

(3) Political emancipation is linked historically with social oppression, since the bourgeoisie established state power in order to guarantee the class interests of the capitalist class against both the feudal past and against the have-nots.

Marx concluded: "Political emancipation is the reduction of man, on the one hand, to the status of being a member of bourgeois society, an egoistic and independent individual; and, on the other hand, a citizen, an ethical person.

"Human emancipation is realized only when man has recognized and mobilized his own forces as social forces and thus no longer alienates social power from himself in the form of political power."[4]

Political emancipation, of the kind that the bourgeoisie has achieved in the struggle against feudalism, is only one necessary stage (despite the illusions on which it rests and those which it engenders) in human emancipation from all alienation, an emancipation that only socialism can fully realize.

The state in all its forms is a class state, the product of the class struggle, the instrument of exploitation of the oppressed class. Its power becomes the more repressive as the class struggle sharpens. It is always in the form of the dictatorship of one class.

From this, it follows that the power of the working class must necessarily take the form of a dictatorship of the proletariat. This is a recurrent theme with Marx. He had already defined its significance with respect to the theory of class struggle. Marx recalled that this theory had been formulated by French historians of the Restoration, and that its real importance consisted essentially in pointing out "that the class struggle necessarily leads to the *dictatorship of the proletariat*."[5] He reverts to this notion again and again. In an article written in 1873, he wrote: "When the political struggle of the working class takes on a revolutionary form, when the workers substitute their own revolutionary dictatorship for the dictatorship of the bourgeoisie in order to break its resistance, they give to the state a revolutionary and transitional form rather than using their weapons to abolish the state."[6]

In the *Critique of the Gotha Programme*, Marx wrote with unmistakable clarity: "Between capitalist and communist society, lies the period of the revolutionary transformation of one into the other. There corresponds to this also a political transition period in which the state can be nothing but the *revolutionary dictatorship of the proletariat.*"[7]

In *The Communist Manifesto*, after extracting from his great historical synthesis the definition of the state as the organ of class domination, he had shown that the proletariat could not arrive at the overthrow of the bourgeoisie without first taking political power and transforming the state "i.e., of the proletariat organized as the ruling class."[8]

The goal of the dictatorship of the proletariat, as Marx had already pointed out in *The Poverty of Philosophy*, is to put an end to class antagonisms, and consequently to render the state itself unnecessary. To put an end to class antagonisms which engender the alienation of the state is to prepare the conditions for transcending the state itself.

The state is not eternal. It did not exist in primitive society, before the birth of classes. It will disappear with the disappearance of classes, since it has no other function than to assure the domination of a class.

Moreover, the possibility that the transition of bourgeois dictatorship to proletarian dictatorship may come about peaceably is not excluded. Marx had explicitly envisaged this possibility of the peaceful transition to socialism in his address of September 8, 1872, in Amsterdam. After the Congress of the International at The Hague, where he had vigorously opposed Bakunin and the opportunistic leaders of the British trade unions, Marx asserted in a lecture on the occasion of the closing of the congress that the conquest of power by the proletariat was a necessary condition of the transition to socialism. "We have by no means claimed that the means for arriving at this goal were identical. We know the part that must be assigned to the institutions, the mores and the traditions of various countries; and we do not deny that there exist countries like America, England and, if I knew your institutions better, I might add Holland, where the workers might arrive at their goal by peaceful means."[9]

Engels in the *Critique of the Erfurt Programme* expanded on this theme in 1891: "One can conceive that the old society will be able to evolve peacefully toward the new in countries where popular representation concentrates all the power within itself or, if, in ac-

cordance with a constitution, the people can do what it wants when
the majority of the nation is behind it; in democratic republics
such as France and America, in monarchies like England, where
the imminent removal of royalty is debated daily in the press and
where royalty is powerless against the people's will. But in Germany, where the government is practically all-powerful, where the
Reichstag and the other representative bodies are without effective
power, to assert such things in Germany gratuitously is to remove
the figleaf from absolutism and to cover its nudity with its own
body."[10]

But whatever may be the form of the transition, peaceful or
violent, it would not consist of a simple change in the personnel of
the state. The machinery of the state has to be destroyed, since up
to that time, Marx wrote in *The 18th Brumaire of Louis Bonaparte,*
"All the revolutions perfected this machine instead of smashing
it up."[11]

The experience of the Paris Commune taught Marx the elements
of a concrete conception of the dictatorship of the proletariat. He
had stressed in the preface of June 24, 1872, to *The Communist
Manifesto* that this experience had rendered null and void certain
passages of the Manifesto: "One thing especially was proved by
the Commune, *viz.,* that 'the working class cannot simply lay hold
of the ready-made state machinery, and wield it for its own purposes.' "[12] In his letter to Kugelmann of April 12, 1871,[13] he
stressed the continuity of his thinking between the thesis developed
in *The 18th Brumaire* and its experiential verification in the Commune of Paris.

In *The Civil War in France,* Marx emphasized the radical
originality of the Commune, which was not a republic designed
solely to suppress the monarchical form of class domination, but
class domination itself.

In putting an end to the alienation of executive power in its
relation to national representation, and of the parliament in relation
to the workers and to the nation, it realized in an original form the
most authentic democracy—not a democracy for the privileged, like
the ancient democracy of the Athenians, which was democratic
only for the owners of slaves; or like the bourgeois democracies,
where the privileges of money permit the full exercise of democracy

only for the owners. Terminating the alienation of the state as the dominant organism of society, the dictatorship of the proletariat is already the most authentic form of democracy, even before the extinction of the state. "Freedom," wrote Marx, "consists in converting the state from an organ standing above society into one completely subordinated to it."[14]

Marx, Founder of Communist and Workers' Parties

In the course of his life, Marx was on two occasions the director and organizer of the political struggles of the working class of his time—with the creation of the Communist League during the revolutions of 1848, and then of the First International from 1864 on.

This multiple experience permitted him to forge the theoretical foundation of the existing communist and workers' parties on the basis of the principles of his doctrine. Three essential features characterized his concept:

(1) As opposed to utopian, reformist or conspiratorial conceptions, these were parties based on a clear consciousness of their class content.

(2) As opposed to a cult of spontaneity, these were parties founded on a scientific conception of the world and the teachings of historical materialism.

(3) This fusion of the workers' movement and the application of scientific socialism made possible the creation of these parties as battle formations capable of effectively leading the assault against the political power of the bourgeoisie with a precise objective: the dictatorship of the proletariat.

The basic *class character* of these parties was strongly emphasized by Marx in the General Rules of the International: "The emancipation of the working classes must be won by the working classes themselves."[1] Such a clear formulation was a triumph of scientific, Marxist socialism in opposition to Mazzini's tendencies to reject the class struggle and adhere to the organizational forms of the *Carbonari*; it was also in opposition to the petty-bourgeois reformism of the Proudhonists.

Marx, who had for some years refused to participate in any movement, emerged from his retirement and accepted collaboration in the creation of the International "because it involves a matter where it is possible to do some important work."[2] He explained to Engels: "I knew that this time real 'powers' were involved both on the London and Paris sides and therefore decided to waive my usual standing rule to decline any such invitations."[3] This time Marx entered into working relations with the active leaders of a real movement; his associates had the merit of representing their class and no longer little adventurous and conspiratorial sects: "The International was founded in order to replace the Socialist or semi-Socialist sects by a real organization of the working class for struggle. The original Statutes and the Inaugural Address show this at the first glance. On the other hand, the Internationalists could not have maintained themselves if the course of history had not already smashed up the sectarian system. The development of the system of Socialist sects and that of the real workers' movement always stand in inverse ratio to each other. So long as the sects are (historically) justified, the working class is not yet ripe for an independent historic movement. As soon as it has attained this maturity, all sects are essentially reactionary. Nevertheless, what history has shown everywhere was repeated within the International. The antiquated makes an attempt to reestablish and maintain itself within the newly achieved form.

"The history of the International was a continual *struggle on the part of the General Council* against the sects and amateur experiments which attempted to assert themselves within the International itself against the genuine movement of the working class."[4]

The whole history of the working class movement since Marx has been characterized by this ideological and political struggle to prevent the working class from falling under the influence of the petty bourgeoisie.

This was Marx's underlying concept of the party. The lessons which Marx drew from the experiences of the revolutions of 1848 for the working class are reflected in his Address of the Central Committee to the Communist League, in March 1850: "The workers' party . . . must act in the most organized, most unanimous and most independent fashion possible if it is not to be exploited and taken in tow again by the bourgeoisie as in 1848." Putting the communists on guard against petty-bourgeois democrats who preached unity and reconcilation in a single great party of opposition, Marx insisted that unity ought not to be achieved in such a form as would make the proletariat a balance wheel for the liberal bourgeoisie, and he warned the workers not to allow themselves "to be seduced for a single moment by the hypocritical phrases of the democratic petty bourgeoisie into refraining from the independent organization of the party of the proletariat."[5]

Thirty years later in a "Circular letter to Bebel, Liebknecht, Bracke and others," at a moment when many intellectuals were turning toward socialism, Marx and Engels denounced "attempts to bring superficially adopted socialist ideas into harmony with the most theoretical standpoints which these gentlemen have brought with them from the university or elsewhere," giving this counsel: "If people of this kind from other classes join in the proletarian movement, the first condition is that they should not bring any remnants of bourgeois, petty-bourgeois, etc., prejudices with them but should whole-heartedly adopt the proletarian point of view."[6]

What was at stake was the creation of a class organization founded on a scientific theory and the instituting of the discipline of a combat army.

The scientific character of this conception of the working class was signalized by Marx's struggle against the Proudhonist idea of spontaneity. Here we are at the opposite pole of the bourgeois and social-democratic conceptions of "freedom" and "democracy" based on the "spontaneity" of the masses. This idea of spontaneity is closely linked to the bourgeois notion according to which freedom is a native characteristic of man, an eternal attribute which is opposed to necessity.

Proudhon was one of the first to oppose vigorously what he calls "governmental socialism" to "democratic socialism,"[7] "the revolution from on high, by dictatorship" to the "social revolution from below, by the initiative of the masses."[8] He fought the

"Jacobin idea" by which "social revolution is the goal; political revolution (i.e., the displacement of authority) is the means."[9]

According to Proudhon, socialism cannot be built by the dictatorship of the proletariat, by taking political power in the way in which the bourgeoisie established its dictatorship to liberate capitalism from feudal shackles.

"Socialism," he wrote, "has fully exposed the Jacobin illusion."[10] He formulated his program thus: "No more party. No more authority. Absolute liberty of man as citizen. In three words, that is our profession of political and social faith."[11]

The claim that socialism can be built without a working-class and socialist party, and without the dictatorship of the proletariat, is today made frequently enough so that the refutation of Proudhonism has by no means lost its relevance: "It implies a contradiction," wrote Proudhon, "to believe that the government can ever be revolutionary—for the simple reason that it is government. Society itself, the masses infused with intelligence can be revolutionized, because society alone can rationally deploy its spontaneity. . . . All revolutions have been achieved by the spontaneous action of the people."[12]

The Proudhonian cult of spontaneity has a mystical base. He did not know how to discover by a scientific analysis of ideologies and their social roots that "the dominant ideas are those of the dominant class," and that, as a result, depending on spontaneity would open the way for the triumph of the ideas of the dominant class.

Thus, making an abstraction of the role of the ideology of the dominant class in the thought and action of the dominated masses, he imparts to their spontaneity a sort of providential and mysterious virtue. "It is the people," he writes, "that in the long run, without theory, by their spontaneous creations, modify, reform, absorb political projects and philosophical doctrines; in creating eternally a new reality, they incessantly change the base of politics and philosophy."[13]

According to Proudhon, there was a development of history comparable to the evolution of nature: a fresh, organic germination in virtue of the "eternal laws of order" and "the law of development, the logic immanent in humanity."[14]

From this act of faith in indwelling reason in the providential development of history, Proudhon's basic conclusion arises: "A revolution is an explosion of organic force, an evolution of society from inside out; it is not legitimate except as it is spontaneous, peaceful and traditional."[15]

Thus, because he failed to concern himself with the fundamental criticism of ideologies and thereby the recognition of class roots, Proudhon found himself tied to bourgeois ideology, both because of his *anarchism*, which translated into slogans of spurious rebellion the individualism that is the very law of bourgeois society; and because of his *reformism*, which gave the name revolution to what was only adaptation and the necessary patching-up job done by bourgeois capitalist society when it tries to overcome, without negating itself, the contradictions that arise at various stages of its development.

This petty-bourgeois spirit criticizes capitalism not "from the left" by showing the contradictions that threaten it and their necessary resolution by the transition to its opposite, socialism, but "from the right" by preaching conciliation and the attenuation of contradictions—that is, an idyllic and impossible return to an artisan or liberal stage of capitalism (whose own laws lead to concentrated acquisition and to pitiless imperialism).

The party, according to Marx, is formed and forged in a permanent struggle against the petty-bourgeois ideology to which Proudhon gave systematic form.* Instead of abandoning the working class to spontaneity, to irrationality, to blind instinct that is in reality only the result of the pressure of prejudices inculcated in the masses by the ruling class, Marx put the accent on the role of consciousness and of science. The party is the conscious interpretation of the real historical movement. To recall his definition: "The question is not what this or that proletarian, or even the whole of the proletariat at the moment *considers* as its aim. The question is *what the prole-*

---

* It is interesting, from this point of view, to follow (in the journal *Egalité* of Jules Guesde, 1877) the polemic against Proudhon that preceded the creation of the French Workers' Party in 1879 at the Congress of Marseilles, and to note the victory of Marxist principles in the program adopted at the Congress of Havre, November 16, 1880, the preamble of whose program was written by Marx.

tariat is, and what, consequent on that *being*, it will be compelled to do."[16]

The party is therefore not the mechanical resultant, the simple aggregate of the spontaneous desires of each of its members conceived as isolated individuals, in the manner of the bourgeoisie. Nor is it the sum total of organizations conceived on this model. It is a system, a "whole," a living organism.

The dictatorship of the proletariat is its goal. The Marxist-Leninist science of the objective laws of development enables it to discover the means to attain this end. Such is the basis of the unity of the party.

It is this unity alone which makes possible the orientation of the working class at each moment by giving it a consciousness of its unity as a class and mobilizing it to accomplish its historical task.

Through the party the class takes cognizance of itself and its role. The working class is not only an aggregation of workers playing the same economic role as producers of surplus value in the totality of the capitalist system; it is, thanks to the party and to its socialist consciousness, a unique power directed toward the destruction of this system, as its negation. With a party that realizes "the fusion of socialism and the working class movement," the class is no longer solely "in itself," it is also "for itself"—to go back to the language of Hegel and Marx. As soon as the links between the working class and its party are broken, the masses of proletarians fall back into the magnetic field of the bourgeoisie.

To the question, What is the working class? Marx replied: It is wherever a man or a group of men has a consciousness of the historical mission of the working class and struggles to achieve this mission.

Between the time of the dissolution of the Communist League and the foundation of the First International, Marx and Engels considered themselves representatives of the "proletarian party," although they were not at the head of any working-class organization at the time. But, as Marx pointed out in 1859, when he was receiving a delegation from the Workers' Club of London, this mandate is "countersigned by both the specific and the generalized hatred" which all the classes of the old world and all its parties felt toward his person.

The character of a fighting organization for the party was strongly stressed by Marx in his *Critique of the Gotha Programme.* "The political movement of the working class has as its object, of course, the conquest of political power for the working class and for this it is naturally necessary that a previous organization of the working class . . . [had] been developed. . . . Where the working class is not yet far enough advanced in its organization to undertake a decisive campaign against the collective power, i.e., the political power of the ruling classes, it must at any rate be trained for this by continual agitation against and a hostile attitude towards the policy of the ruling classes. Otherwise it will remain a plaything in their hands."[17]

The organizational forms of the party did not result from an arbitrary choice; they correspond at each stage of historical development to the aims which the working class adopts. For example, "the party of the new type" which was created in Russia under the inspiration of Lenin was born of the necessity for adapting the strategy, tactics and methods of organization of the working class party to the revolutionary possibilities opened up by the decay of capitalism and by imperialism.

The underlying idea of the Marxist conception of the party is that the principles and methods of organization arise from the objective to be attained, i.e., the dictatorship of the proletariat.

The party is an organization of action. But this action has a specific character: It is oriented to a consciousness of the objective laws of historical development which delineate the perspectives of the working class and enable it to discover scientifically, by the analysis of objective conditions, the means to achieve victory. That is why discipline, in a fighting, action organization such as this, cannot be founded on the irrational mystique of a leader, but only on the clear consciousness of the end, the science and the critique of the means, the objective analysis of conditions.

This discipline, composed of consciousness and clarity, assures the maximum cohesion of the party, by demanding a constant heightening of the level of consciousness and culture of each member, in order to forge the instruments for the liberation of the proletariat.

How could such a party have achieved full efficiency in action if it had not acted as an organized whole, if it had tolerated individuals or groups who made pacts with the enemy, or who, consciously or unconsciously, peddled the enemy's ideology and played a disruptive role within the party?

The class enemy—the boss in the shop or the power of the state—constitutes an organized whole. The dispersion of our own forces would lead to failure. The weakness of the proletariat comes precisely from this dispersion as well as from the splitting role that the patronage system plays in building up competition between the workers. Out of this arises the constant necessity for struggle against opportunism, which, in all its forms, always expresses the penetration of the ideology of the ruling class into the ranks of the working class.

The fundamental task of the party is therefore to struggle constantly to build and to rebuild the unity of the class; to transform the identity arising from its condition as producer of surplus value, the mechanical, practically abstract unity of the class, into a living unity and an act of consciousness and free will, oriented toward the struggle for the destruction of capitalism and the building of socialism.

By its very principles such a conception of the party precludes all dogmatism. "There can be no dogmatism," writes Lenin, "where the supreme and sole criterion of a doctrine is whether or not it corresponds to the actual process of social and economic development."[18] Dogmatism would reduce the working class party to impotence, because it would render it incapable of determining its strategy and tactics in terms of a concrete analysis of the realities of the moment. This concrete analysis requires the participation of all, the attentive utilization of the characteristic experience of each. The party then has the superior advantages of cognition that assimilates the specific experiences of each of its members, thanks to the scientific method common to all. Criticism and self-criticism are the law of development of this knowledge—which is the condition for effective action, for the victory of the working class.

CONCLUSION

Marx's life is indivisibly the life of a scholar and a militant. It is a life of poverty and exile. During the years when he pursued his researches for the writing of *Capital* at the British Museum library in London, Marx knew the cruelest deprivation. Inflexibly refusing the offers of the Prussian government and Bismarck, who wanted to buy out his genius, having only sporadic payments like those for the articles he wrote for the *New York Tribune*,* Marx and his family would have succumbed without the help that Engels unfailingly brought them.

After having sold the silverware of the Dukes of Argyll to pay the debts of the *Neue Rhenische Zeitung* and then the furniture that was his wife's dowry, living in the worst hovels, hounded by creditors, in 1851 he had to borrow money to buy a cradle for his youngest daughter and, a year later, to borrow again to pay for her funeral. His wife followed him valiantly into this hell, where one day the bailiffs put seals on the beds, the cradles, even on the children's toys, and where his family lay shivering with cold and fever on the floor. Mrs. Marx, worn out, nursed one of her children. "In his last days, he fell prey to violent convulsions," she wrote. "He shook so violently when he was taken with these spells that he wounded my breast and my blood flowed into his trembling little mouth." She added: "I only know we are not alone in the struggle, and that I am still among the elect, the fortunate. . . . What kills me is to think that my companion must suffer through such sordid cares when so many others had found in him an inspiration, an aid, a refuge."

The love of Jenny Marx and the friendship of Engels enabled Marx to accomplish his work and to go on with his achievements even beyond his death, for, when he died in London, March 14,

* The New York daily founded in 1841 by Horace Greeley. At the request of Charles Anderson Dana, then its managing editor, Marx was the *Tribune's* European correspondent from 1851 to 1862.—*Ed.*

1883, Engels, putting aside his personal affairs, devoted the remaining 12 years of his life to putting the works of his friend into order for publication. Such was the style of Marx's life: the style of greatness, of action and of love.

His work had a magnificent destiny. After having brought a most fundamental regeneration to philosophy, the greatest it had known since the birth of rational thought, he founded scientific political economy, elaborated the methodology of history and the human sciences, endowed the proletariat with the science of the transformation of the world, taught it the art of prevailing in the class struggle. For a century he has been the living leader of the world working-class struggle.

His posthumous triumph is without precedent. In June 1848, the rebellion of the rising working class held the streets of Paris for only three days. In 1871 the Commune, the first dictatorship of the proletariat, survived three months. The Revolution of October 1917 inscribed the victory of Marxism indelibly, irreversibly on history; it was thenceforth a force against which all the assaults of the capitalist world were broken—in 1917–20, as well as in 1941–45. In contrast to the vitality of Marxism, for a half century capitalism has not been able to produce anything but rear-guard actions in Europe, Asia and even in the Caribbean.

Marxism in our day has achieved a universality that no spiritual, political or philosophical movement has ever known; not only because one man in three in the world already lives in a society that is building socialism according to the teachings of Marx, but because Marxism has become the point of reference against which all thought and all action are measured. Are you for it or against it?

Nevertheless for a century Marxism has experienced many vicissitudes; its enemies have tried, first, to crush it; then they have had to denounce it with fury by presenting it in a horrible caricature. Today they are reduced to trying to emasculate or burlesque it, according to the philosophical fashions of the day, in order to channelize its dynamism.

"There is a well-known saying," writes Lenin, "that if geometrical axioms affected human interests, attempts would certainly be made to refute them. Theories of natural history which conflicted with the old prejudices of theology provoked, and still provoke, the most rabid opposition. No wonder, therefore, that the Marxian doctrine, which directly serves to enlighten and organise the advanced class in modern society, indicates the tasks facing this class and demonstrates the inevitable replacement (by virtue of economic development) of the present system by a new order—no wonder that this doctrine had to fight at every step forward in the course of its life."[1]

The struggle of Marx and Engels against the young Hegelians, against Proudhonism, against Bakunin, against the positivism of Dühring· for a half century (1840–90) ended in the victory of Marxism in the working-class movement.

But at the end of the century an anti-Marxist current commenced to develop in the very heart of Marxism. The revisionism of Bernstein (in philosophy, economics and politics) was the most systematic expression of this. His example since then has been followed many times. It is in the struggle against all revisionists that Marxism is constantly strengthened, affirmed and developed.

The struggle led by Lenin and the Bolshevik Party against revisionism and opportunism made the October Revolution possible. The most consistent historical experience has shown that when Marxism is abandoned, the socialists in power cannot establish socialism: From England to Austria, from New Zealand to Germany and Scandinavia, non-Marxist socialism has been revealed as a mere variation of the rule of fundamentally capitalist interests.

Wherever private ownership of the means of production has been abolished, and a true socialist revolution achieved, it was along the paths indicated by a Marxist party and by the dictatorship of the proletariat, whatever the diversity of the forms of this dictatorship and whatever the diversity of means, violent or pacific, of its establishment.

The most striking successes of Marxism have been at times hobbled and twisted by distortions of Marxist thought. For a quarter of a century, the heroic and long-suffering builders of socialism— against which the capitalist world imposed a barbed-wire policy— had to live in a veritable state of seige, demanding maximum vigilance and centralization of forces. This state of war led to the development of political and intellectual phenomena which constituted flagrant violations of the principles of Marxism and the essence of a socialist regime: the cult of the personality, bureaucracy, dogmatic sclerosis of thought, intellectual isolation. This led, on the ideological plane, during the epoch dominated by the personality of Stalin, to grave distortions of Marxism, regression toward a pre-Marxist, scientist materialism, speculative conceptions of dialectics, reducing it to the pronouncement of four "immutable characteristics" and the mechanical conception of relations between the base and the superstructure, and rupture with the living practice of the sciences and arts. The consequences of this schematism and this hardening are formidable. Marxism, when it becomes dogma, ceases to be a guide to action or to thought. In the name of already known laws of dialectics, scientific problems in biology, physics, psychology, were "solved" *a priori*; certain forms of artistic expression were condemned *a priori*; certain historical possibilities were excluded.

The example, without historical precedent, of public self-criticism presented by the first and greatest of the socialist countries made possible a veritable renascence of Marxist thought and created the conditions for a great creative development.

The development of Marxism in the sense in which Marx conceived it helps us to take cognizance of its profound actuality. Marxism is the conception of the world in accord with the spirit of our times.

Unlike earlier conceptions of the world, such as that embodied in Christian thought, which was elaborated a long time before the birth of the modern world and in accordance with other historical conditions, and which could not begin to adjust itself to the thinking of the new intellectual elites who questioned its basic principles; unlike doctrines such as existentialism, born in the anguish of a society in full metamorphosis, of which it reflects only a partial aspect in mystified form, Marxism was engendered organically from the totality of the conditions of the modern world, the consciousness and the living soul of which it expresses.

It is the inheritor of the Promethean humanism of the French Revolution; of the confirmation of the all-powerfulness of man and his freedom that German philosophy, from Kant to Fichte, from Goethe to Hegel, had not ceased to investigate. It is the inheritor also of that conception of society as a collective organization of the crea-

tive labor of man, whose exploration the classical economists of
England had begun, and of which French socialism, particularly
Saint-Simon, had outlined the demiurgic perspectives.

By discovering in the working class the heir and bearer of all
antecedent culture and all human civilization; by discovering the
roots of the fundamental alienation of the creative labor of man; by
discovering, finally, through the scientific study of the development
of societies, the dialectical laws of the historical transcendence of
alienation by the class struggle, Marx laid the foundations of a
philosophy that expressed the movement of an entire historical epoch
—an epoch that began with the struggle against capitalism and
continued on to the building of socialism and communism.

Marx's underlying thesis persists—from his first works to his last
struggles. It is the key to his philosophy, to his economics, to his
politics: It is to make of each man a man, that is to say, a creator.
The young Marx, heir of Fichte and Hegel, evoked this creative
power to oppose all forms of alienation. Creation is the opposite of
alienation. Scientific analysis, both economic and historical, enabled
Marx to resolve alienation into its concrete forms—exploitation and
class oppression, and to discover a real method for its transcendence
—the class struggle. His communism did not rest on a philosophical
base alone but, first and foremost, on a scientific foundation, the
historical reality of classes and their struggles. This profound humanism was to live on and to be increasingly confirmed—not as a
philosophical or ethical imperative, still resembling utopianism, but
as the objective law of the development of proletarian struggle to
surmount and destroy the alienation engendered by class systems, to
endow each man with the possibility of being a man, a creator, a
"poet," in the deepest sense of the word, in that full sense that made
Maxim Gorki say: "Esthetics is the ethics of the future."

This profound reflection of the creative action of man, by which
Marx succeeded in putting back on its feet in a concrete historical
and materialist perspective Fichte's philosophy of creation, makes
possible the founding of a total and militant humanism. Making
practice (according to Fichte's teachings but demystifying it) the
source and criterion of all truth and all value, Marx not only wrought
the most radical revolution in philosophy by rooting it in the soil of
humanity, but he opened new perspectives of the continual transfor-

mation of nature, society and man, in their most profound reality.

Marxism, far from reverting to a "precritical" stage of philosophy, extended and developed the fundamental movement of modern philosophy which had started with Descartes and which, with the critique of Kant, attained full consciousness of itself: Man can *comprehend* only what he has *made*. Fichte led to its ultimate expression the primordial demand of modern rationalism, rejecting the dogmatic affirmation of "something given," and making the point of departure for his thinking not a fact but an act. What enables Marxism essentially to escape from all dogmatism is that it reversed and demystified the Fichtean conception, gave a concrete, historical, materialist meaning to the primacy of practice.

The demands of the primordial struggle for the social emancipation of man led Marx to develop fully in his major works—in *The Communist Manifesto*, in *Capital*, in his historical books like *The 18th Brumaire of Louis Bonaparte*—that which constitutes its decisive content: a methodology of historic initiative.

He has not left us a system of laws but the dialectical art of discovering them and of founding our creative action on them.

The work of Marx contains the seed of the principles of an exploration of man in all his dimensions—not only the historical and militant dimension to which he consecrated the major portion of his researches, but the dimension of subjectivity and creativeness (which theology generally designates under the name of transcendence). An immense field is open for Marxist research in the age of the victory of socialism, for the exploration of all dimensions in "putting back on their feet," and thereby integrating, all the discoveries realized in these domains but mystified by non-Marxist researchers.

Marxism alone enables us to seize in their totality the tremendous changes in our world and our times.

From the scientific point of view, all the bonds on the free unfolding of investigation must be broken; materialism, while insisting on reference to a reality external to our thought, implies a permanent attitude of ground-breaking and receptivity; a continuous rejection of speculation, dogmatism and closed systems; it reminds dialectics that it is not only a system of concepts but of an inexhaustible reality in motion which envisions concepts beyond itself—an eternal dialectics of practice and of human creation, with the reward of a world to win.

From the esthetic standpoint, it opens to theoretical creation an unlimited perspective by defining art not solely as a means of cognition but primarily as a way of doing things, never defining realism as a carbon copy of real appearances, but as the grasp of the profound laws of development in the process of becoming and of a man in the process of creating himself.

From the ethical point of view, it opposes to an ethics of revelation or of tradition founded on eternal commandments and immutable ideals, to the sophistications of the individual, and to freedom confounded with what is arbitrary and fortuitous, a historical conception of man, developing, breaking down, integrating and transcending the norms of his action and limited only by the movement of continual creation.

Marxism is not only *a* philosophy of our time. It is our time's *sense*.

REFERENCE NOTES

Reference Notes

(Where English editions are available of the works cited by the author, the quotations are given from these editions, and are so noted. Otherwise, the quotations from the French editions used by the author are translated and his sources given. In the case of Marx and Engels, The German Ideology, the two editions available in English are used, viz., abridged edition, Parts I and III, International Publishers, New York, 1947; and the unabridged edition, Progress Publishers, Moscow, 1964, and so indicated.)

I. MARX BEFORE MARXISM

THE SUNRISE OF THE FRENCH REVOLUTION

1. Georg Wilhelm Friedrich Hegel, *The Philosophy of History*, tr. by J. Sibree, London, 1857; revised edition, New York, 1899.

2. E. Gans, *Rückblicke auf Personen und Zustände*, pp. 99–101; cited by Auguste Cornu, *Karl Marx et Frédéric Engels*, tome I, Paris, 1955, p. 88.

3. For the full letter, *see* Marx-Engels, *Gesamtausgabe* (hereinafter referred to as MEGA), erste abteilung, band 1, zweiter halbband, Berlin, 1929, p. 213.

4. "*Differenz der demokritischen und epikureischen Naturphilosophie nebst einem Anhange*," MEGA, I, 1, erste halbband, Frankfurt, 1927, pp. 5*ff*.

THE FAUSTIAN DREAM

1. Heinrich Heine, *Religion and Philosophy in Germany*, tr. by John Snodgrass, Boston, 1882.

2. Frederick Engels, *La Revolution démocratique bourgeoise en Allegmagne*, Preface of 1874, Paris, p. 23.

3. Karl Marx, "Contribution to the Critique of Hegel's Philosophy of Right," Marx and Engels, *On Religion*, Moscow, 1955, p. 45.

4. Marx, Foreword to thesis, "Differences Between the Natural Philosophy of Democritus and the Natural Philosophy of Epicurus," *On Religion*, p. 13.

5. Cornu, *Marx et Engels*. t. I, p. 140. For an understanding of the origins of Marx's thinking, the three volumes of the great work of Auguste Cornu constitute an indispensable working tool, the only work that was inspired by scientific preoccupations alone.

6. For the preparatory notes, *see* MEGA, I, 1, erste halbband, pp. 84*ff*.

7. Marx, *The Economic and Philosophic Manuscripts of 1844*, New York, 1964.

THE STREAM OF FIRE: *"Feuer-Bach"*

1. Ludwig Feuerbach, *Provisional Theses for the Reform of Philosophy*, 1842, Theses 45 and 53.

2. *Ibid.*, Theses 33 and 37.

3. Engels, *Ludwig Feuerbach*, New York, 1941, p. 18.

4. Marx, "*Luther als Schiedsrichter zwischen Strauss und Feuerbach,*" MEGA, I, 1, erste halbband, pp. 151*ff.*

5. Feuerbach, *Provisional Theses,* Thesis 52.

6. Feuerbach, *Essence of Christianity,* tr. by Marian Evans (George Eliot), 2nd edition, London 1881, pp. 29*f.* On the origin of the meaning of alienation in Hegel, *see* Roger Garaudy, *Dieu est mort,* Paris, 1962, especially pp. 67–9.

7. Jean Yves Calvez, *La Pensée de Karl Marx,* Paris, 1956.

8. Feuerbach, *Principles of the Philosophy of the Future,* paragraph 5.

9. *Ibid.,* paragraph 32.

10. MEGA, I, 1, zweiter halbband, p. 306.

11. Marx and Engels, *The German Ideology,* New York, 1947, p. 37.

12. Marx, "Theses on Feuerbach," IV, in Engels, *Ludwig Feuerbach,* p. 83.

13. Engels, *The Condition of the Working Class in England,* Marx and Engels, *On Britain,* Moscow, 1953, p. 4.

14. MEGA, I, 1, zweite halbband, pp. 118*ff.*

15. MEGA, I, 1, erste halbband, pp. 403*ff.*

16. Marx, *Contribution to the Critique of Political Economy,* Introduction, as quoted in Howard Selsam and Harry Martel, eds., *Reader in Marxist Philosophy,* New York, 1963, p. 186.

THE FICHTEAN HERITAGE AND THE HERESY OF PROMETHEUS

1. Engels, *Socialism: Utopian and Scientific,* Introduction to first German edition, New York, 1935, p. 6.

2. Cornu, *Marx et Engels,* t. 1, pp. 34–5.

3. Fichte, Letter to Baggesen, April 1795.

4. MEGA, I, 1, zweite halbband, pp. 297*ff.*

5. Marx and Engels, *On Religion,* p. 38.

6. This analysis is based on an unpublished study by M. Guéroult, "The Fichtean Antecedents of Existentialism," Communication to the International Congress of Philosophy, Mexico, 1963.

7. Marx, *The 18th Brumaire of Louis Bonaparte,* New York, 1963, p. 15.

8. J. G. Fichte, *Rapport clair comme le jour au grand public sur la veritable nature de la philosophie,* p. 88.

9. Marx, *The Holy Family,* Moscow, 1956.

10. Marx and Engels, *The German Ideology,* unabridged edition, Moscow, 1964, p. 286*n.*

11. Fichte, *Sittenlehre,* IV, paragraph 18.

12. Fichte, *The Characteristic Traits of Our Epoch,* 1805.

II. MARXISM: A REVOLUTION IN PHILOSOPHY

THE THREE SOURCES

1. V. I. Lenin, "The Three Sources and Three Component Parts of Marxism," *The Teachings of Karl Marx,* New York, 1964, p. 43.

2. Marx, "The Jewish Question," MEGA, I, 1, erste halbband, pp. 576*ff.*

3. Max Stirner, *The Ego and His Own,* tr. by S. T. Byington, New York, n.d.

4. Marx, "Contribution to the Critique of Hegel's Philosophy of Right," *loc. cit.,* p. 50.

5. *Ibid.,* pp. 51–2.

6. *Ibid.*, p. 57. This passage is translated anew.
7. *Ibid.*, pp. 57–8.
8. *Ibid.*, p. 58.
9. Engels, "Journey from Paris to Berne," Marx-Engels, *Werke*, band 5, Dietz Verlag, Berlin, 1959, pp. 463*ff*.
10. Marx to Joseph Weydemeyer, March 5, 1852, Marx and Engels, *Selected Correspondence 1846–1895*, New York, 1942, p. 57.
11. Marx, *The Holy Family*, p. 113.
12. Unpublished manuscript by Marx, Bibliothèque Nationale, *Manuscrits de Blanqui 9.594, feuillet 310*. Cited by R. Garaudy in *Les Sources françaises du socialisme scientifique*, 2nd edition, Paris, 1949, p. 218.
13. These were published from March 1839 to April 1841 in *Telegraph für Deutschland*; MEGA, I, 2, Marx-Engels Verlag, Berlin, 1930, pp. 23*ff*.
14. Engels, "On the History of the Communist League," Marx and Engels, *Selected Works*, Vol. 2, New York, 1951, p. 311.
15. Marx and Engels, *The German Ideology*, New York, p. 40.
16. Marx, *Manuscripts of 1844*, Appendix, pp. 197–226.

THE ALIENATION OF LABOR

1. Marx, *Manuscripts of 1844*, p. 136.
2. *Ibid.*, p. 179.
3. *Ibid.*, p. 177.
4. *Ibid.*, p. 173.
5. *Ibid.*, p. 177.
6. *Ibid.*, p. 175.
7. *Ibid.*, p. 117.
8. *Ibid.*, pp. 153–4.
9. Marx, *Capital*, Vol. 2, New York, 1967, p. 125.
10. Marx, *Capital*, Vol. 3, New York, 1967, p. 830.
11. Marx, *Capital*, Vol. 1, New York, 1967, p. 550.
12. Marx to Engels, August 2, 1862, Marx and Engels, *Selected Correspondence*, p. 131.
13. Marx, *Capital*, Vol. 2, p. 219.
14. *Ibid.*, p. 225.
15. Marx, Lecture Notes on James Mill.
16. Marx, *Manuscripts of 1844*, p. 106.
17. Marx and Engels, *The German Ideology*, New York, p. 20.
18. Marx, *Manuscripts of 1844*, p. 168.
19. *Ibid.*, p. 174.
20 Marx, *The Holy Family*, p. 73.
21. Marx and Engels, *The German Ideology*, New York, p. 34.
22. Marx, *Manuscripts of 1844*, pp. 109–10.
23. *Ibid.*, p. 135.

PRACTICE AND THE "RECONVERSION" OF SPECULATIVE CONCEPTS

1. Marx, Thesis XI on Feuerbach, Engels, *Ludwig Feuerbach*, p. 84.
2. On this ambiguity in *The Economic and Philosophic Manuscripts of 1844*, see the suggestive article by Maurice Godelier, "Political Economy and Philosophy," in *La Pensée*, Paris, No. 111, October 1963.
3. Marx and Engels, *The German Ideology*, New York, p. 15.

HISTORICAL MATERIALISM

1. Marx, *Contribution to the Critique of Political Economy*, Chicago, 1904, pp. 11–12.
2. *Ibid.*, p. 13.
3. Marx, *The Holy Family*, p. 30.
4. Marx and Engels, *The German Ideology*, New York, p. 14.
5. *Ibid.*, p. 14.
6. Marx, *The 18th Brumaire of Louis Bonaparte*, p. 15.
7. Marx, *Manuscripts of 1844*, pp. 113–14.
8. Marx and Engels, *The German Ideology*, New York, p. 74.
9. Engels, *Ludwig Feuerbach*, p. 8.
10. Marx and Engels, *The German Ideology*, New York, p. 13.
11. *Ibid.*, p. 15.
12. Marx, *Pre-Capitalist Economic Formations*, edited by Eric J. Hobsbawn, New York, 1965. This is from a much larger manuscript written by Marx in preparation for his *Critique of Political Economy* and *Capital*. His complete notes were published as *Grundrisse der Kritik der Politische Ökonomie* in Moscow, 1939–41. A German edition was published in Berlin in 1953.
13. Joseph Stalin, *Dialectical and Historical Materialism*, New York, 1940.
14. Cited in an unpublished study by Maurice Godelier on the "Asiatic mode of production," upon which the author has drawn heavily.
15. Marx and Engels, *The German Ideology*, New York, p. 59.
16. *Ibid.*, p. 40.
17. *Ibid.*, p. 26. For the further exposition of historical materialism by Marx, *see*, in addition to *The German Ideology*, the preface to the *Contribution to the Critique of Political Economy*, and the letter to Annenkov, December 28, 1846, in Marx and Engels, *Selected Correspondence*, p. 5.
18. Marx and Engels, *The German Ideology*, New York, p. 27.
19. *Ibid.*, p. 74.
20. Marx and Engels, *The German Ideology*, unabridged edition, Moscow, p. 430.
21. *Ibid.*, p. 483.
22. Marx, *The Poverty of Philosophy*, New York, 1963, p. 109.
23. Marx and Engels, *The German Ideology*, New York, p. 14.
24. Marx and Engels, *Selected Correspondence*, p. 477.
25. *Ibid.*, pp. 477*ff*.
26. Marx, *Critique of Political Economy*, pp. 311–12.
27. Marx, *Theories of Surplus Value*, Part I, Moscow, n.d., p. 277.
28. Engels to Conrad Schmidt, August 5, 1890, Marx and Engels, *Selected Correspondence*, p. 473.

MARX'S MATERIALISM

1. Marx, Thesis I on Feuerbach, in Engels, *Ludwig Feuerbach*, p. 82.
2. Marx, *The Holy Family*, p. 176.
3. *Ibid.*, p. 173
4. Marx, Thesis I on Feuerbach, *loc. cit.*
5. Engels, *Ludwig Feuerbach*, p. 25.
6. Marx, *Manuscripts of 1844*, p. 181.
7. Lenin, "Philosophical Notebooks," *Collected Works*, Vol. 38, Moscow, 1961, p. 292.

8. Marx and Engels, *The German Ideology*, New York, p. 35.
9. *Ibid.*, pp. 37–8.
10. *Ibid.*, p. 36.
11. Marx, *Manuscripts of 1844*, pp. 142–3.
12. Marx, *Critique of Political Economy*, p. 194.
13. Marx, *Manuscripts of 1844*, p. 169.
14. Marx, *Capital*, Volume 1, p. 57.
15. Marx and Engels, *The German Ideology*, New York, pp. 36–7.
16. Marx, *Manuscripts of 1844*, p. 144.
17. *Ibid.*, p. 145.
18. Marx, *The Holy Family*, p. 79.
19. *Ibid*, p. 82.
20. Marx, *Manuscripts of 1844*, p. 172.
21. Feuerbach, *Contribution à la critique de la philosophie de Hegel* (1839), in *Manifestes philosophiques*, Althusser translation, pp. 32–3.
22. Marx and Engels, *The German Ideology*, Moscow, p. 254.
23. Marx, *Manuscripts of 1844*, pp. 180–81.
24. *Ibid.*, p. 181.
25. Engels, *Anti-Dühring*, New York, 1939.
26. Feuerbach, *Oeuvres*, t. III, p. 142.

MARX'S DIALECTICS

1. Hegel, *History of Philosophy*, tr. by E. S. Haldane and H. Simson, London, 1896, Volume III, p. 451.
2. Marx, *The Holy Family*, p. 172.
3. *See* Garaudy, *Dieu est mort*.
4. Lenin, "Philosophical Notebooks," as quoted in Selsam and Martel, editors, *Reader in Marxist Philosophy*, p. 331.
5. Marx, *Capital*, Vol. 1, p. 309.
6. Marx to Engels, June 22, 1867, Marx and Engels, *Selected Correspondence*, p. 223.

DIALECTICS AND FREEDOM

1. Engels to Starkenbourg, January 25, 1894, Marx and Engels, *Selected Correspondence*, p. 517.
2. Marx to Kugelmann, May 13, 1871, *ibid.*, p. 311.
3. Johann Wolfgang von Goethe, *Wilhelm Meister*, tr. by Henry G. Bohn, London, 1855, p. 59.
4. Marx and Engels, *The German Ideology*, Moscow, p. 225.
5. Montesquieu, *Cahiers* (Notebooks), Grasset, 1942, pp. 100–01.
6. Marx and Engels, *The German Ideology*, Moscow, p. 410.
7. Marx, *The Holy Family*, pp. 156–7.
8. Marx, *Capital*, Vol. 3, p. 828.
9. Helvetius, *De l'Esprit, Discours II*, Chapters 18 and 24.
10. Marx and Engels, *The German Ideology*, Moscow, p. 275.
11. *Ibid.*, p. 330.
12. *Ibid.*, p. 331.
13. *Ibid.*, p. 316.
14. Marx, *Capital*, Vol. 1, p. 78.
15. Marx, *Critique of Political Economy*, p. 13.

16. Engels, *Ludwig Feuerbach*, p. 11.
17. Marx, *Capital*, Vol. 3, p. 820.
18. Marx, *Capital*, Vol. 1, p. 372n.

III. MARX AND POLITICAL ECONOMY

MARX'S METHOD IN *Capital*

1. Lenin, "Philosophical Notebooks," *loc. cit.*, p. 319.
2. Marx, *Capital*, Vol. 1, p. 316.
3. Marx to Engels, June 27, 1867, MEGA, III, 3, pp. 403*f*; *see also* letter of April 30, 1868, *Selected Correspondence*, pp. 240*f*.
4. Marx, *Capital*, Vol. 3, p. 814.
5. *Ibid.*, Chapter 1, "Cost-Price and Profit."
6. *Ibid.*, pp. 26, 28.
7. Marx, *Capital*, Vol. 1, pp. 306–7.
8. Marx, *Capital*, Vol. 3, p. 188.
9. *Ibid.*, p. 25.
10. *Ibid.*, p. 831.
11. *The Works of B. Franklin*, edited by Sparks, Boston, 1836, Vol. 2, p. 267. Cited in Marx, *Capital*, Vol. 1, p. 51n.
12. Adam Smith, *The Wealth of Nations* (American Home Library), Vol. 1, p. 75.
13. David Ricardo, *Principles of Political Economy and Taxation*, London, 1821, p. 1.
14. See Marx, *Theories of Surplus Value: Selections*, G. A. Bonner and Emile Burns, editors, New York, 1952, especially "Ricardo's Conception of Surplus Value," pp. 283*ff*.
15. H. C. Carey, *The Past, The Present and The Future*, Philadelphia, 1859, pp. 74–5.
16. Ricardo, *Principles of Political Economy and Taxation*, p. 86.
17. Marx, *Theories of Surplus Value*, New York, p. 302.
18. Ricardo, *Principles of Political Economy and Taxation*, pp. 467–8.
19. Marx, *Capital*, Vol. 3, p. 242.
20. *Ibid.*, p. 259.
21. Marx, *Capital*, Vol. 1, "Afterword to the Second German Edition," p. 14.
22. *Ibid.*, p. 76.
23. Cited by Mandel, *Traité d'économie marxiste*, t. I, Juillard, Paris, 1962, p. 101.
24. Marx, *Capital*, Vol. 1, p. 77.
25. *Ibid.*, p. 540.
26. *Ibid.*, "The Two-fold Character of the Labour Embodied in Commodities," pp. 41*ff*.
27. Marx, *Capital*, Vol. 3, p. 382.
28. Marx, *Manuscripts of 1844*, p. 129.
29. Marx, *Wage-Labor and Capital*, New York, 1933, pp. 30, 29, 28.
30. Marx, *Critique of Political Economy*, p. 293.
31. Marx, *Theories of Surplus Value*, New York, p. 29.
32. Lenin, "Philosophical Notebooks," *loc. cit.*, p. 319.
33. Marx, *Capital*, Vol. 1, p. 216n.

34. Marx, *Capital,* Vol. 3, p. 43.
35. Marx, *Critique of Political Economy,* p. 296.
36. Marx and Engels, *Selected Correspondence,* pp. 108–9.
37. On this subject, *see* the very interesting ethnographic and historical material, the result of contemporary research, in Mandel, *Traité d'économie marxiste.*
38. Marx, *Capital,* Vol. 3, p. 177.
39. Marx, *Critique of Political Economy,* pp. 303–4.
40. Marx, *Capital,* Vol. 1, pp. 714–5.
41. Marx, *Critique of Political Economy,* p. 300.
42. Marx, *Capital,* Vol. 3, p. 25.
43. Marx, *Critique of Political Economy,* p. 291.
44. Engels, "Karl Marx's 'Contribution to the Critique of Political Economy,'" *Ludwig Feuerbach,* p. 79.
45. Marx and Engels, *Selected Correspondence,* p. 105.
46. *Ibid.,* p. 495.
47. Marx, *Capital,* Vol. 1, p. 35.
48. *Ibid.,* p. 88.
49. *Ibid.,* p. 86.
50. *Ibid.,* p. 103.
51. *Ibid.,* p. 144.
52. *Ibid.,* p. 154.
53. *Ibid.,* p. 488.
54. *Ibid.,* p. 167.
55. *Ibid.,* p. 763.

MARX'S GREAT DISCOVERIES AND THEIR SIGNIFICANCE

1. Cited by Marx, *Critique of Political Economy,* p. 59n.
2. Engels, "Preface to the English Edition," Marx, *Capital,* Vol. 1, p. 5.
3. W. Stanley Jevons, *The Theory of Political Economy,* London, 1911, p. vi.
4. Lionel Robbins, *Essay on the Nature and Significance of Economic Science,* London, 1937.
5. Keynes, *Essays in Persuasion,* London, 1931, p. 300.
6. Marx, *Capital,* Vol. 1, p. 189.
7. Marx, *Capital,* Vol. 2, pp. 424–5.
8. Marx, *Capital,* Vol. 1, p. 218.
9. *Ibid.,* p. 763.
10. *Ibid.,* p. 166.
11. *Ibid.,* pp. 630, 631, 632.
12. *Ibid.,* p. 645.
13. *Ibid.,* p. 618.
14. *Ibid.,* p. 171. *See also* in Marx, *Critique of the Gotha Programme* (New York, 1938, pp. 14f, 30), the refutation of the so-called Lassalle "iron law" recently revived in a new variation under the name of the "wage-price spiral."
15. Marx, *Wage-Labor and Capital,* p. 37.
16. John Strachey, *Contemporary Capitalism,* London, 1957, p. 133.
17. Based on U.S. Department of Commerce, *Historical Statistics of the United States, 1789–1939; Statistical Abstract, 1958,* as cited by Mandel, *op. cit.*
18. Maurice Dobb, *Wages,* London and Cambridge, 1946, p. 71.

19. Marx, *Wage-Labor and Capital*, p. 40; *see also* Marx, *Capital*, Vol. I, Chapter XXV, "The General Law of Capitalist Accumulation."
20. Marx, *Manuscripts of 1844*, pp. 117–8.
21. Marx, *Capital*, Vol. 3, p. 250.
22. *Ibid.*, p. 223.
23. Laurence R. Klein, *The Keynesian Revolution*, New York, 1947, p. 68.
24. Based on U.S. Department of Commerce, *Historical Statistics of the United States, 1789–1939; Statistical Abstract, 1958*, as cited by Mandel, *op. cit.*
25. Marx, *Capital*, Vol. 1, p. 627.
26. Data for 1880–1939, from Spurgeon Belle, *Productivity, Wages and National Income*; for 1950–57, from *Statistical Abstract, 1958*, cited by Mandel, *op. cit.*
27. Marx, *Capital*, Vol. 3, p. 484.
28. Engels, *Anti-Dühring*, pp. 301–2.
29. Mandel, *Traité d'économie marxiste*, t. II, pp. 431–2.
30. *U.S. News and World Report*, February 13, 1961, p. 78.
31. *See* Marx, *Capital*, Vol. 3, pp. 386–8.

IV. KARL MARX AND POLITICAL STRUGGLES

1. Marx, *Capital*, Vol. 1, p. 10.
2. Marx, *Herr Vogt*, 1860, in Marx-Engels, *Werke*, band 14, Berlin, 1961.

FROM UTOPIA TO THE CLASS STRUGGLE

3. Marx and Engels, *The Communist Manifesto*, New York, 1948, p. 43.
4. *Ibid.*, p. 19.
5. *See* Marx, *The Class Struggles in France*, New York, 1964; *The 18th Brumaire of Louis Napoleon*; and *The Civil War in France*, New York, 1940.
6. Marx, *The Holy Family*, p. 53.
7. Marx, *The Poverty of Philosophy*, pp. 172–3.
8. Letter to Sorge, October 19, 1877, Marx and Engels, *Selected Correspondence*, p. 350.
9. Marx and Engels, *The German Ideology*, New York, p. 40.
10. Pierre Joseph Proudhon, *De la justice dans la Révolution et dans l'Eglise*, 1858, t. II, p. 407.
11. Proudhon, *Correspondance*, t. IV, p. 261.
12. *Ibid.*, t. VII, p. 357.
13. Marx, *Poverty of Philosophy*, p. 126.
14. Marx to Kugelmann, October 9, 1866, *Selected Correspondence*, p. 214.
15. Marx-Engels, *Werke*, band 7, Dietz Verlag, Berlin, 1960, pp. 266ff.
16. *See* Engels, "On the History of the Communist League," Marx and Engels, *Selected Works*, Vol. 2, Moscow, 1958, pp. 338–57.
17. Marx and Engels, *The Communist Manifesto*, pp. 43–4.

STRATEGY AND TACTICS

1. *See* John Lewis, *The Life and Teaching of Karl Marx*, New York, 1965, p. 98.
2. Marx, *Critique of the Gotha Programme*, p. 12.

3. For Marx's writings in the *Neue Rheinische Zeitung*, see Marx-Engels, *Werke*, band 7.

4. Engels, "Marx and the *Neue Rheinische Zeitung* (1848–1849)," Marx and Engels, *Selected Works*, Vol. 2, Moscow, 1958, pp. 330–31.

5. Franz Mehring, *Karl Marx*, New York, 1935, p. 233.

6. Marx to Bracke, May 5, 1875, *Critique of the Gotha Programme*, pp. 34–5.

THE STATE

1. Marx and Engels, *Selected Works*, Vol. 1, Moscow, 1958, p. 389.

2. Engels, *The Origin of the Family, Private Property and the State*, New York, 1942.

3. "The Jewish Question," Marx-Engels, *Werke*, band 1, Berlin, 1958, pp. 347*ff*.

4. *Ibid.*

5. Marx to Weydemeyer, March 5, 1852, Marx and Engels, *Selected Correspondence*, p. 57.

6. Marx, "Indifference in Political Matters," in *Almanach républicain de 1874*, Lodi, 1873, p. 141.

7. Marx, *Critique of the Gotha Programme*, p. 18.

8. Marx and Engels, *The Communist Manifesto*, p. 30.

9. "Speech in the Hague Congress"; the text as published in *La Liberté*, No. 37, September 15, 1872, is given in Marx-Engels, *Werke*, band 18, Berlin, 1962, pp. 159–61.

10. Marx-Engels, *Werke*, band 22, Berlin, 1963, pp. 225*ff*.

11. Marx, *The 18th Brumaire of Louis Bonaparte*, p. 122.

12. Marx and Engels, *Selected Works*, Vol. 1, Moscow, 1958, p. 22.

13. Marx and Engels, *Selected Correspondence*, p. 309.

14. Marx, *Critique of the Gotha Programme*, p. 17.

MARX, FOUNDER OF COMMUNIST AND WORKERS' PARTIES

1. Marx and Engels, *Selected Works*, Vol. 1, Moscow, 1958, p. 386.

2. Marx to Weydemeyer, November 29, 1864, Marx and Engels, *Letters to Americans*, New York, 1953, p. 65.

3. Marx to Engels, November 4, 1864, *Selected Correspondence*, p. 160.

4. Marx to Bolte, November 23, 1871, *ibid.*, pp. 315–6.

5. Marx and Engels, *Selected Works*, Volume 1, Moscow, 1958, pp. 107, 117.

6. Marx and Engels, *Selected Correspondence*, pp. 375, 376.

7. Proudhon, *Confessions d'un Révolutionnaire*, p. 200.

8. *Ibid.*, pp. 81–2.

9. *Ibid.*, p. 79.

10. *Ibid.*, p. 82.

11. *Ibid.*, p. 80.

12. *Ibid.*, p. 82.

13. *Ibid.*, p. 76.

14. *Ibid.*, p. 77.

15. *Ibid.*, p. 113.

16. Marx, *The Holy Family*, p. 53.

17. Marx to Bolte, November 29, 1871, Marx and Engels, *Selected Correspondence*, p. 319.

18. Lenin, "Who the 'Friends of the People' Are," Lenin, *Selected Works*, 12 vols., New York, 1943, Vol. 1, p. 452.

CONCLUSION

1. Lenin, "Marxism and Revisionism," *Selected Works*, 3 vols., New York, 1967, Vol. 1, p. 72.

For a Chronology of events in the life of Karl Marx and of his books, articles and other writings, *see* John Lewis, *The Life and Teaching of Karl Marx*, New York, 1965, pp. 275–82.

Index

A Report Clear as Day, 33
All-German Workers' League,
　185n
Anti-Dühring, 88, 161
Aristotle, 95

BABEUF, FRANÇOIS NOËL, 49
Bacon, Francis, 79
Bakunin, Mikhail, 50, 188, 201
Bastiat, Frédéric, 115, 126
Bauer, Bruno, 26, 34, 46
Bebel, August, 185n, 192
Bentham, Jeremy, 143
Bettelheim, Charles, 151
Bismarck, Otto von, 199
Blanc, Louis, 50
Blanqui, Louis Auguste, 49, 172n
Bloch, Joseph, 76
Böhm-Bawerk, Eugen, 119
Bohme, Jacob, 89
Boisguilbert, Pierre le Pesant, 51
Bolshevik Party, 201
Botticelli, Sandro, 109
Bowles, Chester, 165
Bulletin des Sociétés financières,
　164

CABET, ÉTIENNE, 49
Calvez, R. P., 28
Campanella, Tommaso, 36
Capital, 60f, 65n, 72, 77, 83, 107,
　109, 111ff, 142, 145, 166, 169f,
　185, 199, 204
Carbonari, 49, 191
Carey, Henry Charles, 116
Carnot, Sadi, 132f

Charles X, 17
Chartist movement, 22, 50, 90,
　173, 179
Chrysostom, St. John, 123
*Class Struggles in France,
　1848–50*, 170, 184n
Congress of Vienna, 49
*Contribution to the Critique of
　Political Economy*, 76, 128, 134
*Contribution to the Critique of
　Hegel's Philosophy of Right*,
　25, 28, 30f, 45, 47, 73,
　170, 186
Copernicus, Nicholas, 36, 72, 152
Cornu, Auguste, 33
*Critique of the Erfurt
　Programme*, 188
*Critique of the Gotha
　Programme*, 179, 185,
　187, 196
"Critique of the Hegelian
　Dialectic and Philosophy as
　a Whole," 53
Customs Union of 1834, 17

DANA, CHARLES ANDERSON, 199n
Dante Alighieri, 109
Danton, Georges Jacques, 21
Democratic International
　Association, 178
Democritus, 19, 24, 79f
Demosthenes, 123
Descartes, René, 79, 87, 129,
　133, 204
Deutsche-Französishe Jahrbücher,
　see *Franco-Prussian Annals*

219

Dézamy, Theodore, 49
*Dialectical and Historical
Materialism*, 72
Diderot, Denis, 79, 95
Doctrine of Science, 35, 35*n*,
39*f*, 43
Dühring, Eugen, 201
Durkheim, Émile, 74

EAST INDIA COMPANY, 118, 118*n*
*Economic and Philosophic
Manuscripts of 1844*, 24, 28*f*,
48, 51, 59, 62*ff*, 65*n*, 84,
157, 186
Egalité, 194*n*
Engels, Frederick, 17, 21*f*, 28,
50*f*, 68, 71, 75*ff*, 79*f*, 88, 98,
102, 135, 137*f*, 142, 161,
179*n*, 186, 188, 195, 199*ff*
Epicurus, 19, 24
Essence of Christianity, 25
Euclid, 95

Faust, 18*ff*
Feuerbach, Ludwig Andreas,
24*ff*, 33, 51*f*, 62, 64, 78*ff*,
85*f*, 88, 103
Fichte, Johann Gottlieb, 21,
33*ff*, 52*f*, 65*f*, 68, 79*f*, 83,
84*n*, 88, 90, 202*f*
First International, *see*
International Working
Men's Association
Fourier, Charles, 33, 157
Franco-Prussian Annals, 47, 51
Franklin, Benjamin, 115
French Revolution, 15*f*, 20, 35,
48*f*, 182
French Workers' Party, 194*n*
Friends of Poland Club, 17

GALL, LUDWIG, 17
Gans, E., 15*ff*
Gassendi, Pierre, 80
German Legion, 180
German Reformation, 179
German Workingman's Club,
180
Goethe, Johann Wolfgang von,
18*f*, 95, 100, 202
Gorki, Maxim, 203
Gotschalk, 181, 183*f*
Greeley, Horace, 199*n*
Grotius, Hugo, 36
Grün, Karl, 64
Grundlage, 84*n*
Guesde, Jules, 194*n*
Guizot, François, 48

HAILEYBURY COLLEGE, 118*n*
Hegel, Georg Wilhelm
Friedrich, 13, 15*f*, 19*ff*, 36,
50, 52*ff*, 62, 65*f*, 78*ff*, 82*f*, 85,
87, 89*ff*, 100, 103, 111,
127, 130, 138, 195, 202*f*
Heidegger, Martin, 38
Heine, Heinrich, 21, 50
Helvetius, Claude Adrien, 79, 106
Heraclitus, 127
Herwegh, Georg, 50, 180
Hess, Moses, 30*f*, 46, 62
History of Philosophy, 24, 89
Hobbes, Thomas, 36
Holbach, Paul Henri Thiry, 79
Holy Alliance, 16*ff*, 22, 49, 178
Homer, 15
Husserl, Edmund, 82*f*, 133
Hutton, James, 95

INSURRECTION OF CRACOW, 178
International Working Men's
Association, 186, 188,
190*ff*, 195

Jaurès, Jean, 35n
Jevons, Stanley, 143
Justice in the Revolution and the Church, 174

Kant, Immanuel, 12, 20f, 33, 35f, 39ff, 65f, 79f, 87ff, 95f, 111, 127, 202, 204
Karl Marx, 183n
Kekulé von Stradonitz, Friedrich August, 131
Keynes, John Maynard, 144f, 164
Kierkegaard, Soren, 37, 39
Korean War, 164
Kriege, Hermann, 173
Kugelmann, Dr. L., 189

La Mettrie, Julien Offray de, 79f
Lamarck, Jean Baptiste Pierre Antoine de Monet, 95
Lamartine, Alphonse Marie Louis de, 180
Laplace, Pierre Simon, 95
Lassalle, Ferdinand, 43, 154, 179
League of the Just, 172n, 176
Lenin, V. I., 45, 73, 81, 93, 112, 131, 138, 196, 200f
Leroux, Pierre, 50
Lessing, Gotthold Ephraim, 77
Letters From Wuppertal, 50
Lewis, John, 183n
Liebknecht, Wilhelm, 185n, 192
Life of Jesus, 23
Locke, John, 128
Ludwig Feuerbach, 28, 80
Lyell, Sir Charles, 95

MacCulloch, John R., 51, 119

Machiavelli, Nicolò, 36

Malthus, Thomas Robert, 118ff
Manchester Guardian, 144
"Manuscripts of 1843," see *Contribution to the Critique of Hegel's Philosophy of Right*
Maréchal, Sylvain, 63
Marx, Hirschel, 15
Marx, Karl, 5ff; student days, 15ff; doctor's dissertation, 19f, 24; Young Hegelians, 20ff, 45f, 64; *Rheinische Zeitung* editor, 30f; Paris days, 47ff; Communist League, 176ff; First International, 186ff
Marx's Thought, 28
Maxwell, James Clerk, 131
Mazzini, Giuseppe, 16, 190
Mehring, Franz, 183n
Mignet, François Auguste Marie, 48
Mill, James, 51
Mill, John Stuart, 143
Montesquieu, 104
Münzer, Thomas, 179n

Napoleon III, 174
Neue Rheinische Zeitung, 36, 175, 181, 184, 199
New York Tribune, 199, 199n
Newton, Isaac, 95
Notebooks of Kreuznach, 30

October Revolution, 201
"Outline of a Critique of Political Economy," 51
Owen, Robert, 33

Paris Commune, 171, 189, 200
Peasants' War of 1525, 179, 179n

222

INDEX

Petty, William, 115, 142
Phenomenology of Mind,
53, 111, 127
"Philosophy of Law," 32
Philosophy of Right, 31
Piedelièvre, Professor, 157
Plato, 108
*Pre-Capitalist Economic
Formations,* 72
*Preface to the Philosophy of
History,* 34
*Principles of Political Economy
and Taxation,* 116, 119
*Principles of the Philosophy of
the Future,* 25
Proudhon, Pierre Joseph, 49*f*,
124, 173*ff*, 192*ff*, 194*n*
*Provisional Theses for the
Reform of Philosophy,* 25

*Religion and Philosophy in
Germany,* 21
"Remarks on the Regimentation
of Prussian Censorship," 36
Rheinische Zeitung, 30, 32
Ricardo, David, 51, 54*f*, 66,
114, 116*ff*, 119*n*, 128*f*, 142,
150
Robbins, Lionel, 145
Robespierre, Maximilien
François Marie Isidore de, 21
Rostow, Walt W., 165
Rousseau, Jean Jacques, 15,
36, 52
Ruge, Arnold, 29, 46*f*

Saint-Simon, Comte de,
15*ff*, 33, 66
Say, Jean-Baptiste, 51, 115, 126
Schiller, Johann Christoph
Friedrich von, 18

Schmidt, Conrad, 76, 138
Science of Logic, 93, 111, 127
Senior, Nassau, 143
Shakespeare, William, 15
Sismondi, Jean Charles Léonard
Simonde de, 162
Skarbek, Frédéric, 51
Smith, Adam, 51, 54*f*, 66,
114*f*, 120, 128, 142
Social Democratic Workers'
Party of Germany, 185*n*
Société de saisons, 172*n*
Society for the Rights of Man
and Citizen, 180
Socrates, 108
Spinoza, Baruch, 36, 103
Stalin, Joseph, 13, 72*f*, 166, 202
Stirner, Max, 38*f*, 46
Strachey, John, 156
Strauss, David Friedrich, 23, 25

The Civil War in France, 189
"The Closed Commercial
State," 35
The Communist League, 176,
178, 180*f*, 184
The Communist Manifesto, 70,
103, 165, 169*f*, 176, 178*f*,
183, 188*f*, 204
*The Condition of the Working-
Class in England,* 50, 102
"The Differences between the
Natural Philosophy of
Democritus and the Natural
Philosophy of Epicurus," *see*
Marx, Karl, doctor's
dissertation
The Ego and His Own, 46
*The Eighteenth Brumaire of
Louis Bonaparte,* 76, 170,
189, 204

The Evangelist of the Poor Fisherman, 173

The General Theory of Employment, Interest and Money, 144

The German Ideology, 38, 41, 51, 67*f*, 71*ff*, 75*ff*, 103, 172

The Holy Family, 38, 68, 79, 85

"The Jewish Question," 45, 73, 186

The Life and Teaching of Karl Marx, 183*n*

Theoretical and Practical Problems of Planning, 151

Theories of Surplus Value, 77

"The Origins of German Socialism," 35*n*

The Origins of the Family, Private Property and the State, 186

The Peasant War in Germany, 179*n*

The Poverty of Philosophy, 75, 171, 173*f*, 188

The Social Contract, 52

The Stages of Economic Growth: A Non-Communist Manifesto, 165

The Theory of Political Economy, 143

The Theory of Property, 174

Thierry, Augustin, 48

Thiers, Adolphe, 48

Tracy, Destutt de, 51

UNIVERSITY OF BERLIN, 15

VOLTAIRE, 15, 77*n*

Von Cieszkowski, 34

Von Mises, Ludwig, 145

WEITLING, WILHELM, 172*f*

Westphalen, Jenny von, 15, 18, 199

Westphalen, Ludwig von, 15

Wiener, Norbert, 131

Workers' Club of London, 195

Workingmen's Union of Cologne, 180

XENOPHON, 123

"YOUNG EUROPE," 16, 16*n*

ZASULICH, VERA, 73